THE NEW COLORED PEOPLE

Jon Michael Spencer

with a Foreword by
Richard E. van der Ross

THE NEW
COLORED PEOPLE

*The Mixed-Race
Movement in America*

NEW YORK UNIVERSITY PRESS
New York and London

NEW YORK UNIVERSITY PRESS
New York and London

©1997 by Jon Michael Spencer

Library of Congress Cataloging-in-Publication Data
Spencer, Jon Michael.
The new colored people: the mixed-race movement in America / Jon
Michael Spencer; with a foreword by Richard E. van der Ross.
p.   cm.
Includes bibliographical references and index.
ISBN 0-8147-8071-7 (alk. paper)
1. Racially mixed people—United States. I. Title.
E184.A1S7 1997   96-45791
973'.04—dc21   CIP

New York University Press books are printed on acid-free paper,
and their binding materials are chosen for strength and durability.

Manufactured in the United States of America

10 9 8 7 6 5 4 3 2 1

TO
NICOLE WALIGORA

[CONTENTS]

Over thirty years ago (I believe it was the year 1962), I had the honor of sharing a platform with Dr. Martin Luther King, Jr. In the course of my remarks, I told the audience that we, the oppressed in South Africa, were watching the American civil rights movement closely. I stated rather dramatically: If you succeed, we can succeed; if you fail, we will fail. Little did I think that over thirty years later a black American would be saying to the people of South Africa: We in the United States need to learn from you, for we want to replicate your successes and not your mistakes of history.

In this book, the result of the author's inquiries into South African history, bold, frontal attention is given to a highly sensitive and very complex issue—the mixed-race or "multiracial" movement in the United States. This is a movement led by interracial parents and mixed-race people who are dissatisfied with the current racial classifications and seek to have a new racial category added to the existing four. They argue that mixed-race people are "multiracial," and they have petitioned the United States government to add "multiracial" to the federal census. In developing his position against legislating a new racial classification, the author draws parallels between the would-be multiracial group in America and the Coloured people of South Africa.

But most of all, Professor Spencer argues that Americans are uninformed about the tragic consequences of the former white South African government legally classifying all mixed-race people as "Coloureds." Oddly enough, the American multiracials are requesting to be legally classified, whereas South Africa's mixed-race people have never made such a request. We just slid into the position of an intermediary category, having the classification of

"Coloured" semilegislated after the emancipation of slaves in 1834, and having it further legislated to our disadvantage in 1948.

Where do I stand with regard to the idea of the United States government establishing a category of "multiracial"? Having weighed the author's arguments for and against, and having considered the historical situation of the Coloured people of South Africa, I concur with the author's position: While I have great respect for the multiracials striving to strengthen their mixed-race identity and to obliterate their societal invisibility, it is an inescapable fact that the legal classification of "Coloured" provided the lever for the white South African government to introduce all manner of discrimination against the group once it was legally identified.

It is true that a sense of mixed-race identity could be a powerful factor in raising the awareness of all mixed-race people; but it is also true that if raised to the status of a legal category, that which is well intentioned could become a tragedy. This may appear to leave the American people at an impasse, but from this book Americans can walk away with an informed resolution of this quandary.

—RICHARD E. VAN DER ROSS
Cape Town, South Africa

[PREFACE]

Most Americans are rather oblivious to the fact that there is a new racial movement silently shifting the earth beneath their feet as they walk confidently toward the twenty-first century. We may have seen some mention of this movement in the media, particularly the struggle of interracial parents in local school systems that have refused to permit their children to claim a mixed racial background on school forms. However, most of us are hardly aware that a good number of these same parents, out of frustrations regarding the identity and treatment of their mixed-race children, have begun a movement to see a classification of "multiracial" added to the United States census.

Legislating a new classification and thereby establishing a new race could have a profound effect on race relations in this country and therefore affect the lives of us all. But whether or not my alarm is accurate, and whether or not the new classification is adopted for the census of 2000 or 2010, I want to confront the multiracialists (the staunch advocates of the multiracial identity) on their racial logic. Chief among these multiracialists I hope to challenge are the interracial parents of mixed-race children. These multiracialists are, for reasons I will explain in chapters 1 and 2, the real backbone behind the multiracial movement.

The issue I will discuss in this book may also be of interest to whites (not just those in interracial marriages), for it will confront them with some of the issues they may think about when they run across interracial families: the ethicality of such relationships, the status of the offspring of interracial unions, the question of who is and is not black or white, and the uncertainty of whether or not to allow people with partial white ancestry to increase their proximity to whites through a mixed-race classification.

So this book addresses Americans of mixed-race parentage and the multiracialists who wish for mixed-race people to join ranks under the racial rubric of multiracial. But my central target for this book is the group of people I sometimes refer to in shorthand as "mixed-race blacks"—for instance, people of immediate black-white, black-Asian, and black–Native American parentage. Some of what I have to say is particularly relevant to the largest segment of mixed-race blacks—those of black and white parentage. Regarding this group, I address what one woman of such parentage calls the "always painful contradictions" of being black mixed with white.[1]

In addition, this book is written for all black Americans, those 29.9 million who comprise 12 percent of the 250 million citizens in this country. This book should interest the nation's black citizenry (of which I am a member) because officials of the United States Bureau of the Census estimate that at least 75 percent of the black population are ancestrally multiracial.[2] At present, only a small percentage of the black population, those of immediate mixed-race parentage, would be considered mixed race by the multiracialists heading the multiracial movement. But in the future, in the census of 2010 or 2020, that could change.

Finally, in this book I am pushing for an answer to the question historian Joel Williamson raises in the closing pages of *New People: Miscegenation and Mulattoes in the United States* (1980). Williamson says that American blacks, at that time numbering around 22 million, constitute one of the largest communities of blacks outside of Africa and are the richest, probably the most powerful in the world, and are here to stay. "The only question is," he asks, "in what manner shall they stay?"[3] Williamson continues with his prophecy of the year 2000:

> No one can say what the Negro children of 1975 will be as men and women. Nevertheless, it seems probable that they will be much more at ease with both their whiteness and their blackness than their parents have been with theirs. Indeed, the next generation . . . might well be a cultural mutation, a new stage in a long and significant line that has struggled to join black and white comfortably together in America. He and she might well be, in fact, the first

fully evolved, smoothly functioning model of a people who have transcended both an exclusive whiteness and an exclusive blackness and moved into a world in which they accept and value themselves for themselves alone—as new and unique, as, indeed, a new people in the human universe.[4]

These "new people" are the so-called interracial, biracial, multiracial, or mixed-race people I am writing about. But will they be the first fully evolved and smoothly functioning model of a people to transcend an exclusive whiteness and blackness and move into a twenty-first century in which they accept and value themselves as "new people"?

To answer this question I take a South African panorama on the multiracial movement: I draw on the experience of the heterogeneous community of mixed-race people in South Africa, the coloured people. In order to understand the coloured experience in South Africa, for the sake of anticipating the potential results of a multiracial race in the United States, I made research trips to Cape Town in 1994 and 1995. I spent some time at the Institute for Historical Research at the University of the Western Cape looking at the papers of coloured scholar Richard Ernest van der Ross and of coloured theologian and clergyman Allan Boesak, both of whom I interviewed. At the university I also interviewed students, staff, and faculty, both coloured and black, about their views on the multiracial movement in the United States. Among these interviewees were people involved in monoracial and interracial relationships. I also interviewed three men whom I identify throughout the book as "coloured nationalists," people who advocate for not only the continued existence of the coloured people as a community but for a separate coloured nation or homeland in the Cape. I also benefited greatly from my lengthy talk with the Reverend David Botha, a white Afrikaans minister of the Dutch Reformed Mission Church, whose congregation Allan Boesak co-pastored from 1976 to 1985. Thus I interviewed a wide variety of people from the coloured community.

I have drawn a fair amount from the thought of Richard van der Ross. Born in Cape Town in 1921, van der Ross is one of the most important intellectuals to have written on the coloured experience. From 1975 to 1986 he served as the first coloured rector (president) of a South African university—the University of the Western Cape, which was created for coloureds under apartheid legislation in 1960. It was under his presidency that Allan Boesak served from 1976 to 1985 as the student chaplain at the University. In addition, from 1958 to 1965 van der Ross served as the first coloured columnist for the white-owned *Cape Times* and from 1965 to 1966 as editor of the coloured newspaper called the *Cape Herald*. Van der Ross's thought especially assists me in this book because he has visited the United States about a dozen times since his first four-month trip in January 1957, on which occasion he met Ralph Bunche (the first "colored" American nobel laureate).

Similarly, coloured sociologist James (Jimmy) Ellis, who has been a professor at the University of the Western Cape since 1973, proved to be a great help in my comparisons of South Africa and the United States. Ellis's frequent visits to the United States and knowledge of American race relations meant that he, like van der Ross, would be able to speak knowledgeably about the parallels between the coloured experience in South Africa and possible race relations in the twenty-first-century United States if the multiracial movement succeeds.

Given my gratitude to the coloured intellectuals I admire and the coloured acquaintances I made and my respect for them, it should be understood that it is not out of disrespect that I use a lower-cased spelling for "coloured" (which I spell like South Africans spell it). I simply concur with coloured historian Roy du Pre that a lower-cased spelling of "coloured" permits us to avoid the racist implications of the designation as capitalized under apartheid legislation.[5] For that matter, I also use lower-cased spelling for the words "black," "white," and "multiracial" (especially "multiracial," since capitalization would suggest that the group is already a legislated classification). On the other hand, I follow protocol by capitalizing ethnic designations, such as "Xhosa," "Zulu," "Khoi," "Afrikaner," and "English." In fact, I use "Afrikaans"—the Afrikaans people—instead of "Afrikaner," since the latter is associated with apartheid and the debate continues about the usage of this word in this post-apartheid era.

There is another matter I should clear up as well before proceeding to the business of challenging the multiracial movement. That is, although the word "multiracial" is acknowledged by the multiracialists as the "politically correct" term for people who are biracial or interracial, I use that particular term mostly when articulating the views of the multiracialists. In order to avoid the suggestion that I am a multiracialist myself, I have chosen to use the term "mixed race." The term is in the title of several recent books authored by mixed-race people—Naomi Zack's *Race and Mixed Race* (1993) and Carol Camper's *Miscegenation Blues: Voices of Mixed Race Women* (1994), to name just two. One of the mixed-race contributors to the latter book even suggests that "mixed race" is "trendy."[6]

I must say one final word of a qualifying nature, this time about racial designations. I agree that the designations "white," "black," "coloured," and so forth are inaccurate or inconsistent when we speak of the amorphous concept of race.[7] But I do not go as far as sociologist Yehudi Webster in his insistence that people should not even talk about racism until they clarify what is meant by "black people" or "white people."[8] My immediate response to Webster, when I heard him say this on a radio talk show on which both of us appeared, was intended to indicate that I would not be sidetracked by such so-called logical thinking. I gave Webster a definition of black that was good enough for me to get on with the point of the discussion—the multiracial movement—and which is good enough for me to get on with the point of this book. As I defined it that day to Webster, "a black person, to paraphrase Du Bois, is a person who is viewed with jaundiced eye by a white man in a truck with a confederate flag." Du Bois's exact words, equally adequate for this project, were that the black person is "a person who must ride 'Jim Crow' in Georgia."[9] I also concur with Richard van der Ross's definition of a white person, which, although given in 1960, makes the point of identity just as clearly today. Van der Ross wrote, "A fair definition, I would say, is that a White person is a person who can buy a cup of tea in a Cape Town department store without getting his picture in the newspaper for it."[10]

Thus, let me be as clear as I can be about who I am speaking of when I speak of a mixed-race people. In South Africa they are people who in 1960 were not black but still could not get a cup of tea in a Cape Town department store without getting their pictures in the newspaper for doing so. In the United States, mixed-race people are, to give the principal example that concerns this book, people who have a black parent who, in the Georgia of Du Bois's day, would have had to ride Jim Crow, and a white parent who would not have had to ride Jim Crow.

Having made these clarifications, I would like to thank Nicole Waligora, a young, up-and-coming genius of black and white parentage, for reading this book and making invaluable improvements. After her corrections were made, I returned to Cape Town, where the manuscript was read by Richard van der Ross, Jimmy Ellis, Hendrik W. van der Merwe, two of the coloured women I interviewed, and by the young mixed-race American woman from the United States whom I had also interviewed in South Africa. I am solely responsible for whatever inaccuracies remain.

THE NEW COLORED PEOPLE

[INTRODUCTION]

Black people and white people had intermixed in Africa and Europe long before the New World—"America"—was ever "discovered." Thus, black was never purely black, and white was never purely white, and our uses of these racial designations has been merely relative. While race has some relationship to biological makeup, it is primarily a sociopolitical construct, one that was created and has been maintained and modified by the powerful to sustain their group as a privileged caste. In the United States the powerful have done such a thorough job at sewing the idea of race into the social fabric of the nation, that Americans have always treated race as though it were something that defined the very nature of people. Americans have especially treated race as though it defined the essence of black and white people, who generally have been viewed as opposites during the course of their shared history in the New World.

Because black and white people have been viewed as pure opposites, Americans have been confused about the consequence of black and white intermixing (miscegenation). For part of American history, on and off between 1870 and 1920, the term "mulatto" was used to describe people of this particular interracial mixture. In 1920 the category "mulatto" was dropped and "black" was used to cover everyone with any known black ancestry. By including mulattoes under the category of black, it was clear (and has been clear ever since) that "black" and its earlier synonyms no longer denoted a people who were "pure." Rather, it referred to a people who were not white and who had at least "one drop" of black "blood."

The acceptance of the "one drop rule" by black people (the rule that says "one drop" of black blood makes one black) was more than merely a passive internalizing of the system of oppression fashioned by the powerful. Certainly race is a tool of oppression in the hand of the powerful. But, unable to escape from racial labeling, blacks chose to wield race for their liberation by nurturing a sense of common identity and then fashioning unified social and political action. Thus, the ideas of "black pride" and "black power" of the 1960s, logical successors to the New Negro movement that came to wide public attention in the 1920s, brought lighter- and darker-skinned blacks into even closer alliance. Thus, in 1960, when the United States Bureau of the Census commenced the practice of the head of the household defining the race of its members, there was no significant change in the numbers of blacks reported. Even with the coming of the biracial baby boom that started after the last antimiscegenation laws were repealed in 1967, the result was an increase in the number of blacks in the United States.

When the 1970s came, rather than the country moving away from racial categorization, where people are judged by the content of their character rather than by the color of their skin, the sociopolitical construct of race became even more interwoven into the societal fabric. Some scholars blame this on the establishment of a federal document called Statistical Directive No. 15. Issued by the Office of Management and Budget (OMB), Directive No. 15 provides standard classifications for recording, collecting, and presenting data on race and ethnicity at the federal level, so that data acquired by one agency can be used by other agencies for their particular purposes. The current consequence of Directive No. 15 is that there exists a tension between racial identification as requisite for the legal protection of minorities and, on the other hand, racial identification as a traditional tool that whites have used to maintain power by relegating certain races to particular levels of the social ladder.

The history of Directive No. 15 began in 1973 when Caspar Weinberger, then the Secretary of Health, Education, and Welfare, asked the Federal Interagency Committee on Education (FICE) to develop standards for classifying race and ethnicity. The ad hoc committee started its work in 1974, and in 1977 the OMB adopted the FICE recommendations almost verbatim. From that point on there would be, according to Statistical Directive No. 15, four racial groups recognized by the United States government— White, Black, Asian and Pacific Islander, and American Indian and Alaskan Native. The instructions of Directive No. 15 to the parents of those biracial baby boomers of the late 1960s and beyond is that they are to select the racial category that most closely reflects the way their community sees them: "The category which most closely reflects the individual's recognition in his community should be used for purposes of reporting on persons who are of mixed racial and/or ethnic origins."

The census data gathered in compliance with Directive No. 15 are for the purposes of tracking demographic shifts in the country. For instance, we can see that between 1980 and 1990 the black population increased 13 percent, from 26.5 million people to 29.9 million. The white population increased 6 percent, up to 199.7 million people, making up 80.3 percent of the entire population. In addition to tracking demographic shifts of this kind, the census permits the government to be able to measure the racial makeup of the country in order to develop the appropriate public policies and federal services. For instance, the data have been used to address the requirements of the civil rights laws—establishing and evaluating federal affirmative action plans and desegregation plans in schools, and evaluating workforce participation and state redistricting plans for the protection of minority voting rights. Even the Center for Control of Diseases uses the categories of Directive No. 15 to do research on whether certain segments of the population are susceptible to certain diseases. Indeed, a great many programs intended to counter historical and systemic discrimination require demographic information about racial and ethnic groups. Thus, a careful counting of the population has become increasingly important over the last several decades, especially due to the demands on dwindling government resources.

As a result of the racial classification system of Directive No. 15 and societal custom that labeled mixed-race blacks as monoracially black, African Americans became the largest minority group in the United States. Because of the laws that more or less protected those that the classification system identified as black, African Americans increasingly became a political presence to be reckoned with. Much of that political clout was harnessed and organized by the black church, which was the spiritual backbone to the cohesiveness of the black community.

Notwithstanding this black cohesiveness and despite the seemingly important legal and programmatic uses of the data on race and ethnicity collected by the Census Bureau, there is some tension between having racial categories that serve the legislative and programmatic needs of the federal government and having categories that reflect the self-perception of American citizens.[1] There is a growing population of Americans who feel Directive No. 15 props up traditional notions of bigotry with regard to "race mixing" and that this is detrimental to the offspring of such interracial unions.[2] These people believe the four racial groups established by the federal government do not permit mixed-race people to have a name that recognizes their mixed racial parentage. The census instructions directing them to select the racial category most closely reflecting the way their "community" sees them may seem rather liberal, but the "community"—whether black or white, segregated or integrated—has traditionally seen mixed-race blacks as monoracially black.

Many of the complainants who want a change in Directive No. 15 are the people of the biracial baby boom that resulted from the doubling of interracial marriages (from 1 percent to 2 percent) and the tripling of interracial births (from 1 percent to 3 percent) between 1970 and 1990. In 1990, the year the multiracial movement especially picked up momentum, the Census Bureau received a substantial number of inquiries from persons of mixed-race background and from parents in interracial marriages, who did not want to identify themselves or their children monoracially. Whereas in 1970 only 720,000 people (less than one-half of 1 percent of the population) indicated some other category on the census, in 1990 ten million people (about 4 percent of the entire population) checked the official "other" category, which first appeared that year. Of the 8 million write-ins under the "other" category, 253,000 people gave such identifications as "multiracial" or "interracial" or specifically as "black-white" or "Asian-white," and so forth.[3] In most cases the Census Bureau simply reassigned these individuals (those who had specified their biracial makeup) under monoracial categories. For instance, while people who wrote "multiracial" or "biracial" were left in the "other" race classification, those who wrote "white-black" were classified as white and those who wrote "black-white" were classified as black.[4] Those who wrote "creole" on the 1990 census were also classified as black.

Since 1990 the growth in the number of interracial marriages and births has continued to increase, as has the growth in the number of advocacy groups for interracial couples and mixed-race people. Today, most states have support groups for interracial families and mixed-race individuals, and there are two national magazines that address the blessings and curses of interracial living. These advocacy groups and magazines have helped organize the frustrations of interracial parents and mixed-race people into the multiracial movement, which seeks an appropriate and recognized racial identity for mixed-race people.

We should understand that mixed-race people are not the only ones who view themselves different from what the government calls them, and that the multiracialists are not the only ones trying to convince the OMB to modify the racial categories on Directive No. 15. For instance, the Census Bureau and the OMB have received suggestions that the term "African American" be substituted for "Black," that "Native American" be substituted for "American Indian,"[5] and that "European American"[6] be substituted for "White." A number of organizations representing Arab Americans wish to see their constituency removed from the "white" category.

Louis Massery, an Arab American attorney from Boston who testified before the OMB as a representative of the Arab Anti-Discrimination Committee, said Arabs and other Middle Easterners who are American citizens are the only groups from the Third World who do not hold protected status as minorities. Massery also argued that classifying Arab Americans as if they were a white European ethnic group is absurd, since the Arab world neither lies in Europe nor traces its ancestry to Europe.[7] Hamzi Moghrabi, representing the Colorado branch of the Arab Anti-Discrimination Committee, told the OMB that by identifying Arab Americans as white they are denied the benefits of a minority group. He said Arabs are a people whose history and culture are ridiculed by whites in the nation's classrooms and whose well-being is threatened by the bigotry and hate crimes of whites.[8]

A result of the effort of some Arabs not to be classified as white is that there are now some white groups that would like to eliminate the "white" classification. They seek this change because the category of white has, since the 1970 census, included North Africans and Southwest Asians along with European Americans. Perhaps this suggests a possible change for the better in white self-perception, such as we see among some white South Africans who went by the name "Afrikaner" during the era of white minority rule but who now prefer to be called "Afrikaans people." This was an appellation coined only after the downfall of apartheid, like the term "European American" was coined after the official end of segregation. However, whites may also prefer "European-American" to further protect white "purity" and privilege.

The attempt to protect white purity and privilege seems to be favored by those whites who feel that the term "white" is no longer synonymous with "European American."[9] For instance, Dale Warner, representing Irish, Scottish, and Welsh groups before the OMB, said his constituency does not want to be classified as white because it includes peoples originating from North Africa and Southwest Asia (the Middle East).[10] Joseph Fallon, who testified similarly before the OMB as a representative of the National European American Society and the Society for German-American Studies, said that "European American" would refer specifically to Americans whose ethnic origins derive from peoples of Europe, such as the English, Germans, Irish, Italians, and

Polish.[11] Fallon is also concerned that European Americans are being labeled by false portrayals. For instance, he told the OMB that when Hispanics are victims of hate crimes the Federal Bureau of Investigation (FBI) lists them as Hispanic, but when they are the perpetrators of hate crimes the FBI lists them as white. He complains that this classification hides the "true identities" of the perpetrators of hate crimes and inflates the criminal statistics against European Americans in a way that is "libelous" to their race.[12]

Gerhard Holford, co-moderator of the Conference of Americans of Germanic Heritage, also wants the category of white eliminated because of the political and social ideology the term carries. First, Holford argues that few of the people categorized by the government as white really consider their culture, language, or history to be "white culture," "white language," or "white history." "If anything," he remarks, "the notion of whiteness is a political idea or a state of mind." To this Holford adds that from time to time the idea of whiteness has been a factor in both pro-white and anti-white political movements, but due to changes in political ideas and states of mind the number of people identifying themselves as white has decreased.[13] Among these changed political ideas and states of mind, according to Holford, is the idea of white supremacy. Many European Americans reject the term "white," he argues, because of the stereotype that suggests that any people calling themselves by that name are white supremacists. For similar reasons, Holford suggests that the Conference of Americans of Germanic Heritage advocates omitting references to a "majority race" in Directive No. 15, in that such a term suggests that the white race is more dominant, superior, and more powerful than the other races that are not white.[14]

Another representative of this view, Donald Freiberg, a San Jose attorney, submitted a written testimony to the OMB, which said of the term "European American" what blacks have long said about the term "African American": "It enriches us with a history, culture, and continent of origin. Other groups choose a continental label because they wish to embody more than a mere color. European Americans wish to do the same, yet we are constantly slapped with a bland, lifeless color 'white' that we did not choose." Freiberg also said that the term "European American" would permit whites to distance themselves from the likes of David Duke, the Louisiana politician who uses the term "white" in a way that implies white supremacy.[15]

These efforts at racial name changes are part of the context in which the multiracial movement is situated. While certain groups feel they want an identity more fitting than the "white" label, the multiracialists now feel that people of mixed racial ancestry deserve a fitting appellation since they are the country's least recognized people in a period when racial and ethnic pride and cultural awareness are at an all-time high.[16]

Aware of the complaints of the various groups of Americans who wish to have a federal name change, Thomas Sawyer, chair of the House subcommittee that addressed the census, said that the problem with the categories of Directive No. 15 is that they have remained constant at a time when the country is changing in significant ways.[17] Indeed, today's reality of greater interaction between the existing racial categories suggests to many people a need for modification, not to mention that those interacting across racial lines and those offspring who are the product of that interaction are developing a new self-perception.

The increased interaction across racial lines and the new self-perception that mixed-race people have of themselves descended on most Americans so quickly that we have not had much time to think about the possible consequences. Indeed, views have changed so rapidly that it was just a few years ago, in 1991, that sociologist F. James Davis concluded that the "one-drop rule" was here to stay for the foreseeable future. Davis raised a question about whether or not a change in the "one-drop rule" might not result in the adoption of one of the world's other status rules for mixed-race people (such as in South Africa). He answered that the potential for the establishment of a "middle-minority position" that has occurred in other parts of the world, even in the early history of this country, "seems to be nil."[18] Davis summarizes, "We can only conclude that none of the world's known alternatives to the American definition of who is black now seems at all likely to be given serious consideration in the United States."[19] Perhaps in 1991 most Americans would have come to the same conclusion as Davis, but today a movement is spreading among the community of interracial parents and their mixed-race offspring whose goal is to see "multiracial" established as a new racial classification on the United States census for the year 2000. If this does not happen, then efforts will likely be made to reach this goal in 2010.

Some may be surprised by the rapid rise of the multiracial movement. After all, the Census Bureau has been trying to accommodate those who wish to identify themselves in myriad ways by allowing them to check the category "other" and write in a racial identification not included in the standard classifications. Furthermore, many of us know mixed-race people who prefer the "other" category—people like Roy Harrison, founder of a California support and advocacy group called Mixed Race People of Color. Harrison testified at the OMB hearings that he prefers "other" because it allows him to be more specific.[20] Nonetheless, for the multiracialists the "other" category is unsatisfactory in that it signifies a nonidentity that relegates mixed-race people to nonpersonhood. In addition, some of the multiracialists do not like the fact that the Bureau recategorizes those "others" into the four principal monoracial categories. This reclassification becomes necessary because "other" is used in the census but not in those administrative records that need to know who those "others" are. Since the figures gathered by the census are used to enforce certain legislation that depends on precise numbers, the Bureau cannot leave nearly 10 million "others" outside the standard racial categories.

The multiracialists who are challenging the one-drop rule prefer the word "multiracial" over "biracial" because there are many instances where a person's ancestry includes more than two racial or ethnic groups. Some prefer "colored," a name that for a time referred only to mulattoes (especially lighter ones) but later was used to identify all blacks. As I will discuss in chapter 1, some South African coloureds would like mixed-race Americans to join them in using the name "coloured" because of the similarity they see between mixed-race Americans and themselves as mixed-race South Africans.

The coloured people of South Africa, whose experience forms an important part of this book, are principally of black (African) and white ancestry, but also of black-Asian, white-Asian, and black-coloured ancestry. Until 1950, birth certificates referred to coloureds as "mixed," while after 1950 the term "coloured" was required by law, thus grouping together people who are heterogeneous in terms of ethnicity, culture, color, class, and so forth.[21] Most of the coloured people can trace some ancestry to the indigenous peoples of the Cape called the Khoikhoi (herdsmen whom whites called Hottentots) and the Khoisan (hunters whom whites called Bushmen). The Khoi peoples settled in the Cape hundreds of years before the Dutch came in 1652, at which time the Khoi were partly wiped out and the remaining peoples were subordinated. To solve their labor problems, Dutch settlers brought in Malay and Indian slaves from Asia, and some slaves from other parts of Africa. Because of a shortage of white women, the settlers intermixed and sometimes intermarried with subordinate groups. From the intermixture of these groups—Dutch, French, British, Khoi, Malay, and Indian—came the coloured people. During the early nineteenth century, many among this group fled the Cape to escape the intensifying racism of the whites, and they met up and intermixed with Khoikhoi and Khoisan tribes that had also fled. This group became the Griqua nation, which settled beyond the northwest and later the northeast borders of the Cape colony. When whites discovered diamonds in Griqua territory in 1867, the Griqua were dispossessed of their land and later became part of the coloured group under apartheid. All of the coloured subcultures began to intermingle and intermarry after 1949, since the Prohibition of Mixed Marriages Act of 1949 forbade interracial marriage between the racial groups (whites, blacks, coloureds, and Asians) and the Immorality Act of 1950 forbade sex across racial lines.

Because the mixed-race people of the United States share some history with the coloureds of South Africa, as the multiracialists themselves have argued in order to legitimize their movement, Richard van der Ross suggests a definition for "coloured" that sounds fitting as a definition for the American multiracial as well:

> There exists in South Africa a number of persons who vary in number according to [the] basis by which they are calculated. They are the product of intermixture between people from various racial groups from Europe, Africa and the East, in proportions varying from person to person. As a result of this varying mixture, these people also vary from one another just as the racial groups from which they originate, vary. At the same time a section of this total group has emerged having what appear to be common physical characteristics. These people . . . have for many years been subjected to a process of economic and political discrimination, and have suffered economically and politically as a minority group which was also a socially marginal group. The result of this marginality was that there was on the one hand a striving towards the rights and privileges of the more privileged section of society, and on the other hand—where the numbers were overwhelming—these people have been influenced by the less privileged section of society. . . . In the course of time, too, they have acquired a legal identity insofar as it was possible for the law to identify them using vague and often subjective criteria of descent, appearance and association. Insofar as the law succeeds in defining and identifying them, it deals with them as members of a group. These people are known as "the Coloured people."[22]

The premise of this book is that the coloured people of South Africa and the proposed category of "multiracial" people of the United States are parallel groups that allow for a cross-cultural analysis. Historian George Fredrickson, who has done comparative studies of race in the United States and South Africa, says that what makes a comparison between these two countries possible are the "broad similarities" in white attitudes, ideologies, and policies, and the fact that both countries were colonized by northwest European Protestants.[23] In other words, the United States is also a "pigmentocracy," to use a South African term long favored by Allan Boesak.[24] This "pigmentocracy," according to Boesak, reached an all-time low during the Reagan era, when racism received presidential validation through a denial of its existence. Like the Afrikaner-dominated Nationalist Party that took control of the South African government in 1948, having run on the platform of "apartheid" or "separate development," the United States has also had a long history of political segregationism.

On the other hand, there is also a major historical difference between the United States and South Africa. South Africa was not involved in a civil rights movement, because there was no Bill of Rights to appeal to and no Supreme Court to underwrite the call for freedom, justice, and equality. Unlike the United States, then, South Africa went through a true struggle for liberation.[25] The result was that on November 17, 1993, President F. W. de Klerk and African National Congress (ANC) leader Nelson Mandela ratified an interim constitution that made blacks, who comprise three-fourths of the South African population, citizens for the first time. This was certified in the final version of the constitution, which was completed in May 1996. Even though there are some differences between the histories of the United States and South Africa, with regard to the multiracial movement the phenomenon of miscegenation and the problem of the status of mixed-race people lend themselves to comparison because race mixture in the United States and South Africa first occurred under similar social and political conditions. Moreover, in both societies a general strategy for managing racial mixture developed early in their history and became deeply rooted in the form of the color line that separated whites from those of mixed origin.[26]

Several scholars, on the other hand, have preferred to compare the coloured people to black Americans, as George Fredrickson has done.[27] Though Fredrickson does not address the multiracial movement because it comes after his research had been conducted, he could defend his position by making the simple point that the coloured people, like black Americans, are a product of the mixing of different racial types over hundreds of years, while the multiracials in the United States are people of an immediate mixture of the different racial groups enumerated on Directive No. 15.

Sociologist Everett Stonequist also prefers this comparison because he believes black Americans, like coloured South Africans (as described above by van der Ross), have no traditional culture of their own making. He claims that American slavery completely uprooted blacks from their antecedant African cultures.[28] But I disagree. Black Americans may be somewhat culturally marginal in the sense that Stonequist suggests, that is, they may be caught between devotion to white cultural forms and black cultural substance. But black Americans are not racially marginal like the coloured people, who, because of apartheid legislation, are caught between the opposing white and black racial groups.

Thus there is a parallel between the mixed-race people in the United States and the coloured people in South Africa. If some of the multiracialists get their way, the multiracial classification they seek could be the beginning of a global pan-colouredism, where "brown" (mixed-race) peoples take their place along white and black peoples of the world. Because the multiracial movement may have national and global significance, it may surprise us that we did not see it coming long before now. But some movements seem to work that way: we do not see them coming, but when they are here we can see that they were coming all along. This multiracial movement, then, was no sudden development, even though sociologist F. James Davis had not yet seen it coming only a few years earlier in 1991.

At any rate, it is here, and we should understand it as fully as possible. I will present in chapter 1, as sympathetically as I can, the multiracialists' argument for a new multiracial classification. This then becomes the data against which we will weigh the challenges to the movement in chapters 2 and 3. Chapter 2 provides a direct challenge to the ideas of chapter 1, mostly using the voices of people inside and outside the multiracial movement who are familiar with the debate. In chapter 3, I address the social and political experience of marginality that the coloured people in South Africa know well, in order to point out the potential negative social and political consequences of the United States pursuing such a system of racial classification. In chapter 4, I present my conclusion, based on the information of the previous three chapters. I suggest how mixed-race people should identify in a way that is best for themselves, best for black people, and best for the country.

[ONE]

The Rainbow People
of God

In 1993 Richard van der Ross, the South African coloured scholar, raised the question of whether or not coloured people exist, and if they do exist, then how that existence can be known. His answer was that they do exist and that this can be known because they can be seen.[1] When I met van der Ross in Cape Town the following year, he said something similar: that whether or not people identify individuals such as himself as coloured, the existence of coloured people cannot be denied. "They are recognizable," he added, "if not all that definable." Coloured people are a community, concluded van der Ross, for everyone knows them when they see them, and they know so themselves. A young coloured woman of Xhosa, German, and English ancestry concurred with van der Ross when she told me that it was evident that she was coloured because she looked coloured. "I just look that way," she stated. Because coloureds exist as readily "recognizable" and "seen" people, van der Ross also said that they should assert themselves and claim their rights, not because they are allies of some big brother but because they are full-fledged South Africans.[2]

I have pointed this out because we can ask the same question about mixed-race people in America: Do they exist? The answer is yes—not so much because they can be seen (as of yet) but because they can be defined. Sometimes they look monoracial, taking after only one of their interracial parents. But at other times they can be seen as well, as told by Teja Arboleda in a poem he submitted for the records when he testified before the Office of Management and Budget (OMB). Arboleda tells us that his mother's father is Danish and his mother's mother is German, while his father's father is Filipino and Chinese and his father's mother is African American and Native American. This is why he, born in New York and raised in Germany and Japan, is called by so many people "Ethnic Man." Being "not quite black as black" and "not quite white as white," he writes, he can "leap from race to race in a single bound." He says jokingly, "I am not mixed up, just mixed."[3] Arboleda finishes his poem with a postscript that tells us to look at his face, and he asks if we can honestly say "without disgrace" that he is of "pure race." He concludes with the cadence, "I rest my case."[4] As the coloured woman of Xhosa, German, and English ancestry said of herself in terms of her coloured look, so Arboleda essentially says of himself in terms of his mixed-race look: "I just look that way."

Mixed-race people therefore exist in the United States, and the multiracialists may rest their case! But how did they come to exist so prominently and to the degree that they could defy sociologist F. James Davis's decree only a few years earlier that the one-drop rule would not be seriously challenged in the near future?[5] In this chapter I will answer that question. I will detail the emergence of the multiracial movement from the late 1970s to now, when it is lobbying for a multiracial classification to be added to the United States census. I will also detail the diverse concerns and goals of those involved in the movement, first articulated in the late 1970s. During this time interracial couples began expressing their dismay about school forms that imposed the one-drop rule on their children by disallowing complete recognition of their multiracial background. They also wanted to make sure their children would not be hurt because the parents chose to marry interracially.[6] It was during this period and with these concerns that numerous local and national multiracialist advocacy groups were founded.

Before I introduce some of the multiracialist advocacy groups that began emerging in the late 1970s, the reader should know that their precursors predated them by as much as three-quarters of a century. The earliest support group for blacks in interracial marriages, some of whom were soldiers returning to the United States with foreign wives or "war brides," was the Manassa Society. This group was organized in Milwaukee in 1890 and later spread to Chicago. In New York a group called the Penguin Club was organized in 1936. More groups emerged following World War Two, including a club started in Washington, D.C., in 1947 called the Club Internationale. By 1950 the membership of this latter club included fourteen couples—ten black ex-servicemen with war brides, two white men with black wives, one Filipino with a black wife, and an Indian Hindu with a Moslem wife. In subsequent years a similar club was started in Los Angeles, called Club Miscegenation. In 1950 this club had a membership of twenty-three couples, thirteen of whom had married during the war years and more than half of whom had children. Detroit had a club called the Club of Tomorrow, which in 1950 had a half-dozen interracially married members.[7]

Club Miscegenation and the Club of Tomorrow existed to help interracial parents deal with concerns over raising biracial children. One member (a black man married to a white woman), speaking at a club meeting in November 1950, articulated the very concerns that are fueling multiracialist advocacy groups today: "We've got to teach our children Negro history and white history and Mexican history. They've got to be proud of every part of their background." Another black man (married to a Mexican woman) made a remark in that same meeting which is just as likely to be heard today from multiracialists. He said, "We teach our children they are members of the human race. We try to make them realize all people are one—white, black or brown."[8]

As we will see, these are the very same concerns interracial parents express today in their advocacy groups. What has changed is that several of today's groups are national in scope and the number and diversity of the organizations has increased. The most prominent of these contemporary advocacy groups are the American Association of Multi-Ethnic Americans (AMEA) and Project

RACE (Reclassify All Children Equally). Both of these are pressing the federal government to add a multiracial classification to the United States census through a modification of Directive No. 15.

The AMEA, the only national confederation of local multiracial and multiethnic groups, was founded in November 1988 by representatives of local multiracial and multiethnic advocacy groups. These groups began forming in the late 1970s and early 1980s to address the identification of their multiracial children in the public schools. The founding president of the organization was Carlos Fernandez, a San Francisco attorney who is himself half Mexican and half white. Project RACE, founded in the fall of 1991, advocates nationwide for multiracial children and adults through education, community awareness, and legislation. The organization attempts to bring about the day when a multiracial classification is required on all state and federal forms that request racial identification. The founder and executive director of Project RACE is Susan Graham, a white woman married to Gordon Graham, the black television anchorman for Headline News on the Cable News Network (CNN) station.[9]

There are uncountable other organizations with the same goals as the AMEA and Project RACE which work at the local and national level, a few of which I will mention as a means of illustrating the diversity and tenacity of the multiracial movement. One of these organizations is I-Pride (Interracial/International Pride) of Berkeley, California, a founding chapter of the AMEA. The organization began in Berkeley in February 1979 when parents, teachers, and social workers met to discuss and challenge the monoracial classification system in the city's public schools, which have a high proportion of multiracial and multiethnic students. Today the organization's goal is to educate both the immediate community and the entire American citizenry about multiracial identity and interculturalism and to fight racism aimed at multiracials. The organization sponsors forums, support groups, a biracial adults group, and an interracial couples group. It also publishes a newsletter to inform its members of current matters related to the multiracial and multiethnic community.

A Place For Us is a national advocacy group founded by inter-racial couple Steve (who is white) and Ruth (who is black) White. The Whites founded the group after Steve's minister refused to marry them. Disgusted by such blatant racism, the Whites, after they were married elsewhere, decided to become certified Christian counselors. In 1988 they were ordained as nondenominational ministers, and since then their ministerial mission has been to break down the barriers of racism so that people may be judged by their character rather than color. When their mission is accomplished, they say, interracial couples and their multiracial children will be accepted unconditionally by society. Until then, their tasks include sponsoring workshops, social events, and rap sessions, counseling, and networking with other multicultural ministries and support organizations across the country. Their goal is to help monoracial families understand and accept people of all nationalities, cultures, and ethnicities. Their motto is "Unity Without Compromise," and they sell T-shirts and buttons proclaiming "We're Color Blind."

Another group with a Christian core to its mission is the Brick by Brick Church, led by pastor Kenneth Simpson in Lexington, Kentucky. Simpson, of mixed black and white parentage, founded the church in order to meet the spiritual and social needs of multiracial people. The membership comprises interracial couples and their children, white parents of adopted black and biracial children, and other black and white families and individuals who wish to share in the church's interracial ministry. One of the church's activities is its sponsorship of a social group called Shades, a group that seeks to transcend society's color lines by bringing people of all "shades" together.[10] The Brick by Brick ministry is similar to the Interracial Family Alliance of Augusta (Georgia), a social outreach group started at St. Alban's Episcopal Church in May 1988.

Unlike any of the above organizations is the Interracial Lifestyle Connection, located in Fort Smith, Arizona. This group is a correspondence club for interracial families and people who wish to write to one another across racial boundaries. The goal is for people to develop friendships and meet one another for interracial dating.

Political activism is the major factor that distinguishes the contemporary multiracialist groups from the groups that existed in the earlier part of the century. Both the AMEA and Project RACE have done what the members of the Manassa Society, Penguin Club, Club Internationale, Club Miscegenation, and the Club of Tomorrow would never have dreamed of doing: in 1993 and 1994 they testified before federal legislative bodies in the hope of having mixed-race people recognized in the United States census. In 1993 they testified before the subcommittee on the census in the House of Representatives, which eventually made a recommendation to the OMB on the needed modifications in Directive No. 15. In 1994 they testified before the OMB itself, since it is responsible for any modifications in the racial categories of the directive.

The aim of the "census movement" of the multiracialists is to convince the federal government to identify mixed-race people correctly as "multiracial" rather than forcing them into choosing monoracial categories. By counting multiracial people, the multiracialists say, the government will put an end to the historical invisibility of multiracial people in this country. Specifically, the AMEA and Project RACE want the racial classifications of Directive No. 15 to add the category "multiracial," which Project RACE wants defined as "a person whose parents have origins in two or more of the above [existent] racial and ethnic categories."[11]

Carlos Fernandez told the House subcommittee on the census that failure to recognize and count multiracial people (preferably in the way that the multiracialists outlined) prevents the government and other agencies from discovering and assessing the needs of this population of people, needs that may require legislative or judicial action "if congress deems such to be appropriate."[12] However, that legislative or programmatic actions may be required of the federal government specifically to protect multiracial people does not preclude the multiracial classification from being decompounded and dispersed into the four traditional racial categories around which current laws are built. According to the AMEA and Project RACE, following the multiracial category on the census form could be a list of the existing categories on which multiracial people could check off their particular racial combination. Thus, for the opponents of the census movement who worry that the multiracial category would dilute the count of minority groups and diminish the benefits going to these groups, Fernandez gave the House subcommittee on the census a ready response: "Since many multiracial people have traditionally been discriminated against as if they were monoracial, their continued inclusion in at least some of these programs would seem justifiable."[13] Sociologist Reginald Daniel, a multiracialist of black and white parentage, also feels that a breakdown of the multiracial classification into the traditional racial categories would not only be justifiable but necessary: "We must devise a means of statistically enumerating individuals who identify themselves as multiracial in a manner that does not negatively affect the measuring of African American demographics, potentially undermining already besieged policies designed to redress the continuing effects of past racial inequities. Otherwise, we may very well reverse even further those gains achieved by the civil rights movement that now makes the recognition of multiracial identity a possibility."[14] Sally Katzen, the administrator of the OMB, responded that a breakdown of a multiracial classification was a possibility, so that "multiracial" would be a basic category with subcategories that could be dispersed into the monoracial categories.[15]

Besides these attempts by the AMEA and Project RACE to work out the practical matters of a multiracial classification so the government's statistical needs can be met, the directors of these organizations have spoken fervently about the needs of their constituency. Carlos Fernandez told the House subcommittee on the census that the government had no business forcing multiracial people to select a monoracial classification and thereby to favor one parent over the other when multiracial people should have the right to respect each of their parents equally. With particular regard to multiracial youth, Fernandez said: "Such a requirement offends personal dignity and interferes in a negative way with the development of self-esteem of multiracial/ethnic students."[16] Susan Graham made a similar comment when she took her House testimony before the American public on a radio talk show in August 1994. "Self-esteem is really the basis for this entire movement," she remarked. "If a multiracial child has to walk out of the door in the morning and deny that his mother is his mother or his father is his father, then that's obviously going to affect their self-esteem. And we don't think that's a good choice for a child to have to make."[17] Graham has also pointed out that the name changes that black Americans have gone through over the centuries are evidence of the importance of an appropriate identification for esteem purposes—even for multiracial children.[18]

This basic tenet of the multiracial movement, faithfully held to by interracial parents such as Graham, has been confirmed at the grassroots level by mixed-race people themselves. A biracial man named Phil Vernon believes that having to choose one racial heritage over another is not a good choice for an adult, let alone a child, in that it evokes feelings of incongruity and disloyalty. He cannot look to Norway for his complete ancestry without rejecting his black father, Vernon holds, and he cannot look to Africa for his complete ancestry without rejecting his white mother.[19] Roy Harrison, founder of the California support and advocacy group called Mixed Race People of Color, said the same thing in his testimony before the OMB. Harrison commented that in the 1960s his mother felt rebuffed when he defined himself as black rather than as both black and white, and that he personally felt that he had betrayed her after all the years of love she had given him. But in the 1960s, Harrison concluded, he did not feel he had any choice about defining himself as black.[20] These feelings expressed by Vernon and Harrison are quite legitimate and must be expected. As sociologist F. James Davis points out, it is often an affront to the personal dignity of the white parent for multiracial offspring to be forced automatically into a black identity by the one-drop rule. "It is as if the child has only African ancestors," says Davis, "as if the white parent's family and white ancestry do not exist."[21]

Some multiracialists have also seen fit to point out instances of hypocrisy in the one-drop rule. For instance, Lora Pierce complained that on the television show *A Different World*, the character of Dwayne Wayne (played by black actor Kadeem Hardison) dated the character named Whitley (played by mixed-race/black-identified Jasmine Guy), but their relationship was not portrayed as interracial. The hypocrisy, Pierce points out, is that if a white male were to date Whitley on the show it would have been treated as an interracial relationship, even though the same actress is not only part black but part white.[22]

Susan Graham decided that she would succumb neither to the insult nor to the hypocrisy of the one-drop rule and does not want her multiracial children to adhere to it. When she testified before the House subcommittee on the census, she told a story about receiving the 1990 census form and feeling confused about how to identify her children. She called the Census Bureau, she said, which instructed her to check the race of the mother, since the mother of a child (and not always the father) is always known. Around the same time, when enrolling her son in a Georgia kindergarten, she left the race selection box blank because there were only monoracial categories. In this instance a teacher "eyeballed" her child and officially labeled him black. "Ironically," Graham concluded, "my child has been white on the United States Census, black at school, and multiracial at home, all at the same time."[23] Graham also pointed out the fact that some states identify multiracial children by the race of the mother (as the Census Bureau instructed her to do), while other states go by the race of the father, so that without the guidance of the federal government there would continue to be confusion at the state level about the procedure for identifying multiracial children.

It was Graham's objection to this confusion and the negative impact she felt it had on her own children as well as on others that led her to found Project RACE and eventually to testify before the House subcommittee on the census: "Whether I like it or not, I realize that self-esteem is directly tied to accurate racial identity. More and more parents all over our country are instilling new pride in our multiracial children. Can we say we have succeeded if our children leave home only to be denied an equal place in our society?"[24] Senator William Keating supported this position in his brief remarks before the OMB. He said that by having a multiracial category people can feel that their family is a unit and recognized as such by society.[25] Within the educational arena, the Massachusetts Parent Teacher Student Association (Massachusetts PTA), which has a membership of 15,000, told the OMB that they endorse the use of a multiracial category so that students do not have to deny one parent.[26]

Mark Mathabane, a black South African novelist, and his white American wife are among the interracial parents who are instilling new pride in their multiracial children. Mathabane said to his firstborn daughter: "Your father is black. . . . And your mother is white. You unite the best in both of us. You're a testament to our belief in the oneness of humankind. Never allow society to force you to choose between one or the other. You're both, you're beautiful and be proud."[27] Being proud of being "both" is also what Graham has taught her children, who are now legally "multiracial" in Georgia due to the legislation Project RACE helped sponsor in that state. In fact, Graham had her proud eight-year-old son Ryan tell the House subcommittee on the census just how happy he was to be multiracial and how sorry he was for children whose states do not yet permit them to be identified as such. Ryan said, "I feel great because I am multiracial. . . . I like being multiracial and I feel good about it. . . . I think we need multiracial on forms for all kids like me and my little sister now because I think it's the right thing to do."[28]

The old school form that Susan Graham had to fill out for her son Ryan did not even have an "other" category. But even if it had, most sympathizers of the multiracial movement understand why that particular category is offensive to many mixed-race people. Jan Haley, president of the Colorado Congress of Parents and Teachers (Colorado PTA), said that their membership of 40,000 feels that "other" implies "not identifiable."[29] George Dailey, former coordinator of the elementary and secondary education program for the

Census Bureau, argued in his testimony before the OMB that "other" fails to be a celebration of the diversity of America's citizenry because it makes people feel they are "second class."[30] He remarked of the category, "It's not about including someone, it's about excluding someone."[31]

With the arguments made by Susan Graham and her son Ryan, by Jan Haley, George Dailey, and other previously mentioned multiracialists, Project RACE was able to help legislators in Ohio, Illinois, and Georgia pass laws mandating that all forms in the primary and secondary schools carry the category "multiracial." For instance, in Georgia, as of July 1, 1994, every school form and employment application in every state agency must carry the multiracial category. The Georgia legislation, according to Senate Bill 149, still allows for some dispersal of the state's multiracial population into the existing racial categories when those data are needed. The bill reads as follows:

> In any instance in which it is required that racial data collected by a state agency be reported to a federal agency, the computation of all persons designated on state forms or other documents as multiracial shall be reported by such state agency as multiracial. However, if any such federal agency deems the multiracial designation unacceptable, then the reporting state agency shall, upon resubmission of such data, redesignate the multiracial population by allocating a percentage of the number of persons comprising such population to each federally acceptable racial or ethnic classification.[32]

Similar legislation sponsored by Project RACE has been introduced in Michigan and New York, and without the assistance of Project RACE a similar law has already been passed in Wyoming. By whatever means, the goal of Project RACE is to see every state enact legislation mandating a multiracial category and to see "multiracial" become an accepted classification on the 2000 census. In addition, Project RACE announced in the fall of 1994 that they are considering filing class-action complaints with the Office of Civil Rights for people who feel that they or their children have been hurt by past or present methods of racial classification.[33] With this kind of momentum and support behind them, specifically with parents, educators, legislators, and the myriad multiracialist groups working to make the term "multiracial" a positive identification, increasing numbers of interracial parents throughout the country have been instilling in their children pride in being multiracial. Thus, the idea of having multiracial people check the appropriate combination of monoracial boxes on the United States census without being able to identify themselves first as multiracial is not satisfactory to Graham.[34] "I object to any format that does not include the term 'multiracial,'" Graham said adamantly to the House subcommittee on the census.[35] "Parents, school districts, state legislatures and organizations are showing us what they want. They want an accurate category for multiracial children, not 'mixed,' not 'other,' but 'multiracial.'"[36] Graham also wrote a poem to this effect, which she published in *New People* magazine. Titled "I'm Not an 'Other,'" Graham ends the last stanza with the couplet: "And if you cannot check one box/don't check two."[37]

Graham also argued before the House subcommittee that the multiracial category is no less valid than the other census categories, in part because all multiracial people feel a kinship and historical bond. She pointed to the support groups for multiracial people and interracial families that have emerged in most states, in major cities, and on college campuses, groups she said were formed because multiracial people share similar historical, cultural, and social characteristics.[38] Fernandez similarly argued before the census subcommittee that he considers multiracial and multiethnic people to be a "community" that deserves recognition and respect like any other community.[39] Cynthia Chamble, of Brooklyn, concurs and endearingly refers to the multiracial community as the "Interrace Nation."[40]

Many blacks frown upon the entire multiracial movement and feel that it is simply a lack of self-esteem on the part of white parents to want their mixed-race children to claim a part-white identity alongside their black identity. Blacks feel this way particularly in light of the fact that this racist society will still view mixed-race children as black. But the feelings Graham displays, feelings that prompted her political activism, are natural human responses. We can see this in an instance where the tides are turned. In November 1993, television talk show host Sally Jessy Raphael interviewed several biracial girls who had rejected half of their racial background. Two of the girls had rejected being part black and one rejected being part white. One of the girls, Latoya, who rejected being part black, prompted the same kind of response from her black mother that often comes from white parents whose biracial children choose or are forced into the monoracial black identity. Latoya's mother said it is hard to accept the fact that her daughter has decided that she wants to turn her back on the black race because it makes her feel that Latoya has also turned her back on her as a black woman. Latoya's mother continued, "I'm Mom, first and foremost. . . . Just because you're biracial doesn't mean that you can just automatically divorce me, you know?"[41]

Just as there are many blacks who have not considered the natural feelings of white parents who feel left out of the racial identity of their children, so are there many blacks who will feel appalled at Latoya's behavior. But another thing we should understand about multiracial identity is that Latoya is just as likely to fluctuate in her identity during the course of her lifetime. Let us take twenty-two-year-old Danielle Williams as an example. Danielle's white mother and black father were divorced when she was young, and Danielle was raised by her mother. Even though her mother's white family had disowned her mother for marrying a black man, the irresponsibility of Danielle's father in paying child support and his overall disinterest in the family left Danielle with a negative impression of blacks. On the other hand, Danielle's mother never disappointed her, not to mention that she (like so many other young daughters) wanted to be like and look like her mother. Due to these factors, and especially because she was raised by her mother in a white neighborhood, white identity became Danielle's orientation.[42] Moreover, Danielle's mother was able to shield her from the racism of whites who recognized that

Danielle was not white (or completely so). For instance, on an occasion when Danielle was in second grade or so, her teacher had each student in the class stand and discuss their family's religion, culture, and ethnicity. Danielle stood and said she was (like her mother) Irish-Catholic. The teacher responded by saying in front of the class that Danielle obviously did not know what she was talking about and needed to go home and ask her mother for the truth.[43] Despite such experiences of racial insensitivity, if not outright racism, Danielle could still be raised as white because she was under the careful protection of her mother. But later in her life outside the home, to show how identities may fluctuate for mixed-race people, Danielle made a complete turn and became oriented to a black identity. It happened at a women's college where she was treated badly by white females but nicely by black females. As a result of these dynamics, Danielle started learning more about black history and culture, which had the surprising effect of building some distance between her and her white mother and white friends. In fact, Danielle became frustrated with her mother because she could not understand what it meant to be the object of racism. At the same time, however, there were some blacks who still felt that Danielle was not black enough, perhaps partly because she had difficulty accepting the black separatist ideology and the idea that all whites be loathed. In the end, because of these cross-pressures, Danielle started moving toward a median identity by calling herself a "black/biracial" woman.[44]

There are still many blacks who would feel somewhat disappointed by Danielle's watered-down black identity and appalled by the kind of behavior displayed by Latoya but who would not feel at all concerned if either of them had rejected their white ancestry. Such blacks evidently feel that mixed-race people with one black parent should automatically and unconditionally reject the white side of their lineage because whites have been the traditional oppressors of blacks. But it is this very attitude—a narrow black nationalism that places limitations on what it means to be black—which is partly responsible for the multiracial movement. The multiracialists especially detest this kind of attitude because it overlooks the fact that mixed-race people sometimes have unique experiences that result in their taking an identity other than or in addition to black. The narrow black nationalist attitude overlooks the fact that while some mixed-race people settle on a monoracial identity, others, as a result of being raised in an interracial home, have fluid identities that adjust to the immediate context. Such a person may feel biracial at home, white among accepting white grandparents, and black among black relatives or in an all-white classroom.

Psychologist Christine Iijima Hall, herself of black and Japanese parentage, confirmed, through her interview of thirty mixed-race people of black and Japanese parentage, that mixed-race people have different experiences that go into determining which part of their ancestry they identify with. She points out that many black-Japanese intermarriages took place among black servicemen located in Japan, and that with the black father away on duty sometimes for six to nine months a year, some of the children of these marriages grow up culturally Japanese and almost completely unfamiliar with the African American heritage.[45] For instance, one of Hall's interviewees chose to identify solely as Japanese because she had lived in Japan most of her life.[46] In general, Hall found that black-Japanese biracials who were older, less knowledgeable of black culture, had fewer black friends, and felt accepted by Japanese Americans tended to choose a category other than black. On the other hand, those who were young, had knowledge of black culture, had predominantly black friends, and felt unaccepted by Japanese Americans tended to identify as black.[47]

There are thus very legitimate factors that can explain why a mixed-race person with partial black ancestry might choose an identity other than or in addition to black. One of these reasons is the post-1960s surge in black nationalism, which has continued to this day to define black very narrowly and sometimes even arrogantly. While we can understand how this black nationalism arose and even why it has been necessary in order to push those on the political right toward more compromising positions, we can still see how narrow definitions of black have isolated those mixed-race people whose experiences have not been so narrow. We can also see where insisting that mixed-race people spurn the white half of their family and identity could be difficult. Just as it is said by some coloured South Africans that they could never fully shun the white Afrikaans people who are part of themselves and whose white "blood" flows in their veins, so is it that many mixed-race people of black and white parentage cannot shun whites because they would be condemning half of themselves.

The difficulty people of mixed race have in disowning their partial white ancestry and the people whose white lineage they share is evidenced in South African history. During the black consciousness movement in South Africa, many coloured people were choosing to become black, but in doing so were really cutting against the grain of kinship they had historically shared with whites, particularly the white Afrikaans people. Nonetheless, up until 1990 blacks and coloureds were somewhat unified (as unified as they had ever been). But on February 2, 1990, President F. W. de Klerk depleted some of the impetus behind the black consciousness movement with his famous speech that unbanned the political organizations (including the African National Congress), announced the release of Nelson Mandela from prison, and that in general began the process that led up to the April 1994 elections. This speech took the wind out of the sails of the black consciousness movement because it suggested to coloured people that South Africa's racial climate was changing and that it was the white Afrikaans people (of the National Party) who had begun that process of change. But the Reverend David Botha, a white Afrikaans minister of the then-coloured Dutch Reformed Mission Church who long advocated the integration of white and coloured Afrikaans people, insisted that the coloured people were not simply manipulated politically into rekindling their faith in whites as governmental leaders. He told me that their move away from black consciousness following de Klerk's 1990 speech was the result of the feeling of most coloured people that they are very close to the white Afrikaans people and culture, so close that given the right conditions (such as those set by de Klerk's speech) the coloured people would always choose to side with their white Afrikaans kindred over the blacks. Botha said that he knew all along that when the white Afrikaans people apologized and welcomed them back, the coloured people would rush to those open arms no matter how intense was the history of their pain.

Coloured historian Roy du Pre verifies Botha's views about the way coloured people feel toward their white kindred. Du Pre calls coloureds the "blood brothers" of the white Afrikaans people, blood brothers who were really a part of the "European nation" in South Africa and different from whites only in skin color and so-called mixed blood.[48] Like Botha, du Pre also says that despite the way whites have treated the coloured people, "blood is thicker than water." He explains, "No matter how they fight and squabble, a family stands together in the face of danger or destruction and whites and coloureds are, and have always been, family."[49] The coloured nationalists I spoke with in Cape Town also said that while black South Africans have been trying to get coloured people away from the whites and have accused coloured people of wanting to "play white," the fact is that there is an ancestral, historical, and cultural linkage between the white and coloured Afrikaans communities.

The April 1994 election seems to prove Botha and du Pre right. The backlash of de Klerk's speech was that many coloured people felt that perhaps they were no longer being rejected by the white Afrikaans community and therefore no longer had to join forces with blacks. One significant result is that the coloured vote went to the National Party, thus making the Western Cape the only province to have a white premier (governor). Hence, the political identity of blackness championed by the black-consciousness movement (political because blackness embraced all of the politically disenfranchised people) was not sufficient to sustain unity between blacks and a mixed people who did not truly identify as black. The political identity of black was thus a thin veneer that could be easily scraped away when the political climate changed. With this example perhaps we can see that the insistence that mixed-race blacks have a particular political orientation (Democrat rather than Republican), a particular cultural proclivity (celebrate Kwanzaa instead of the "white" Christmas), or a certain religious affiliation (Baptist rather than Episcopalian) has made "black" rather repressive, if not repulsive, to some mixed-race people.

This selective defining of black has been occurring for a good part of black American history, so there is much for us to rethink in terms of our behavior. For instance, because some blacks persisted in remaining members of historically white denominations, such as the Episcopal church, early scholars of the black church tended to question their black identity. E. Franklin Frazier claimed that members of the new black middle class sought to separate themselves from their black roots by severing relationships with the black Baptist and Methodist churches and joining the white-dominated Episcopal, Presbyterian, and Congregational churches whose cultured worship permitted escape from lower-class black status.[50] Booker T. Washington claimed that if blacks were anything but Baptist or Methodist, then white Christians had been tampering with their minds.[51] Naturally, blacks in non-black denominations resented being viewed as elites who were attempting to elude the black community and the Southern idiosyncrasies of black religion. We can imagine that mixed-race people, too, with their more varied cultural experiences resulting from the transgressing of two racial worlds, are equally resentful when asked to be black in a certain prescribed way.

Some of the pressure on mixed-race blacks to deny part of who they are in favor of accepting only the black side of their ancestry comes from certain Afrocentrists. In an article entitled "Racing to Leave the Race," Afrocentrist Molefi Asante says that such multiracialist magazines as *Interrace* and *New People* give him the impression that self-hatred among some blacks is at an all-time high, insofar as both magazines advocate for the creation of a third race in addition to black and white. In the context of a racist society, continues Asante, white parents want their mixed children to have the same privileges they enjoy, but these children are by tradition considered black. Because in this racist society blackness is viewed as negative, concludes Asante, the multiracialists attempt

to minimize the effects of this negativity by claiming they are neither black nor white, but multiracial.[52] This kind of Afrocentric
criticism is bothersome to the multiracialists.

Edwin Darden, an African American with two multiracial children, also founder of the Interracial Family Circle in Washington,
D.C., feels that one of the problems of Afrocentrism is its assumption that mixed-race blacks are solely black.[53] Similarly, Reginald
Daniel contends that if we are to move away from Eurocentrism
then we should also move completely away from the European
"either-or" worldview that has dominated Western thought for
centuries. This "either-or" perspective should be replaced with a
worldview that incorporates the concept of "both/and," says
Daniel, so that someone such as himself can be both black and
white. The error of Afrocentrism, he concludes, is that it often
wishes to replace Eurocentric half-truths with Afrocentric half-
truths.[54] The replacement of black truths for white truths is
exactly what mixed-race people sometimes get when they hear the
public rhetoric of black nationalist figures. Thus, Francis Wardle,
a white psychologist married to a black woman who is the mother
of their biracial child, expresses the sentiment of many multiracial
people when he criticizes the anti-white speeches of the radical
black Muslim, Khalid Muhammad. Wardle says that by definition
an anti-white speech is anti-multiracial when part of the genetic
and cultural ancestry of the multiracial person is white.[55]

In an article entitled "The Melanin Myth," Rainier Spencer, a
young man of black and white parentage, similarly criticizes Professor Leonard Jeffries for his Afrocentric claims about melanin
making blacks (the so-called sun people) more friendly, coopera-
tive, and superior than the melanin-deficient whites (the so-called
ice people). "What then does this way of thinking imply about
those of us with mixed heritages?" Spencer asks. What it implies,
he answers, is that mixed-race people are inherently defective.
How unfortunate and ironic it is to find a black professor claiming
that race-mixing leads to mongrelization, Spencer chides, since
most black Americans have some degree of European ancestry.
Even if the theory were true, Spencer says, what Jeffries espouses

[33]

would result in a system of judging people not by the content of their character but solely by the color of their skin.[56] After several centuries of racist whites telling blacks they are inferior because of their darkness, Spencer concludes, the last thing we need is a group of racist blacks perpetuating theories that suggest mixed-race blacks are inferior because they are not dark enough.[57]

A lot of this black nationalist rhetoric and black supremacist ideology trickles down into the consciousness of black youths at colleges and universities, the formative years during which such literature is being read (in and out of class) and where ideologues on the lecture circuit propagate their beliefs. The acceptance of these beliefs by black students results in mixed-race blacks being criticized when they reject the racial separatism that is being taught. A college-aged multiracial named Nomathombi Martini said that such black nationalist talk of separatism is bothersome to him because he does not wish to deny either side of his ancestry. Martini feels this way mainly because he does not want to have to choose between his black father and his white mother or between his black and white friends.[58]

However, Martini is not alone in his anxieties. Other mixed-race people, ages twenty-something and up, feel likewise. Lisa Feldstein recalls that she was bothered by the separatist rhetoric of black nationalists in college who insisted she had too many white friends and needed to choose sides between blacks and whites. But skin color and race were never the ultimate test for Lisa in terms of who was or was not faithful to the goals of the black struggle. For after all it was her white (Jewish) father who was involved in the civil rights movement while her black mother was not involved and never had any strong feelings about blacks being unified.[59] Similarly, a multiracial named John Blake confessed that he could not view all whites as evil because his mother is white. Furthermore, as a Christian he could not accept the notion that the white race is inherently evil.[60] Zenobia Kujichagulia said of the stereotypes about whites being evil, that it would have been much easier if her white mother and relatives had been racists. But since they treated her well, she could not simply reject her white ancestry as undeserving of inclusion in her identity.[61] Anne Vespry, a Canadian of black and white parentage, says that what angers her is when people ridicule her for identifying herself as mixed and when they affront half of who she is by belittling all that is white.[62] Nya Patrinos put the latter complaint succinctly when she explained that she could not be militant and loathe whites because she would be abhorring half of herself.[63]

It is such ideology coming from blacks and comparable ideology coming from whites that led one anonymous mixed-race man from Kansas to move toward a median identity, an identity that is free of such troubling aspects of black and white. He says that as a mixed-race person he is too proud to succumb to white or black supremacist ideologies and thereby suffocate himself in either group.[64] Indeed, the black community cannot hold certain people in limbo—uneasy with their interracial marriages or their biracialness—and expect them to wait around for acceptance, an acceptance that is often tenuous. Moreover, mixed-race people do not need to go through life feeling that they are at war with half of themselves or maintaining a double-consciousness that is constantly in a duel with itself. For mixed-race people to embrace their white lineage may be the only way for them to make peace within themselves, and for black people to permit them to do so may be the only way they will ever make peace with the black side of their ancestry.

The real challenge for the black community comes, however, with the fact that many multiracialists are not simply asking blacks to accept mixed-race people as both black and white. What many multiracialists are really asking for, if not demanding, is for mixed-race people to be accepted as a race apart from both the parent races—a race that would be called "multiracial." In this regard, Susan Graham told the House subcommittee on the census that her children have three histories: "They have their father's history, their mother's history, and they have a multiracial history, too, and they do identify with other multiracial people."[65] About her children's multiracial history, Graham said that, like other groups of people, their group is no different in sharing historical characteristics: "The Mestizos of Brazil and Coloureds of South Africa have very specific multiracial histories. . . . During the plantation era, the unions of White plantation owners and Black slave women produced 'mulatto' children in great numbers. Yes, we have shared history." She continued: "Unfortunately, oppression is sometimes the common denominator in shared identity. Historically, oppressed people share close bonds. The reality that multiracial people of numerous racial combinations have been unable to embrace their entire heritage has, indeed, strongly banded them together as a very distinct category."[66]

Some blacks might argue that the oppression that mixed-race people face is not so much due to their being multiracial but because they are not white, and specifically because one of their parents is black and dared to lure someone white into marriage and miscegenation. Perhaps this could account for harassment by racist whites, but part of the history of oppression that mixed-race blacks suffer comes from the hands of blacks themselves. This is an experience that can be especially painful for mixed-race people who identify as black but who look white and are denied recognition and equal treatment in the black community. That such mistreatment comes at the hands of children does not change the fact that this harrassment is black-on-black. In fact, it seems likely that being of mixed-race is more difficult as a child, because children, who have a unidimensional rather than multidimensional view of race, engage in name-calling and other such cruel behaviors.[67] But the fact that adults may tend to be better than children in the treatment of mixed-race people does not necessarily erase the memory of racial abuse as a child. In fact, such memories probably create a sensitivity to the more subtle forms of abuse or bias that mixed-race people face from some blacks when they are adults.

Numerous examples can be provided of mixed-race adults who have not forgotten their racial brutalization by black children when they were young. One mixed-race man, who goes by the pen name of Jamoo, says that based on his experience, blacks are usually more cruel to biracial kids than whites are. He recalled having been called "white boy" by black kids, and he remembered several mixed-race girls who were harassed and beat up. One of these girls was victimized by a black girl who tried to cut off her long hair because she was jealous of her.[68] Emma Baker, a senior mixed-race woman, has never forgotten that as a child blacks called her "half-white bitch" and "half-white monkey."[69] She says, "In my world, you're not quite white and you're not quite black."[70] A young mixed-race woman named Omattee Carrasco similarly recalls being told by black children that she talks like a white girl and even thinks she is white. When she was in college, the adults were more subtle by accusing her of not being black enough.[71] Rosa Emilia Warder, a young woman also of black and white parentage, recalls that as a child black children called her "honkey nigger" and tied her long braided hair to a railing. On the other hand, while her father's black family accepted her white mother, her mother's family never accepted her black father and she has never met any of her white relatives. It is probably due to the experience of marginalization by blacks and whites that Warder sees herself not as black or white, but as both.[72]

Countless books and theories have explained the basis for and the nature of white discrimination against blacks, but far fewer attempts have been made to explain the kind of discrimination blacks practice on their mixed-race kindred. One of the best explanations for this black-on-black harassment is given by Nila Gupta, a mixed-race Canadian of East Indian and French Canadian parentage. Gupta says that black women often accuse mixed-race women of wanting to be white but that such internalized racism, common to all people of color, is merely being projected onto them. That is to say, mixed-race people face the same struggles as black women.[73]

In addition to the discrimination that mixed-race blacks suffer from the internalized racism common to all people of color, mixed-race people have suffered from a history of discrimination resulting from the deeply rooted fear of miscegenation in American society. This fear embraces belief in the degeneracy of mixed offspring and therefore the possibility that society as a whole could become "mongrelized." Indeed, it was only in 1967, on June 12, in the case of *Loving v. Virginia*, that the United States Supreme Court struck down the last antimiscegenation laws that had banned interracial marriage. These laws were still on the books in almost one-third of the states—Virginia, Alabama, Arkansas, Delaware, Florida, Georgia, Kentucky, Louisiana, Mississippi, Missouri, North Carolina, Oklahoma, South Carolina, Tennessee, Texas, and West Virginia. Before this Supreme Court decision, mixed-race people born in these sixteen states were essentially illegitimate. If we look at the racial categories in the U.S. census as a documentation of the social and legal relationships that different groups of citizens represent to the federal government and the nation,[74] then a multiracial classification makes perfect sense, since the federal government did not strike down these antimiscegenation laws earlier.

According to Carlos Fernandez, one of the goals of the AMEA is to eradicate the old fear of miscegenation that prevents Americans from viewing themselves as one people.[75] Indeed, many whites still hold the old views, as an event in Alabama illustrates. At Randolph County High School, in the city of Wedowee, at a school assembly on February 24, 1994, a white principal named Hulond Humphries told students that the annual prom would be canceled if interracial couples attended. When student ReVonda Bowen asked what this meant for her, since her mother is black and her father white, Humphries said his rule was intended to prevent such "mistakes" from recurring. When the school board learned of the remark, it simply suspended the principal with pay, but eventually reinstated him. According to Fernandez, this case proves that the racial classification pursued by the multiracialists is not simply about a new form of racial pride or about baseless social reform, but that multiracial people are discriminated against—in this instance, not because ReVonda Bowen was believed to be black but because she was known to be "mixed."[76]

The principal of this far-south Alabama high school seems to be cut from the same old mold as Elroy Stock, who lives halfway across the country in the far north of Woodbury, Minnesota. Stock has responded to the multiracial movement by arguing that God placed the different human races on different parts of the earth so that the races would be preserved as they were created—unmixed. He concluded, "Interracial sex relations produce mix-race people and are a form of racial genocide—today's holocaust."[77]

It is likely that Stock would not only be opposed to interracial relationships and the birth of mixed-race people but also to the creation of a multiracial category. All historical attempts by mulattoes to gain special class or caste status have met with the disapproval of whites and have made white prejudice more acute and whites more conscious of protecting their social status and racial "purity."[78] Between 1850 and 1915, mulattoes went from trying to assimilate into the white world to building their own world within the black community, because beginning in the 1850s free mulattoes went from being partly accepted by whites to being outright rejected by them.[79] This change in white attitudes accelerated during the Civil War, Reconstruction, and post-Reconstruction, and on into the twentieth century. Concurrent with this changing attitude was their adherence to the one-drop rule, which keeps blacks and everyone mixed with black in the caste that stands in starkest contrast to white. Perhaps the fear of allowing a middle group between the black and white races, for someone like Elroy Stock, is that this social arrangement would result in a greater degree of miscegenation and the eventual browning of America. That is to say that whites, who have always managed to intermix voluntarily with blacks, might be more likely to intermix with multiracials.

These examples provide multiracialists with a way out from the accusations of blacks that mixed-race people with only one black parent have internalized white racism and are trying to escape the stigma and oppression that results from being black. These examples provide a way out because we can see that mixed-race people face their own peculiar brand of racial discrimination.

Another way out from the accusations that mixed-race people just want to deny blackness is the claim of many multiracialists that being of mixed race carries with it the responsibility of being in solidarity with the people of their minority side. This point was articulated by David Kaufman, a mixed-race man of black and white (Jewish) background. Kaufman says that along with the experience and pain of being multiracial, which have sensitized him to oppression, comes a knowledge that he can never see racial discrimination perpetrated against blacks without identifying with it firsthand and having a vested interest in its eradication.[80] Francis Wardle, a white psychologist who is married to a black woman and has a biracial child, concurs because of his belief that multiracial children experience many of the obstacles and insults that black children encounter.[81] Wardle says multiracial people and their multiracialist advocates are natural allies of the black struggle because they know better than any non-black person what the reality of being black is. Wardle goes on to say that the multiracialists, aware of the need to improve conditions for blacks, are puzzled that blacks oppose them when they are not the enemy. "Are we a threat to Blacks and their continual struggle?" he asks. "We don't believe we are. We believe we are strong supporters and advocates. . . . We belong on the same side. We must unite our energy and commitment to attack our common enemies."[82]

The points of Kaufman and Wardle are illustrated in a story told by an eight-year-old girl of black and white parentage named Gabriela. Gabriela was friends with a black girl and a white girl at school. The white girl called the black girl a mean name and said she did not want to play with her because she was black. When Gabriela told the white girl that she was part black and the black girl was her friend, the white girl told Gabriela she did not want to play with her anymore either. Gabriela concludes, "I didn't care because Jackie was prejudiced and I only like to play with people who are nice. Maybe if every kid was Biracial like me they would be nice, too."[83] Gabriela took sides—the side of the oppressed over the prejudiced, which is further evidence to the multiracialists that their quest for racial status is justifiable. That is, it is further evidence to them that their attempts at a new status are by no means merely to find an escape hatch through which mixed-race people can be liberated from the stigma of being black.

As I suggested earlier, the multiracialists can also point to the coloureds of South Africa as an example of mixed-race people who, in not wanting to be black, are not necessarily being racist. Even though there is coloured racism against blacks, many coloured people say they are what they are—which is coloured or "brown." Many also speak of a specific coloured culture, or at least a subculture within the Western-oriented Afrikaans culture. For instance, some coloureds point out their "jazz" dancing, which I was told was not found among black or white South Africans. In this regard, Richard van der Ross told me that in his view the term "coloured" gained its greatest degree of negativity during the apartheid era, and that once the stigma of apartheid is removed the day will come when his people will again pridefully call themselves coloured. I got the same response from a coloured man of some Khoi and Middle Eastern background who is a professor of social work at the University of the Western Cape. He commented that he once rejected the word "coloured" but no longer does so, given that it is no longer a legislated category. He said that there is obviously a complexity about both the coloured situation in South Africa and the multiracial situation in the United States, but if there are deep roots connecting mixed-race people then he would be in favor of the United States implementing a federal classification for this group of Americans.

Thus mixed-race Americans have in coloured South Africans an example of a people who by not wanting to be black are not necessarily racist. For they are not black—they are "brown." They are, I was told by three coloured nationalists in Cape Town, "coloured people"—not "so-called coloured people" but just plain "coloured people." Additionally, not anyone can be coloured, the coloured nationalists explained, even though it is difficult to draw boundaries when it comes to the coloured race. For instance, a Zulu and Xhosa offspring may be ethnically mixed but not coloured, they said, for they are more purely "black" than not black. This means, for example, that "black" cannot be used to refer to oppressed people in South Africa or the third world as a whole, since brown people are also oppressed. Rather, one must speak of "oppressed communities" or "disadvantaged communities." Similarly, as stated earlier, most coloured people are part of the larger Afrikaans community (and also of the English-speaking community), not because they want to be white but because historically coloured and white Afrikaans people are related. The point being made with regard to mixed-race Americans is that those who are part black who say they are not wholly black are not necessarily denying their black ancestry. Historically, they are mixed and, as it were, "brown."

Moreover, being brown, coloured, or multiracial has been viewed by some in the United States and South Africa as being of special importance in race relations. Carlos Fernandez told the House subcommittee on the census that the United States, having drawn on the peoples of the world for its community, should especially set an exemplary standard for multiracial living. "Certainly this is at least the ideal to which we should aspire," he said.[84] He also said that recognizing multiracial and multiethnic people is as American as the nation can get, given that the idea of the "melting pot" is as old as the nation, although the term was initially intended to describe the "melting" of peoples of European descent.[85] This is also what Francis Wardle is getting at when he says interracial marriage is "the purist form of true integration between the races."[86] Similarly, Sandy Cirillo, the multiracial host and producer of the access cable television show in Atlanta, *Interracial Relationships: Crossing the Color Line*, holds the opinion that the words "American" and "multiracial" are sometimes interchangeable. Speaking of her own multiracial children, Cirillo comments, "They are the living example of the 'American Melting Pot' and it is time for our society to acknowledge and accept their biracial and/or multiracial heritage!"[87] Phil Vernon, a multiracial himself, remarked: "We're saying that we are the real product of America—we are the essence of the melting pot."[88] Similarly, a coloured professor of social work at the University of the Western Cape insists that he would have no problem with a child of his being classified as coloured in the absence of apartheid legislation. For he believes that South Africa's citizenry should ideally "colourize"—that is, blacks and whites should reconcile and intermix so that the country increasingly becomes coloured.

Perhaps this, then, answers historian Arthur Schlesinger, Jr.'s complaint in *The Disuniting of America* (1992) that a "cult of ethnicity" has emerged among non-white minorities and non-Anglo whites. Schlesinger protests that, while the "melting pot" or "one people" idea has thus far kept American society intact, this "cult of ethnicity" has arisen to denounce the idea due to their preference for protecting and promoting their separate racial and ethnic heritages.[89] One could perhaps argue that the multiracial movement is an answer to Schlesinger's worry because the multiracialists seem to be the only group pursuing the "melting pot" or "one people" ideal.

The most humanistic argument the multiracialists make in favor of the multiracial category on the United States census is that their movement may be the answer to the question of how to overcome racism. They claim that multiracial children exposed to contrasting cultural traditions from birth are more likely to develop a respect for human diversity. To this effect, Francis Wardle says that transcending racial boundaries, in a way that fulfills the promise of the civil rights movement, begins inside the interracial home where the family learns to respect and be enriched by the components of its interracial history and culture.[90] Kathlyn Gay concludes in her book *The Rainbow Effect* (1987) that interracial families also enhance the communities in which they live and serve as a model of harmony for the American family.[91] Gregory Stephens, a white man married to a black woman and father of a biracial child, says: "People with their feet in more than one group are seen as natural bridge-builders in achieving what Nelson Mandela calls a 'spirit of reconciliation' in the process of multiracial 'nation-building.'"[92] Likewise, Carlos Fernandez espoused these very points when he testified before the House subcommittee on the census. He stated that his organization believes that a positive awareness of interracial identity comprises an important first step toward resolving the problem of race relations in the United States and throughout the world. "We are convinced that our community is uniquely situated to confront these issues," he continued, "because of the special experiences and understanding we acquire in the intimacy of our families and our personalities."[93]

Grey Wolly, a young man of black and white ancestry who was raised by an adoptive black family, reflects that being able to move in both black and white worlds has been beneficial. It has allowed him to see the differences and divisions between those worlds, which he believes are aggravated by the distance between and isolation of the two groups.[94] Conversely, having white and black parents can help biracial children recognize the similarities between the two races, given that in some societies keeping the races separated is part of a "divide and rule" strategy. Here we can draw a parallel between the United States and South Africa by looking at the experience of South African novelist Mark Mathabane, whose father and mother are, respectively, of Venda and Tsonga ethnicity. Mathabane says that the old apartheid government, in following its "divide and rule" strategy, wanted him to believe that his parents' ethnic groups were not only enemies but that it was not beneficial for him to claim both identities. This, he continued, is akin to the United States, where the purveyors of racism want biracial children to believe that blacks and whites are antagonistic and unreconcilable.[95]

In this regard, Reginald Daniel, the mixed-race sociologist, believes multiracialism has the potential to undermine racial categories, which he sees as the very basis of racism insofar as the categories create the delusion that there are boundaries between population groups.[96] He believes adding the classification of multiracial to society's rostrum of races could therefore help people see the connections we all have to one another but have never acknowledged or been permitted to acknowledge. So, though the multiracial category would not be a solution to racism, it would at least open up discussion about black and Native American ancestry in the white community, white and Native American ancestry in the black community, and so forth. "That's what the new multiracial identity is about," Daniel concludes. "It's not about exploding racial identity, but expanding the definition of identity to something more inclusive."[97] Daniel also insists that dealing with racism must parallel any changes that are made, because neither abolishing nor adding racial categories will alone cause the demise of racism.[98]

Carlos Fernandez said before the House subcommittee on the census that by recognizing the existence of multiracial people and the concept of people whose identities transcend traditional racial boundaries, the idea of social unity becomes easier to imagine.[99] "I would make the argument," he stated, "that in fact recognizing multiracial people or people who transcend the boundaries between communities that make up our country in fact in practice represents the unity or the unifying force in society, that anchor that we're all looking for in these very difficult questions." He continued, "And so, I would make the argument that what we're talking about here is really perhaps one of these hidden keystones that we've been looking for in the race question, precisely because we've overlooked it as a taboo."[100] Philosopher Naomi Zack, whose mother was the daughter of Russian Jewish immigrants and whose black and Native American father she did not know, explains Fernandez's point in saying: "An American who identifies herself as mixed black and white is a new person racially, because old racial categories do not allow her to identify herself this way. It is such a person's very newness racially that gives her the option of racelessness. To be raceless in contemporary racial and racist society is, in effect, to be *anti-race*."[101]

A white Afrikaans woman, who grew up in Cape Town during the apartheid era and later married a well-to-do coloured man, told me that she agrees with the foregoing sentiments. She illustrated her agreement with a story. She said that when she was pregnant with her mixed-race child, her white daughter (from a previous relationship) asked what color the new baby would be: "Mommy I'm white, you're white, Daddy's brown; what will the baby be?" The woman told me that neither she nor her husband had an answer to that question, but since the birth of their child they had begun to feel that the child's mixed racial heritage allowed them to meet in the middle. This meeting in the middle was such that she does not feel singularly white anymore, nor he singularly coloured. Furthermore, she believes that her own mixed daughter and all mixed-race children in general are richer because they come from two cultures. They can be the peacemakers of tomorrow, she added, because they can see two points of view due to their background and experience. In this regard, she concluded, she viewed the American multiracial movement favorably.

The idea of these white and coloured parents of a mixed-race child being able to meet in the middle may be one of the ideals to emerge from the multiracial movement. In a sense, this meeting in the middle consummates the marriage vows stating that the woman and the man are to become "one"—which suggests "multiracial." Therefore, an interracial couple is, together, the same as their offspring. This indeed surfaces as a theological argument not unlike the theological arguments some multiracialists are making. For instance, in his testimony before the House subcommittee on the census, Carlos Fernandez posited an argument for establishing the multiracial classification by pointing to the principal tenet of the Baha'i Faith. The "oneness of humanity" is such a principal tenet of the faith in this religious group, he explained, that the group's members are encouraged to marry across racial lines. Therefore, he concluded, forcing the offspring of Baha'i marriages to identify themselves in monoracial categories affronts not only their personal integrity but their religious belief.[102]

Fernandez probably draws his information from an article on the Baha'i Faith that appeared in *Interrace* magazine about a year earlier. In the article, authors Paul and Marcia Lample give a history of the religion, which was founded in Persia (present-day Iran) in 1844 by a Persian named Baha'u'llah. Baha'u'llah's writings, which provide the scriptural basis for the faith, teach that only one God exists, that all religions are one, and that all of humanity comprises one family. Since all humanity is one family and people are to close their eyes to racial differences, all people are free to intermingle. When Baha'u'llah's son, Abdu'l-Baha, came to the United States in 1912, he taught the Baha'i community that the races, even black and white, should intermarry.[103]

A 1991 statement by the National Spiritual Assembly of the Baha'is of the United States commented similarly that diversity of color, culture, and nationality should never be barriers to harmonious relationships, including intermarriage.[104] The document also showed the religious belief in the oneness of humankind to be in concert with the patriotic theme of the oneness of America's citizens. It says that the United States, as the home to many diverse peoples of the world, might be the only country where the promise of societal unity can come to fruition. Moreover, the document admonishes the nation to beware of things to come if the ideals of this faith are not put into practice: "A nation whose ancestry includes every people on earth, whose motto is *E pluribus unum*, whose ideals of freedom under law have inspired millions throughout the world, cannot continue to harbor prejudice against any racial or ethnic group without betraying itself."[105] Today there are an estimated 110,000 Americans of this faith, and the Lamples, an interracial couple themselves, are among them, raising their mixed-race children to be a "new race" that will shun racism and racial segregation.[106]

Despite these foregoing arguments of a patriotic, moral, and religious nature, opponents of the multiracial movement suspect that the movement's real aim is to dismantle the black community. But Sally Katzen of the OMB suggested the opposite, comparing these fears to those expressed when the "other" category was added to the 1990 census. On January 20, 1988, the OMB solicited comments on a plan to include the category of "other" to the existing categories of Directive No. 15, and many of the same arguments made regarding the proposed multiracial category were discussed. The proposed category was supported by many groups representing multiracial and multiethnic people, but opposed by members of minority groups who viewed the proposal as an attempt to provoke internal dissension. It was also opposed by groups who were concerned that the official lower count of their groups would be to their detriment.[107]

Some opponents of the multiracial movement may also suspect that the real aim of the multiracialists, particularly those who have traditionally been viewed as black due to the one-drop rule, is for mixed-race blacks to be able to disassociate themselves from that despised caste. This was my initial response to Susan Graham when in August 1994 we debated the issue with other round-table participants on a radio talk show. I remarked that perhaps Graham does not want her children to be black. I also spoke admirably of a Jewish woman (Jewish like Graham) named Verna Arvey who seemed to take the opposite view of Graham. I recalled that one day, sometime around the year 1950, the daughter of Arvey and her famous husband, black composer William Grant Still, came home from grade school and inquired as to whether their family was white or colored. Her mother responded that they were "colored people," a "colored family."[108]

But the position that I originally held has been widely disputed by the multiracialists. In a written statement to the House subcommittee on the census, Ramona Douglass, then vice president of the Central Region of the AMEA, contested this notion based on her own feelings about being of black and white parentage. She said that she understood this suspicion from outsiders that the motivation of multiracials to have their own identity could be masking a desire to disassociate themselves from blacks. Though she could not speak for everyone in the multiracial community, she continued, finding an escape hatch from blackness is not the intent of the AMEA, for their organization is deeply concerned with both multiracial and monoracial groups that have suffered discrimination.[109] Kendra Wallace, a multiracial woman of black and white ancestry, offered similar testimony to the OMB. Serving as the West Coast representative of Project RACE, Wallace admitted that though she is identified as "colored" on her birth certificate, she grew up identifying as both black and white and in doing so was not trying to deny her minority status or achieve a more privileged position in society.[110]

I accept these arguments now, particularly since I have viewed them from a South African perspective. However, there are other fears and counterarguments to the many positions in favor of the multiracial movement that we have heard in this chapter. The other side of the story, the challenge to the multiracial movement, is the subject of the next chapter.

[T W O]

The Blessings of the
One-Drop Rule

In addition to my initial belief that interracial parents were participating in the multiracial movement because they did not want their biracial children to be black, I, probably like most black people, had taken the "one-drop rule" for granted. I had long presumed that the mixed-race black people I knew, and the others I had seen in passing (with a white parent), were like thirty-four-year-old Pamela Austin. Of black and white parentage, Pamela was raised by black relatives on her father's side of the family and always considered herself black.[1] Or I presumed that all mixed-race blacks were like twenty-eight-year-old Michael Mayson, who was raised by an adoptive black family. Though Michael does not deny that he is half white, he feels no connection with the white side of his ancestry.[2] Similarly, twenty-six-year-old Jacqueline Djanikian considers herself to be black, in part because she and her black mother have a closer bond than she and her white father.[3] Bernette Ford, forty-two years old, always identified as black because her Jewish father and black mother taught her to identify that way, so much so that she naturally married a black man.[4] Camille Hernandez-Ramdwar, a Canadian of black (Trinidadian) and white (Ukrainian-Canadian) parentage said that her white mother loved her and raised her, but upon reaching adulthood she realized there was something important that her mother could not give her — a culture that matched her color. Since she could neither identify with her mother's white

[51]

culture nor acquire her white color, Camille adopted her father's black culture.[5] Jeana Woolley, forty years old, was not aware of her black ancestry until she was twenty, because she was raised as white by her white mother and her white stepfather. But when she did learn she was partly black, Woolley vowed never to forsake the black identity.[6]

Woolley evidently felt on that day of reckoning the way I felt when first coming into contact with the views of multiracialists— that all black people (of "race" and "mixed race") have come this far together and absolutely must stay together until we are all free. Now that I understand the views of the multiracialists as presented in chapter 1, I no longer feel as unyielding about this position. In terms of mixed-race people who are of Jeana Woolley's light complexion but who seemed to prefer disappearing into a multiracial race, I initially felt as Nannie Burroughs did in 1950 when she said of "white Negroes" who disappeared into the white race: "Negroes like that should pitch in and make the race worth belonging to instead of escaping into a race that is already made."[7] Now, of course, I concede that the multiracial "race," with its unique historical struggles, is far from being "already made."

Nonetheless, I must admit having always found racial behavior to be at its best when someone had a choice to identify or associate with a more privileged group but instead opted to identify or associate with the less privileged group. This was often the choice whites made when they married blacks and when they raised their children as black, no matter how white they appeared. For instance, when I first came into contact with the views of the multiracialists, I admired author and poet Hettie Jones, the Jewish ex-wife of writer LeRoi Jones (Amiri Baraka) and mother of cultural critic Lisa Jones. Hettie Jones wrote in *Essence* magazine that she thought a black identity, because of its cultural vibrancy and its historical tradition of overcoming hardships, could only bring her daughters happiness.[8] She always taught her daughters that the black community was "a steady home" and that to abandon this home would mean "to swim with sharks."[9] To be sure, says Hettie Jones, her daughters are black and strong. "And I'm still

this man, even though his family was well-to-do, her biological father completely disowned her before he died, telling her he never wanted to see her again. He disowned her, as it were, just as the white Afrikaans people had disowned their coloured kindred when the National Party took power in 1948 and instituted apartheid. Her mother only started to come around to accepting the marriage when her newlywed daughter became pregnant, but her stepfather remains an "enemy," she said, who hates her marriage "with his whole being." Thus, the woman and her coloured husband have only been to her mother's home on a few occasions and only for brief stays—always in the kitchen. Because of this, she concluded: "I don't really have a family anymore." Such has been the general trend of race relations in the United States as well: the extended black family typically accepts the interracial marriage and the mixed-race offspring, while the white family frequently rejects the interracial family. When this occurs, the white parent constitutes the only white family the mixed-race children ever know.[17]

So, although the consequence of being mixed-race often results in the mixed-race person being the target for hostilities existing between the parent races,[18] blacks have been less likely than other groups to take fatal aim. Despite the fact that black children are sometimes cruel to mixed-race black children and the black community is sometimes tentative about mixed-race adults and interracial marriages, there is a measure of acceptance in the black community that is rarely matched by the whites. As put by Omattee Carrasco, a mixed-race black: "Even though I did get a lot of rejection from Blacks, they were also the only people that accepted me."[19] This very point explains Lisa Jones speaking sarcastically of whites who fail to understand that mixed-race people such as herself would choose to be black rather than white, or even part-white: "What could they possibly think is *in it* for us to be white people? Would it extend refuge or protection, provide moral directive? If it helped us get better jobs and higher salaries, would it offer spiritual community? Would it bring us family?"[20] In other words, who would prefer to swim with sharks? If, for instance, a mixed-race youth of black and Japanese parentage is told by white American kids "remember Pearl Harbor" and by Japanese kids "Hiroshima is your fault,"[21] then what other community is there to accept him but the black community? Certainly if whites were as welcoming of interracial families as blacks generally are in comparison, then gleaning a sense of the insignificance of racial boundaries and achieving a multiracial identity would probably be easier for mixed-race people. But this is far from being the case.

As I have just alluded, I also presume that mixed-race blacks who have an Asian parent are likewise more accepted by the black community than by the Asian American community. As Angelo Ragaza writes in *A. Magazine* for Asian Americans: "Biracial Asian Americans who are half African American . . . represent two minority communities. Because the hierarchy of race in America posits Asians, as the 'model minority,' slightly 'below' whites but 'above' other people of color, many monoracial Asians are even less prepared to accept half black Asian Americans than they are to accept half white Asian Americans." Ragaza continues: "Part of the extent to which this hierarchy has been internalized by the Asian American community stems from negative stereotypes held about people of African descent in Asia. . . . In Vietnam and the Philippines, as in many Asian countries, dark skin is associated with lower socioeconomic class and with ethnic minorities. Such attitudes are carried over into Asian communities in America."[22]

Likewise, Cynthia Nakashima, a sociologist of Japanese and white parentage, confirms Ragaza's point. According to Nakashima, mixed-race Asian Americans have very limited entry into Asian American communities, especially if they are part black.[23] Christine Iijima Hall, a mixed-race psychologist of black and Japanese ancestry, agrees. Having interviewed thirty mixed-race people of black and Japanese parentage, Hall concludes that mixed-race Japanese with a black parent tend to be less acceptable to Japanese Americans than mixed-race Japanese with a white parent. She says this may be a factor in mixed-race Japanese with a black parent choosing to identify with blacks.[24]

Teresa Kay Williams found in her research that the negative views of Africa and black America shared by Japanese and whites have prevented a positive Afro-Asian image from developing in both Japan and the United States.[25] For instance, Williams found that white-Asian biracials tended to see their racial mix as a more glamorous blend than that of black-Asian biracials, while black-Asian biracials tended to find that all mixed-race Asians display a glamorous blend.[26] Williams writes of one black-Japanese biracial who spoke of the three years he had lived in North Carolina after being raised in Japan: "It was awful. We were 'niggers.' Then, we were 'Japs.' Then, we were 'Chinks.' I finally got so mad that I went, 'Make up your minds.' So they settled with 'nigger.'"[27] Thus, we are faced again with this inescapable reality: black is the bottom line with regard to social caste. So mixed-race blacks, no matter what their mix, are always niggers. No wonder many mixed-race people choose to identify with blacks—revolutionary attitude or not, "black and proud" or not.

With the racism mixed-race blacks face from the white and Asian communities in the United States (and elsewhere in the world), it makes sense that the one-drop rule would be viewed by blacks and many mixed-race blacks as a necessity. It makes sense not simply for the sake of mixed-race blacks having a "steady home" but for the sake of the black community being able to maintain a healthy cohesiveness. After all, that cohesiveness has allowed us to fend off the racism that all of us—"race" and "mixed race"—must endure. In other words, I concur with the point of sociologist F. James Davis who writes in his book, *Who Is Black?* (1991), that any suggestion of changing the one-drop rule at this point would impair rather than enhance black unity and racial progress:[28]

> The common experiences shared in this black community provide the basis for ethnic unity and pride and for political and other orga-nized efforts to protect and help its members. The suggestion today that the one-drop rule is an arbitrary social construction that could be changed sounds to the black community like a dangerous idea. If one result of such a change would be to cause some lighter-colored

persons to leave the black community for the white community, the former would lose some of its hard-won political strength, perhaps some of its best leaders, some members of its churches and other community institutions, some business and professional people, and some customers and clients. American blacks now feel they have an important vested interest in a rule that has for centuries been a key instrument in their oppression.[29]

Because I so sympathize with Davis's point, I initially believed that the attempt of the multiracialists to undermine the one-drop rule was part of a conspiracy that earlier had taken aim to explode black racial identity through farfetched rhetoric about achieving a raceless or color-blind society. This conspiracy, as I saw it, was the equivalent of the earlier "melting pot" theory, which postulated that all Americans should melt into a single cultural identity. What made the modern notion of achieving a raceless or color-blind society just as disturbing to me as its "melting pot" precursor was that it too seemed to suggest that black people and other peoples of color have no alternative but to fulfill Frantz Fanon's prophecy in *Black Skin, White Masks* (1952). "However painful it may be for me to accept this conclusion," prophesies Fanon, "I am obliged to state it. For the black man there is only one destiny. And it is white."[30] African American religion professor Alton Pollard seemed to corroborate my assessment, particularly the notion that there are blacks, some of them mixed race and some of them interracially married, who seem eager to rush the black masses toward this singular destiny. Pollard says:

> The belief in "color-blindness" is largely a post-Du Bois condition among African Americans, a quality or approach to establishing a sense of self or identity that implies certain rites (and rights) of social entry without regard to race. For many if not all adherents to this position, rainbow declarations of a "color-full" society (the postmodern recognition of otherness, social heterogeneity, cultural difference, distinctive gender views, and so on) are highly suspect, an odious and irrational deception. . . . The new breed of "color-blind" African American sings a refrain that is distressingly as simple as it

is symptomatic: "Rather than cast our lot with the race, we race to leave the caste."[31]

I still have in mind, as I think Pollard does, such blacks as Yehudi Webster and Kwame Anthony Appiah.

Anthony Appiah, a philosopher of Ghanaian and English parentage, contends that the time has passed for black racialism—that is, black identity based on the concept of race (and the one-drop rule)—to be an intelligent reaction to white racism. He simply does not believe that people of African ancestry can or even should create alliances based on the concept of the black person or that racism can be countered by accepting the categories of race.[32] Such discourse may sound very humanistic, like much of the discourse of the multiracialists. However, this discourse begs to be weighed against the racial realities of this society, which have made black people—both "race" and "mixed race"—feel that they have a vested interest in the one-drop rule. As Houston Baker, Jr., points out with regard to Appiah's suggestion that the gross features of hair, bone, and skin have nothing to do with the illegitimate concept of race: "In a world dramatically conditioned both by the visible and by a perduring discursive formation of 'old' (and doubtless mistaken) racial enunciative statements, such gross features always make a painfully significant difference—perhaps, *the only* significant difference where life and limb are concerned in a perilous world."[33]

So, when radio talk show host Warren Olney asked me during his round-table discussion on the census movement how it was that allowing Susan Graham's children to choose a multiracial identity would explode black racial identity,[34] I should have said that the multiracialists, many of whom are interracially married whites, do not understand the points that I have presented thus far. They do not understand that the black community has been a "steady home" and that being able to maintain a healthy cohesiveness with which to fend off racism has been a blessing of the one-drop rule. In answer to Olney's question, I also could have referred to a remark made by Beverly Smythe of Oakland, California: "It is not coincidental that the woman spearheading a movement for a 'multiracial' category is white. White people have historically had a need to label people of color. I am 'biracial' but I consider myself to be Black. A 'multiracial' category will only serve to elevate mixed race people to a non-Black status. What's so bad about being just Black?" Smythe concludes, "If society had defined Susan Graham's children as White she would not be fighting for a 'multiracial' category. Project RACE? More like Project RACIST!"[35]

In terms of white people having the historical tendency to label peoples of color, when Olney used the term "mixed race" on his radio talkshow, Graham told him the term was "offensive."[36] But for numerous people who are themselves multiracial, the term "mixed race" is not only fitting but "trendy" or stylish.[37] Moreover, in terms of Graham's objection to any modification of Directive No. 15 for mixed-race people which does not include the specific name "multiracial," we get the impression that it is a name rather than a principle that is important. So, once again a white person is trying to tell people who are not white what name to go by. I understand Beverly Smythe's point. Just because Graham has biracial children does not mean she holds the right to push for a legislated category that would name all mixed-race people. She may name her own children, if she wishes, but not the mixed-race children of everyone else. Moreover, since Graham refers to the coloureds of South Africa in order to legitimize the mixed-race category that she wants to name "multiracial," it should be interesting to know that a few coloureds I spoke to find the name "multiracial" unfitting. They would like mixed-race Americans to use the name "coloured"—the very term Graham rejects.[38] The term "coloured," it was argued by three coloured nationalists I spoke with, preceded apartheid legislation in South Africa and is a name once widely used in the United States for mixed-race blacks. Moreover, they pointed out, it is still a name used by the National Association for the Advancement of Colored People (NAACP).

Furthermore, not only does Graham wish to determine the name by which people of color will be known, she wants to determine who can and cannot be "multiracial." She seeks to determine this by narrowly defining the term to include only those persons having parents from two of the existent monoracial categories. The fact is, however, blacks are and have always been a multiracial people, a fact that has long led scholars to draw parallels between black Americans and the mixed-race coloured people of South Africans. Among these scholars are sociologist William Brown in *Race Relations in the American South and in South Africa* (1959), H. F. Dickie-Clark in *The Marginal Situation* (1966), and historian George Fredrickson in *White Supremacy* (1981), to name only a few.[39] All three of these authors recognize that blacks and coloureds are peoples generally comprised of racial mixture that especially dates back to the nineteenth century. The experience of segregation that blacks endured after slavery, beginning between 1890 and 1910 and extending through the first half of the twentieth century, was also experienced by coloureds by law and by custom long before the National Party took office in 1948. Soon thereafter, the apartheid regime in South Africa initiated the Population Registration Act that segregated coloureds and the Immorality Act that outlawed interracial marriage and sex, so that the mixed-race coloureds married and mated among themselves just like black Americans did due to segregation and antimiscegenation laws. Additionally, up until 1991, when racial classification was repealed in South Africa, any offspring of clandestine relationships between whites and coloureds would be coloured children, just as in the United States any offspring between blacks and whites have traditionally been black. This parallel between coloured South Africans and black Americans as people of mixed racial ancestry raises serious questions about Susan Graham's inclination not only to name mixed-race people but then to define narrowly the name she is lobbying for.

In terms of the narrowness with which "multiracial" is being defined by the multiracialists, coloured scholars Richard van der Ross and Jimmy Ellis take the opposing view. Ellis said he was always under the impression that, with a few exceptions, the situation of coloured South Africans was parallel with that of black

Americans. He said that both groups evolved out of slavery during which they mixed with whites, that both speak the language of the white settlers, that both adopted the Christian religion brought by whites, and both had a subculture that existed within the larger Western culture. While black Americans are of mixed race, Ellis added, it is blacks within the African enclaves in the United States (those isolated areas such as the Sea Islands) and Native Americans on the reservations who he believes parallel the indigenous blacks of South Africa. Similarly, van der Ross told me that unlike blacks in South Africa, black Americans do not speak a native tongue, have tribal affiliations, or live in their native land. For essentially the same reasons Ellis pointed out, van der Ross has always recognized commonalities between black Americans (as a mixed race) and coloured South Africans (as a mixed race). He has always recognized commonalities between himself and Ralph Bunche (whom he met upon his first trip to the United States in 1957).

Therefore, African Americans should be included among the "coloured" or multiracial peoples of the world, because they are ancestrally a people of mixed racial background. The multiracialists, according to the three coloured nationalists I spoke to, have too narrow an approach to multiracialism or colouredism, because determining multiraciality must be based on one's ancestral lineage and not simply on one's parentage. If African Americans were to come to South Africa, the coloured nationalists agreed, they would see that they are coloured, not just in appearance but in being of mixed racial lineage. Jimmy Ellis (who is not a coloured nationalist) concurred that for people now to insist that the racial categories of the United States be "refined" so that all biracial people are "multiracial" is to ignore African American history. Likewise, a man of English and Afrikaans parentage married to an Indian woman (a Muslim) whom he met during the anti-apartheid struggle said that limiting multiracial identity to one generation freezes racial identity and creates a new race— which he opposes. American journalist Hanna Rosin similarly remarks that "Graham's definition waters down the definition of race and makes it a one-generation phenomenon, more like an

interest group."[40] In this respect, for the multiracialists to compare mixed-race Americans to the South African coloureds and
yet exclude black Americans is further suggestion that there are
stark problems behind some (if not many) of their positions.

In addition to attempting to name mixed-race people and to define
"multiracial" narrowly while simultaneously drawing parallels
with coloured South Africans, the multiracialists have criticized
those people of mixed-race background who are comfortable with
a monoracial identity (the identity they have selected for themselves). Carlos Fernandez of the AMEA contends that counting
multiracial people in the monoracial categories means that the
monoracial groups are being mischaracterized or misrepresented,
especially the black American group. He says that there are many
mixed-race people who choose to identify as black when they are
really indicating the community with which they most closely
interact or the community whose political interests they wish to
support.[41] But the notion that the government's failure to count
mixed-race people results in monoracial groups being mischaracterized is based on questionable premises. For if coloured people
(the multiracials of South Africa) were classified monoracially as
white (due to their kinship with white Afrikaans people), would
white be mischaracterized? White would only be mischaracterized
if white actually has something to do with a white color or white
genetic purity. Neither is true in South Africa or the United
States—or in Brazil, for that matter. In South Africa many who
were classified as white under apartheid were neither white in
color nor pure in race, since the white Afrikaans people were generally known to have 6 percent to 8 percent mixed ancestry,
which sometimes made them even darker in complexion than
some coloureds. In the United States, Arabs are classified as white
when even they themselves say they are not—not white in ancestry (European), color, or treatment. In Brazil, white "purity" is
not the issue either; white appearance is the issue.

Susan Graham fails to see this and makes a similar point to that
of Fernandez. She says that the question is not how many people

of African descent are purely black but rather how many people who identify as black would rather identify as multiracial. "That is a very very small number," she concludes.[42] The point is not simply how many blacks would rather identify as multiracial, but that multiracialists such as Graham and Fernandez, who are not black, are tampering with the naming and characterization of black people. That is the primary principal and the tricky problem involved.

The secondary principle and problem is that the numbers of blacks wishing to become multiracial may not be "a very very small number" if mixed-race people do not have a choice in the matter of their self-identification. Currently mixed-race people do have a choice in the matter of self-identification, for the federal government does not itself uphold the one-drop rule. The instructions of Directive No. 15 are that mixed-race people should select the racial category that most closely reflects the way their community sees them: "The category which most closely reflects the individual's recognition in his community should be used for purposes of reporting on persons who are of mixed racial and/or ethnic origins." These directions provide enough space for easy defiance of social custom—the "one-drop rule"—for the "individual's community" is a concept that is indefinite enough for broad interpretation. Furthermore, if, as we heard Graham say in chapter 1, the United States Bureau of the Census advised Graham to identify her children after the race of the mother (who is white in this instance), then this too is contrary to the one-drop rule. Thus, in removing the possibility of choice from mixed-race people who prefer to identify as black, removing that choice because monoracial groups are allegedly otherwise "mischaracterized," the multiracialists are establishing a much stricter (indeed an apartheid-like) standard for racial identification.

While Graham says she does not think mixed-race people must choose the new multiracial identity over a monoracial identity,[43] there are multiracialists who argue that being multiracial is not a matter of choice. Candace Mills, editor of *Interrace* magazine, says that race, like sex (male and female), cannot be selected.

"When a Black person and a White person mate, the resulting child is a 'blended' product," she argues. "The Black cannot be separated from the White."[44] So, even though actress Halle Berry identifies as black, Mills insists she is biracial.[45] Similarly, in an article entitled "Where Are All the Dark-skinned Black Women," a multiracial going by the pen-name Jamoo writes that the new black woman for the 1990s is anything but black. He says that anyone looking through such black magazines as *Essence*, *Ebony*, and *Jet*, as well as through corresponding black teenage magazines, will see that there are only a few women who are truly black, since most of the women in the magazines are "light, bright, and damn-near white." He insists that "real sisters," like Anita Baker and Cicely Tyson, should be the models of black beauty that are showcased in magazines rather than mixed-race women like Jasmine Guy and Halle Berry.[46]

The same view is held by Francis Wardle, the white child psychologist and family therapist who is the husband of a black woman and the father of a biracial child. Wardle illustrates this stricter view of racial identity in his criticism of Halle Berry, whose comments about her monoracial black identity he had encountered in an *Essence* magazine interview by Lisa Jones. Jones asked Berry why certain media had identified her as multiracial, and Berry responded (to Wardle's dismay) that she never once announced that she is biracial but rather always said she is black. Berry went on to say that if someone else wants to identify as multiracial then that is their right to do so, but she identifies as black and feels very comfortable as a member of the black community.[47] As though Berry does not have a choice in the matter of her identity, Wardle comments sarcastically that Berry has made it quite clear in this particular interview that she does not want to be a role model for multiracial kids.[48]

Wardle has similar criticisms for law professor Lani Guinier, the mixed-race black woman whom President Bill Clinton dropped as his first nominee for Assistant Attorney General in charge of civil rights. Wardle even made light of the black leaders who protested Clinton's decision, given that Guinier is really biracial (with a Jewish mother), he argued, and not black.[49] These instances of Berry and Guinier choosing to identify as black disturb Wardle, because in his opinion they convey the message to mixed-race children that they must choose a black identity to succeed.[50] Thus, in response to people who say it is wrong to raise biracial children as white when they are also part black, and to people who feel it is comfortable for an interracial couple to raise their mixed children as black, Wardle says both views impose an identity on mixed children that is inaccurate since the children are inescapably biracial.[51]

So far I have criticized the fact that some multiracialists want to determine the name by which people of color will be known and determine who can and cannot be multiracial. Now we have before us the claim that having a white parent automatically removes offspring from the category of black, even if these individuals select black as their racial identity. Overlooking for the moment the obvious implications of apartheid, this sounds reminiscent of the racial situation in Brazil, where people of any degree of mixture who display some white features cease to be classified as black. Given Brazilian race relations, this would suggest that racial blending (miscegenation) does not necessarily mean there is an absence of racism, since in Brazil there is, as I will explain later, an intentional process of obliterating blackness. Additionally, for Candace Mills, Francis Wardle, and other multiracialists to say that race cannot be a choice for people like Halle Berry and Lani Guinier, is for these multiracialists to essentialize race. That is, it is to say that race is a real thing of nature, when it is really but a sociopolitical construct. Moreover, for the multiracialists to say Berry and Guinier cannot choose their race is for the multiracialists to essentialize racial mixture as though it is held by a few but not by all. So, the more the multiracialists defend their proposition, the more we are plunged deeper into racialization, layer by layer.

Fortunately there are a few among the multiracialists who rebuff this submergence. For instance, Ramona Douglass, the successor of Carlos Fernandez as president of the AMEA, had words of rebuke for Wardle's criticism of mixed-race people who choose a black identity. Douglass, who is herself of black and white ancestry, said that she finds Wardle to be presumptuous in thinking that his interracial marriage and his parenting of biracial children gives him the right to impose his views about racial identity on mixed-race people who choose to identify with only part of their ancestry. She concludes, "I am sensitive enough to the variety of experiences that we as 'mixed-race' people contend with, to respect and accept that choice."[52] In fact, Lois Melina's advice to biological and adoptive parents who are raising mixed-race children to be biracial is that they allow these children the right to develop their own racial identities. She also says that parents should make sure these children do not think they are being disloyal to their white birthparents or adoptive parents if they choose to consider themselves black.[53] Richard van der Ross feels the same about coloured people—that they should have the right to identify with whatever group they wish: "This is a decision which each one must make for himself or herself. In so doing, people will naturally ask where they feel they belong. They must also ask whether the group with which they wish to identify, will accept them. Identity must not be forced."[54]

Not only must identity not be forced, but it would be unfair and apartheid-like to insist that mixed-race blacks such as Jasmine Guy, Halle Berry, and Lani Guinier depart from the black race and cease allowing themselves to be models of black beauty and success. Would not such apartheid-like behavior on the part of blacks be akin to whites saying that these women cannot be models of white beauty and success? Would this not be racism? This is a question that needs to be answered by the multiracialists. On the one hand, they often emphasize the fact that biracials such as Guy, Berry, and Guinier are both black and white. Now some of them are saying these women cannot be black, either by choice or by fact.

If certain of the multiracialists were to succeed in their designs to force the multiracial identity on mixed-race people who allegedly cause the black population to be "mischaracterized," then this would have significant bearing on the number of people who are removed from the black community. There are also other factors that could result in a substantial number of blacks becoming multiracial. Although there may not be millions of blacks who go to the extreme of physically altering their appearance to look white, there might be a substantial number who opt for this non-surgical removal from the category of black. This was essentially the apprehension expressed by Arthur Fletcher, chairperson of the United States Commission on Civil Rights. Fletcher said to the House subcommittee on the census that he is concerned that the multiracial category would attract more blacks than simply those of immediate biracial parentage. He worries that the category would also attract significant numbers from that 70 percent of the black community whose multigenerational lineage is multiracial given the substantial strains of white and Native American ancestry in black people. Fletcher said that in the 1990 census approximately 253,000 people (about 1 percent of the population) made entries under the "other" category, which indicated that they were of mixed racial background. Although this is a relatively small number of people, he continued, the Commission believes that many more blacks would select "multiracial" on the census if it were a choice. This is because a multiracial category would be more likely to appeal to blacks who identify more than one race in the previous generations of their family lineage.[55] Fletcher also worries that a host of blacks, not necessarily those who are of immediate mixed-race background, might opt for "multiracial" in hope of escaping the stigma of black and thereby receiving some economic benefits in corporate America.[56] In that regard, it would certainly be easier for many black people to "pass" for multiracial than to "pass" for white.

According to black South African journalist Mike Siluma, to draw a parallel, some black South Africans, in an effort to escape the worst of apartheid, tried to "play" coloured—including changing their personality, fleeing black townships, adopting Afrikaans or English as their language, and applying skin whiteners. All this was done to look coloured, he says, since they certainly could not "play" white.[57] In fact, there were numerous instances of South Africans who, during the apartheid era, applied to the Race Classification Board for reclassification to the next category up on the social totem. These were blacks who "tried for coloured" and coloureds who "tried for white." Between January 1, 1983, and December 31, 1990, for instance, there were 9,100 applications for racial reclassification. There were 4,539 coloured who successfully applied for white status and 1,083 who were denied it. There were 2,517 blacks who successfully applied for coloured status and 690 who were turned down.[58]

Although I admitted at the close of the previous chapter that I no longer believe the principal motivation of the multiracialists is to provide mixed-race blacks with an escape hatch from blackness, there are some mixed-race people who have made it clear that they wish to steer clear of the degrading stigma of black.[59] There are also sophisticated arguments coming from the multiracialists that suggest the reasonableness of people's flight from the taint of blackness. For instance, mixed-race philosopher Naomi Zack says that since the concept of a black race has no uniform factual foundation and since people who identify as black are coerced to do so and in turn do not receive the same social treatment as whites, then perhaps the day has come to reject the idea of a black race.[60]

For whatever reasons mixed-race people might choose to desert blackness, Susan Graham's low estimate of the number of possible defectors may be incorrect. Roderick Harrison, head of the Census Bureau's Racial Statistics division, says it is reasonable to believe that a multiracial box on the census could result in at least a 10 percent defection from the black category.[61] That is nearly 300,000 people. Additionally, in future generations the number of blacks would decrease with the rise of interracial marriage or mating between blacks and the former mixed-race blacks who defected to the multiracial classification. The numbers of blacks would decrease because a black person who marries a multiracial (even a multiracial with partial black ancestry) will have crossed racial boundaries. Thus, the offspring of such a mixed union would be multiracial rather than black, even though that person would essentially be three-quarters black. This point is also illustrated in the earlier part of this century by an Arizona woman of black and white parentage who went to court to challenge the state's law against interracial marriage, since she could not legally marry someone white or black without crossing racial lines and therefore being involved in illegal miscegenation.[62] Under the old system of racial classification in South Africa, to give another illustration, the offspring of a black and coloured person was automatically mixed and therefore coloured, even though that person might have been essentially three-quarters black. So, given the fact that the offspring of a union between a multiracial and someone from any of the other racial groups would result in an interracial union and a mixed-race child, we essentially have the one-drop rule all over again. Will a one-drop rule now determine who is or is not multiracial?

Given all that has been said in the last several pages, when I was asked by radio talk-show host Warren Olney how allowing Susan Graham's children to choose the multiracial identity causes black racial identity to explode, I could have also referred to a remark by Bernette Ford, a mixed-race adult who has always identified as black. Ford says that the racial situation in the United States is so serious and complicated that this "splinter group" of mixed-race blacks, which does not need to separate, diverts attention from the more serious problems of black people in this country.[63] Similarly, Joy Zarembks, who has a Kenyan mother and a white father, says that since most blacks are already multiracial, she is against the multiracial category because it would do nothing more than break up the black community.[64] Indeed, whites who have multiracial ancestry—say, Native American—are not going to leave the upper-caste of white for the lower-caste of multiracial, so the multiracial classification results in the fragmenting of peoples of color, including the black American population.

I could have also answered Olney's question by saying that, given that approximately 70 percent of the black community has multiracial ancestry, the introduction of a multiracial classification would undoubtedly inject an element of ambiguity into the black community. Black people would have no way of distinguishing blacks from nonblacks (identification that heretofore could be determined visually based on the recognizable remnants of black African phenotype). A mixed-race young woman from the state of Washington, who had been living in Cape Town for nine months when I met her, said she found it comforting to be able to walk down the street and just nod to a black person. But the situation of racial ambiguity of which I was speaking, where blacks can never be certain in the distinctions between blacks and multiracials, would be unsettling to her. Michele Paulse, a South African coloured woman raised in Canada, points out that already there is a lack of trust in the black community for those who appear mixed, given that historically whites have chosen mixed-race people who are part white to guard their systems of power and privilege in countries they have colonized.[65] A separation of blacks of "race" and "mixed race" would, in my estimation, only aggravate black distrust of blacks who look mixed according to stereotypical notions of mixed appearance.

The havoc that would likely be wreaked in the black community by the legislation of a multiracial classification is not worth the effort that might be made by mixed-race people to serve as mediators between the antagonistic races that comprise their ancestry. It is not that such racial mediation is unworthy of attention. It is that it is unrealistic to expect mixed-race people somehow to mediate our own racial problems. No one has successfully attempted to do so for Jews and Christians, Catholics and Protestants, Republicans and Democrats, heterosexuals and homosexuals, males and females. Carol Camper, a Canadian of black, white, and Native American ancestry, finds the idea naive and points out that it unfairly leaves the necessary work of racial reconciliation up to mixed-race people.[66] Similarly, Heather Green, a Canadian of black and white parentage, says that if she were to attempt to be a "wizard mediator" between the black and white races, between the oppressed and the oppressor, she would be sacrificing her entire being. "It is not possible," she insists. "It is not wise. And it makes no sense for any one woman to take on what humanity as a whole is so far from taking seriously—the . . . destruction of white supremacy."[67]

Moreover, the destruction of white supremacy will not occur by further fragmenting the black community or peoples of color. It is for this reason that South African historian Gavin Lewis speaks negatively of the Population Registration Act of apartheid, which, requiring every South African to carry an identification card setting them apart in racial groups, divided blacks and coloureds. Writing in 1987, before apartheid was abolished, Lewis says that many people classified as coloured rejected that categorization because it represented the attempt of the white-supremacist regime to "divide and rule." It divided the oppressed while simultaneously preserving white "purity" by treating coloureds as a separate, homogeneous race apart from both blacks and whites.[68] The same holds true for Brazil, as historian Cleveland Donald, Jr., illustrates:

> while one can condemn the fact of only one category for Blacks in the United States as a technique for the dehumanization of Afro-Americans, in Brazil the presence of infinite variations in color results in the same type of Black dehumanization. During slavery, and to a limited extent even today, the Afro-Brazilian can be born a mulatto, reared a preto [black], live the life of a pardo [mulatto], and be buried a moreno [white]. But this does not mean that white Brazilians regard Blacks as human beings any more than white Americans do; for the power of self-definition in the Brazilian case lies beyond the control of Afro-Brazilians, in the hands of whites. The fact that white Brazilians can define Blacks as they please contributes to the anxiety and frustration that makes possible the easy co-optation and psychological emasculation of Blacks. In this sense, color gradations in the context of the Brazilian cultural milieu are a disadvantage rather than an advantage.[69]

Thus, as anthropologist Angela Gilliam says in comparing Brazil's so-called raceless society to the United States: "I would contend that American blacks, by virtue of the imposed historical definition of *who* is or is not black, may have more advantages. That is, the identifiable . . . black in this country has potential for family/group unity and common goals far exceeding that which is possible in Brazil."[70]

Again, my presumption in coming to the multiracial debate was that within a racist country the one-drop rule has served blacks best, even though this rule allows whites, with their majority status, to hunt down, identify, and discriminate against everyone with that "one drop." The strategy I am suggesting is akin to that used by minority whites when they were in power in South Africa and by the minority whites in Brazil, who are still in power. Both of the minority white populations counted every white or part-white as white in order to buffer their numbers. In the United States, where blacks are in the minority, we need to count every black or part-black as black. So, while whites, with their majority status, hunt down, identify, and discriminate against everyone with that "one drop," the greater number of blacks resulting from the "rule" make it more difficult for our oppressors to maintain the institutions of discrimination. This is no doubt the reason that doing away with the one-drop rule has never been on the civil rights agenda. The threat of an undermining of the one-drop rule is essentially the reason Arthur Fletcher, chairperson of the United States Commission on Civil Rights, told the House subcommittee on the census that the Commission recommends against the addition of a multiracial category to the OMB's Directive No. 15.

In following Fletcher's testimony before the House subcommittee, it might not be so obvious that the root of the Commission's concern about the proposed multiracial classification is the havoc that would be brought upon black racial identity and black solidarity. This is not so obvious because the Commission's principal arguments against the added classification were aimed at the issue of legal and policy protection for the black minority. This is the issue on which they had to concentrate, not only because this is the official domain of concern for the Commission but because this is the issue the OMB finds to be of significance given its official domain of concern—federal law and policy needs. The OMB understands such data to be important because, since 1970, after the civil rights movement and the United States Supreme Court decisions that ensued, the tallying of racial demographics through the census has increased in importance. This is because the statistics are used for monitoring compliance with court decisions involving civil rights and the allocation of government resources to meet the needs of the "protected" minority groups that historically have been discriminated against. The amount of resources that go to the black community relate directly to the number of blacks counted on the census. This is why Fletcher stated that the eight civil rights commissioners he represents did not think adding a new classification to the existing racial categories would produce useful information, but rather would undermine the quality of data currently received on race and ethnicity. This is particularly the case, he said, given the undercounting of minorities in recent census counts.[71]

That a multiracial category on the census could draw numbers from the existent minority groups and therefore lessen the extent of their protection was the fundamental concern of the National Urban League. Billy Tidwell, the director of research for the Urban League, articulated this to the House subcommittee on the census. Tidwell expressed concern about the impact that adding a multiracial classification could have on the representation of blacks and consequently on the gains they have previously accrued under the existing classification system. He said, "It would be an unfortunate circumstance, indeed, if changes in census data collection methodology effectively turned the clock back on the well-being of a group that has had such distinctive and profound experiences with exclusion and deprivation in this society."[72]

Paul Williams, assistant secretary of the Department of Housing and Urban Development (HUD), illustrated before the House subcommittee that the clock could indeed be turned back on the well-being of blacks. According to Williams, the term "multiracial," like the category "other," would not permit HUD to protect that constituency from possible discrimination with regard to mortgage loans. He explained that the 35,000 people who previously filled out "other" on lending applications are the same people who come to HUD asking for help. However, HUD needs specific data on identification, data that the category "other" does not give them in order to protect minorities and ensure their right to fair housing practices.[73] This very kind of problem led one government analyst to say of the movement to procure a multiracial category on Directive No. 15 (and the census), that the multiracialists are evidently not concerned about the possible results of this movement. "What they don't understand," the analyst said, "is that it's going to cost their own groups."[74] While mixed-race people may be classified as multiracial, the analyst and Williams are saying, they may still be treated as black and therefore lose out on needed protection that blacks get.

Though the United States Civil Rights Commission is partly concerned for black racial identity and black solidarity, as I will show, we should not be put off by the fact that the commissioners and other black leaders are concerned about the official count of blacks. It has been by our numbers and unity, both a result of the one-drop rule, that we have made strides in attaining civil rights in this country. In fact, from the days of slavery we were Colored, Negro, Black, Afro-American, and African American together, and together we have come this far "by faith." By that faith and determination black leadership and grassroots activism have pushed the needs of the black community and the ideals of the country to the forefront of the national consciousness and of political agendas. A knowledge of this history is no doubt what led one South African coloured woman of Indian and Cape coloured parentage to say to me that she thought one of the strengths of black Americans was their unity. "Why can't they just call themselves African Americans?" she asked of the multiracials who are part black.

Some of those who wish for a new identity other than black have in fact forgotten: that is my answer. They have forgotten that since the days of slavery blacks have tended to embrace even the whitest of their interracial offspring. Children born out of wedlock from relationships black women have had with white men (by force or compliance) have been accepted or adopted by relatives in the black community in a far higher percentage than the children white women have had from black men (by compliance) have been accepted or adopted by relatives in the white community. Moreover, while the white community has generally abandoned whites who are involved in interracial relationships with blacks, the black community has generally granted those white spouses entry into the black community, though sometimes with some caution and discomfort. For instance, in 1950 one white woman in the Club of Tomorrow, the interracial support group of Detroit that I mentioned in chapter 1, said that though she had been rejected by whites for marrying a black man, she was welcomed in the black community: "I can truthfully say I am not sorry for changing from my race to the Negro race, because it's grand to be loved by so many fine people."[75] Hettie Jones, the white ex-wife of black writer LeRoi Jones (Amiri Baraka) and mother of cultural critic Lisa Jones, also says she found comfort, friends, and generosity in the black community.[76] Similarly, Gail Mathabane, the white American wife of black South African novelist Mark Mathabane, says that the racial discrimination she faces in the United States has made her realize that she has relinquished her privileges as a white person and is now a member of a black family.[77]

"Why can't they just call themselves African Americans?" was a most fitting question by the above-mentioned coloured woman with regard to mixed-race blacks. The coloured woman may also have been considering that it is by our numbers and unity that black Americans were able to help bring an end to apartheid in South Africa, a unity that black and coloured South Africans essentially failed to build because of apartheid. It was black American unity (and therefore influence) that gave the black consciousness movement to South Africa.[78] This is the movement that, beginning in the 1960s, started to bring black and coloured South Africans together in a calculated challenge to the undemocratic rule of the white minority government. Black Americans' unity and influence inspired the black consciousness movement in South

Africa, and probably moved Richard van der Ross to comment, following a two-month trip to the United States in 1962, "Can and will the Coloured man face the problems of minorities as a Black man, or will he persist in constantly being part White?"[79]

During the 1980s and 1990s, black Americans began to reassert the kind of unity and influence they first expressed in the 1950s for the plight of the oppressed South Africans. After the Congressional Black Caucus and Randall Robinson's TransAfrica persuaded Congress to impose its 1986 economic sanctions against the white minority government and presidential candidate Jesse Jackson put the issue of sanctions into the 1988 Democratic platform, the way was paved for Nelson Mandela's eight-city tour of the United States in the summer of 1990. That tour was intended to raise funds for the African National Congress (ANC) and to urge the American government to maintain its economic sanctions. This came less than a year after Mandela's release from twenty-seven years of imprisonment in February 1990. Mandela emphasized the need for continued economic sanctions against South Africa during his speech before the joint session of Congress, and it was the sanctions that eventually led to the legal repeal of apartheid. When little changed, Mandela established the "Democracy Now Tour." In 1991 he invited a delegation of twenty-nine prominent black American leaders and celebrities to South Africa to view the realities firsthand. In a pledge for black Americans to continue to stand behind the oppressed of South Africa, Randall Robinson said to Mandela, "The blood that unites us is thicker than the water that divides us." This is why now-President Mandela, upon his October 1994 visit to President Bill Clinton's White House, took special care in thanking black Americans for their steadfast support.[80] Mandela said, "The Afro-Americans never forgot that Africa is their continent." I heard these words spoken by Mandela on Cable News Network (CNN) while I was in Cape Town, and at that point Arthur Fletcher's worry over the depletion of the black community made sense, even in terms of the history of South African liberation: Black Americans could have been divided against themselves and their unity and political clout undercut, just as black and coloured South Africans were long divided and ruled by their country's white minority government.

Given the way the actual number of black Americans has served to help change history for the better, both in the United States and in South Africa, black leaders such as Arthur Fletcher should not be blamed for seeming more concerned about official population counts than about people's identities. After all, in Latin American countries the only people who are counted as black are unmixed Africans, only slightly mixed blacks, and the very poorest of mulattoes, which greatly reduces the numerical clout of the most oppressed in society. In fact, if the United States used a similar definition for black, which is essentially what the multiracialists are seeking, millions of black Americans would be counted as mulattoes or even as white.[81] In Brazil, for instance, Martin Luther King, Jr., would have been a mulatto (if he wore a suit and tie) and Adam Clayton Powell, Jr. would have been white.[82]

Let us not forget, too, that the multiracialists themselves are concerned about official counts. It is because of the numbers of mixed-race people, which have rapidly increased over the last twenty years, that the multiracialists could stand before the House subcommittee on the census and the OMB portraying their petition for a multiracial classification as urgent. It is also due to these numbers that the multiracialists, if the new classification were adopted, would be able to petition for certain legislation for the mixed population. This petition has already been alluded to by Carlos Fernandez as being next on the agenda of the multiracialists if a multiracial classification were approved.[83]

Not far removed from Paul Williams's concern that the 35,000 people who checked "other" on loan applications are the same people who come to HUD asking for protection against racial discrimination, is the long-standing concern among blacks for the well-being of mixed-race black children. Blacks are concerned that mixed-race black children who are raised as something other than black are being denied the opportunity to learn the survival skills that come with being raised as black, and that one day these children may be traumatized when they learn that society sees them as black. I am thinking of people like Heather Green, a mixed-race black woman from Ontario who says that when she was growing up her adoptive white parents refused to use the words "black," "white," or "race" in their home.[84] Such white parents who have adopted mixed-race black children often prefer to describe their adopted children by some term other than black, evidently believing or hoping that people will overlook the racial mixture in their children and just treat them as human beings. Lois Melina, in an article giving advice to biological or adoptive parents wishing to raise their mixed-race children as biracial, beseeches these parents to examine their motives. "Do you hope that by being viewed as part-white," she asks, "that your child will not encounter negative stereotypes about blacks, or will experience them to a lesser degree?"[85] Children who are well prepared to define themselves as black can experience enough problems with their black identity as is—if less than those who are not at all prepared.[86] Thus, Melina warns biological and adoptive parents of mixed-race children that being biracial does not mean a child can choose to be white or black or can have "the best of both worlds." Rather, being biracial will likely mean that the child will be identified as black.[87]

Carol Camper, who was raised by an adoptive white Canadian family that kept her mixed-race black identity from her, has even stronger words for white women who give birth to black children and raise them outside the black community. Her premise is that the custody of children by mothers, who control and shape their children's identity as no one else will, is rarely challenged, and that in the context of a racist society the mothering of black children by whites might not in this regard be so benign.[88] Camper is not troubled by white women conceiving black children without an enduring relationship to the black men, but she is very angered by the white women she suspects are into the "fad" of having black children as the "fashionable breed." By "fashionable" she means that these white women may be exoticizing their black children in an effort to make some progressive statement about race.[89] In such instances, Camper argues, black children are but another acquired possession of whites, who, even since the days of colonialism and slavery, have been adept at acquiring things and even people that they have wanted.[90] "Why is it still so important to own us?" Camper asks.[91] This ownership of black children by white women disturbs Camper all the more when these white women raise their black children with no connection to the black community to which they will ultimately belong.[92] Such children, she insists, are simply raised as "house niggers"—that is, as blacks stolen away and kept from the community and culture of their black kindred while they are given better opportunities.[93]

Sometimes it sounds as though Susan Graham wants this for all mixed-race people. For instance, Graham said to the House subcommittee on the census that it is "an invasion of privacy with no justification" to have mixed-race people mark the appropriate categories on the census that indicate the multiple sides of their racial ancestry.[94] This sounds as though Graham wishes for mixed-race people (including her own children) to hide something. Is it their partial blackness that she wants them to hide? She almost suggested the same in response to my remarks on the radio talk show we shared. I commented that her children should be privy to historical reality as regards racial identity in this country, a reality that holds her children, no matter what racial designation she chooses for them, to a black identity (at least until racism has been completely eradicated). Graham responded ardently, "My daughter is not black; my daughter is multiracial." Later she qualified the remark by saying that it is not that she does not want her children to be black or white but that they are really multiracial.[95] Still, the multiracialists have declared that mixed-race people are proud of their biraciality and wish to claim the ancestry of both parents. The clinical psychologist whom Graham frequently references for scientific endorsement, Allan C. Carter of Atlanta, has spoken of the importance of mixed-race children "identifying with both races of their parents," of being able "to embrace their total heritage."[96] Is this only theory but not reality? Graham's son Ryan told the House subcommittee on the census that he feels great about being multiracial, but does he feel great about being black and white (especially the former)? Or, better, does he feel great about being black and Jewish—like Sandy Lowe, who says that Jews are not white but are Semites like Arabs?[97]

Ryan Graham is evidently being raised by his mother to think like the mixed-race child who answered a fill-in-the-blank statement in the very way that contradicts the ideals of the multiracialists about biracial identity. The child filled in the blanks of the statement "I used to ___, but now ___" in a way that never allowed the child to deal with his or her complete racial makeup. "I used to think I was white," the child wrote, "but now I know I'm mixed."[98] Such a statement is very different from saying, "I used to think I was white, but now I know I am also black." The original statement shows a coming to grips with not being completely white, but does not show an acceptance of also being black (or whatever the other part of the person's racial ancestry may be). It is comparable to a child saying, "My mother is white but my father is not" or "My mother is from Europe but my father is not." In this regard, I must agree with multiracialist Lawrence Tenzer, who says the term "multiracial" is inadequate because it gives no indication of a person's particular racial makeup.[99] Thus Susan Graham's claim that it is "an invasion of privacy with no justification" to have mixed-race people mark the appropriate racial categories on the census that indicate their racial parentage will help contribute to the raising of "house niggers."

When we speak of "house niggers" as blacks stolen away and kept from the community and the culture of their black kindred, we must also wonder whether the multiracialists are trying to make house niggers out of black historical figures by stealing them away as well, stealing them away for the multiracial history that is to give mixed-race children an exclusive source of self-esteem. Although mixed-race Michael D'Annunzio understands that whites have lost out in their rightful claim to numerous great black Americans who were part white,[100] it appears that many whites in marriages with blacks are trying to claim that black history not for themselves but for their mixed-race children. These white spouses who push multiracial pride know their children cannot have white pride and evidently do not want them to have black pride, so they have to create a pride for them by ransacking black history and renaming it.

The current rhetoric coming from the multiracialist camp suggests that with the initiation of an official multiracial classification might also come more organized attempts to acquiesce black history as multiracial history. This would be accomplished by the multiracialists claiming, as they have already begun to do, that such traditional black historical figures as Frederick Douglass, W. E. B. Du Bois, James Weldon Johnson, Langston Hughes, Malcolm X, Alex Haley, Lena Horne, and General Colin Powell (to cite the ones multiracialists have named) are not black but multiracial.[101] It is interesting in this regard to find multiracialists Edwidge Danticat (a black-white biracial novelist and short story writer) and Daniel Hollis (the white, interracially married co-editor of *New People*) criticizing Afrocentrism for being revisionist history.[102] Are not the multiracialists doing this by now claiming parts of black history to be multiracial history? Indeed, many of them suggest explicitly that this revisionism is appropriate. Gregory Stephens, a white man married to a black woman with a biracial child, says: "In a multiracial democracy we will have to begin moving away from writing history in black and white, towards telling our-story in living color."[103] Mixed-race philosopher Naomi Zack says that one of the requirements in attempting to create a "multiracial" identity based on the history of multiracial people in the United States would be "many intensely deconstructive dialogues with past texts." By that she means a reconstruction of history.[104] So, the multiracials do not need to evolve a historical canon for themselves because the black American canon is being ransacked for them for the best of black tradition.

The United States has a history of this kind of grand larceny, which is why it makes the black community uncomfortable. For instance, during the early twentieth century, black musicians and intellectuals were constantly contesting claims by white scholars that jazz was of Jewish origin, not to mention the claim that white musicians were better interpreters of black music than black people themselves.[105] Now Yvette Walker Hollis, the black co-editor of *New People*, claims that jazz is not black music but is multiracial music. Country and western and rock and roll are white, and rhythm and blues, soul, and rap are black, she says. But jazz, she insists, is multiracial.[106] Jimi Hendrix is also presumed to be no longer black but multiracial, since he was the offspring of a Native American mother and a black American father. An editorialist for *New People* even went so far as to suggest that Hendrix's style of music was not black but "mixed" like he. "With his brown skin and African features," said the writer, "most assumed he was black—but his style of music (although derived from blues and jazz) wasn't the style associated with his black contemporaries."[107] Similarly, in an article that gives advice to interracial parents regarding how to explain Spike Lee's movie *Malcolm X* to multiracial children, Norvella Hickman says Malcolm X was himself multiracial and that it may have been this personal discovery that led him to change his views about hating whites.[108]

What will be said next, then? That the black church is not the black church but is the multiracial church? Or perhaps the multiracialist revisionists will say that the "mainline" black churches (Baptist and Methodist) constitute the colored church, while the "sects" (Holiness and Pentecostal) constitute the "real" black church with its genuine emotional qualities. Thus, is Black History Month to be replaced by Multiracial History Month? Are the African American studies programs at numerous of the nation's colleges and universities to become programs of multiracial studies?

Mixed-race cultural critic Lisa Jones would not doubt that for the multiracialists the answer to these questions would be yes, given the conversation she had with Susan Graham about this whole matter. Jones learned that during Black History Month Graham's son returned home with some information about Langston Hughes and she became disappointed that his teacher had failed to focus on Hughes's multiraciality. Jones says she reminded Graham that black Americans as a whole were multiracial and that while

Hughes never hid the fact that he had white ancestry he nonetheless cast his lot with his darker kin. Graham seemed irritated at the remarks and insisted that the one-drop rule was the only thing that kept Hughes in the black community. Graham even went so far as to say that if Hughes were alive today he would not only choose to be multiracial but would also support the work of her organization, Project RACE.[109] Jones concludes, "Wasn't Graham aware of a rather painful history? One where black people have had their every gift confiscated and attributed to others? Would this now happen in the name of multiracialism?"[110]

A more ominous question to ask is: What would have happened if blacks such as Thurgood Marshall, Mary Church Terrill, Adam Clayton Powell, Jr., and L. Douglas Wilder had been classified as multiracial rather than black? The answer is that there would have been a skimming off of tens or even hundreds of thousands of people from the black community. Among these thousands would have been the countless historical figures who no longer would have been among the foremost intellectual leaders and advocates of blacks. Instead, these talented people would have been struggling for the parity of their own people, the multiracial people, as we saw among the coloured intellectuals and activists of South Africa during the apartheid era. In fact, we can get a sense of what could happen in the United States with the creation of a multiracial classification by examining the reclassification system of South Africa's old apartheid policy. When the white government permitted some coloureds to pass officially as white so that whites could augment their numbers, the government also siphoned off a large proportion of the people who otherwise would have constituted the leadership class in the coloured community. This was the case since the coloureds most likely to be reclassified as white were not simply the ones who had a white appearance but the ones with greater degrees of wealth and education.[111]

So, if blacks such as Marshall, Terrill, Powell, and Wilder had been classified as multiracial rather than black, there would have been a skimming off of some of the best talent in the black community, just as there was a skimming off of some of the best talent among the coloured people by means of apartheid's reclassification system. Such a strategic move on the part of the white minority government fell just short of proposals to co-opt the entire coloured population by granting that population white status or a status close to it, a move that would have left the dispossessed black majority with even fewer allies in their struggle against apartheid.

One person who pushed for the assimilation of the entire coloured population into the white Afrikaans community was the Reverend David Botha, a white Afrikaans minister who was born in the Western Cape in 1925 and whose ministry in the Dutch Reformed Mission Church spanned the years of apartheid, 1948 to 1990. Botha told me that before official apartheid had begun he never saw any difference between the white Afrikaners and the coloured people. He said that in his book of 1960, *Die Opkoms Van Ons Derde Stand (The Rise of Our Third Estate)*, he argued for the complete assimilation of the white and coloured people on sociopolitical grounds. At the same time, however, he presumed the cultural distinctiveness of blacks, with whom he had very little contact. Were it not for the fact that the idea of assimilating whites and coloureds was rejected by the white Afrikaners, who in 1948 completely turned their backs on their coloured kindred, coloured people would have joined whites in their subjugation of blacks. Instead, the black consciousness movement drew in coloured activists and leaders who were an important part of the anti-apartheid struggle, and the black and coloured wings of the Dutch Reformed Church joined forces in 1994 under the name of the Uniting Reformed Church in Southern Africa.[112]

If Thurgood Marshall, Mary Church Terrell, Adam Clayton Powell, Jr., and L. Douglas Wilder had been classified as multiracial, blacks would not have progressed as far as we have. Edward Reuter understood this as far back as 1918. In his book, *The Mulatto in the United States*, Reuter says that to form mulattoes into a separate caste between the white and black races is to lessen the clash between those two races. Such, he continues, would simultaneously deprive the members of the lower caste of a greater chance to advance in society by dispossessing them of leaders who otherwise would protest against the racial policies of whites.[113]

Today a multiracial classification could result in an immediate skimming off of tens or even hundreds of thousands of people from the black community, among whom would certainly be people who otherwise might have become some of the best leaders and advocates of blacks. In other words, the political and economic consequences of such an exodus from blackness could be even greater than the black middle-class exodus from segregated black communities into the suburbs, where they have become increasingly comfortable and forgetful about the truly disadvantaged they have left behind. Fortunately, however, the United States thus far has not been a South Africa. So, from the days of slavery, Frederick Douglass, W. E. B. Du Bois, James Weldon Johnson, Langston Hughes, Malcolm X, Alex Haley, Lena Horne, General Colin Powell, and the rest of us, have been Colored, Negro, Black, Afro-American, and African American together. Together we have come this far "by faith."

But how they have forgotten — "they" being those who now wish to leave black behind. Who are they anyway? Who exactly has forgotten that we have come this far together? In part, it is the white spouses in interracial marriages with blacks, white spouses who have never known our struggle together because our history is not a part of their heritage. These white spouses, like Susan Graham, Francis Wardle, and Daniel Hollis, have never been the caretakers of black history and culture. As a result, they can misconstrue even the meaning of our most precious leaders. For instance, Graham tried to use the words of Martin Luther King, Jr., to argue for her multiracial movement. She ended her testimony before the House subcommittee on the census saying that in 1963 King said "Now is the time to make justice a reality for all God's children" and that she believed King was thinking of multiracial children too. "With your help," concluded Graham, "their time has finally come."[114] For Graham to draw on the words of King is not only for her to put words into King's mouth but the wrong words into his mouth, behavior that is not far removed from the multiracialists who would also like to change King's race to multiracial. However, how can we think of King (the American Mandela)—or for that matter Mandela (the South African King)—and with a clear conscience move deeper into racial classification?

Some of this behavior among interracially married white parents who are trying to revise black history so that it becomes multiracial history is not all about the self-esteem of their mixed-race children. Some of this behavior has to do with the self-esteem of these interracially married white parents who have difficulty accepting their mixed-race children choosing black as an identity. Candace Mills, the interracially married black woman who edits *Interrace* magazine, confesses to this accusation. She says, "The self-esteem of the interracial parents is also an issue here—more an issue than any parent is willing to admit."[115] Indeed, some parents fear that their child may grow up hating them for marrying interracially and giving birth to a child who suffers because of their mixed parentage.[116] But perhaps the greatest fear of these white parents is the possibility of one day hearing something like the remark made by Nila Gupta, the mixed-race Canadian of East Indian and French Canadian parentage. Gupta says that, just as people are sometimes shocked to see a white mother and her mixed-race daughter together, sometimes she herself is shocked to see her own white mother: "I've been in the women of colour community for over a decade, and so I've only been with women of colour. When I see my mother, and I don't see her very often, it's a shock to me that she's my mother."[117]

On the one hand, we can sympathize with the way Gupta's mother might feel upon hearing this. We can also sympathize with the feelings of the mother of Rene-Marlene Rambo, who took a long time to accept the fact that her daughter identified with her father as black. It was so hard for Rambo's mother that her daughter was in fact twenty years old before she could accept her daughter's choice of a black identity.[118] On the other hand, it may be that the interracially married white parents who find it difficult to accept their children being classified as black or identifying as black are not too different from white couples who do not want their sons or daughters to marry someone black. Just as white parents may feel insulted because their children have not chosen to marry people who look like them, so it is possible that some white spouses in interracial marriages may feel insulted when their child identifies with the race of the black spouse. This is Lisa Jones's point about white women who have difficulty seeing her black identity as anything but a rebuff of her white mother: "Deep down I wonder if what they have difficulty picturing is this: not that I could reject, in their minds, my own mother, but that I have no desire to be them."[119]

If the self-esteem of white spouses in interracial marriages is at all part of the impetus behind the multiracial movement, then we must understand that too much is at stake in terms of race relations in the United States for the census movement to continue. Too much is at stake for it to continue just because these white spouses cannot accept their mixed-race children being classified or identifying as black. But could this honestly be the truth—that white spouses in interracial relationships are really behind a movement that could have such grave consequences? Candace Mills unwittingly suggests so, for she not only admits that the self-esteem of the interracial parents is an issue in this identity hopscotch being played around mixed-race people, but that it is interracial parents (principally the ones with this self-esteem problem) who are really behind the multiracial movement. "There is, in fact, no *broad based* movement consisting of biracial/multiracial people," Mills says. "The current fight for a 'multiracial' category is missing this important ingredient as the majority of individuals demanding change and placement as part of such a category are interracial parents."[120]

Given that interracially married whites, for the sake of their racial self-esteem, may be playing identity hopscotch with mixed-race people (at the expense of black people), and given the attempts of multiracialists to steal black history for the people of their proposed multiracial classification, we must reconsider the comment of Francis Wardle (in the previous chapter) that the multiracialists are not the enemy of black people.[121] With Wardle as the example of the interracially married white wishing for blacks to take him as their friend, we must also discount the comment of Carlos Fernandez that intermarriage and multiracial families are good gauges of the degree of racial harmony in society.[122]

For instance, Kathy Russell, Midge Wilson, and Ronald Hall, the authors of *The Color Complex* (1992), argue that whites should no longer be kept ignorant of the color complex in the black community since they have the power to hire, promote, appoint, and elect.[123] But Wardle illustrates that whites can also use this information to divide and rule. He says that the belief that mixed-race blacks are monoracially black reinforces colorism (color prejudice) in the black community through the notion that light-skinned blacks (such as Lani Guinier) are more successful than dark-skinned blacks.[124] First, we wonder if Wardle is not slipping the "mulatto hypothesis" into his argument. Conceived by antebellum whites of the South, the "mulatto hypothesis" holds that blacks with white ancestry are intellectually superior to dark-skinned blacks.[125] Indeed, in claiming our black historical figures, the implication of multiracialists such as Wardle is that few "really black" people have done anything historically. Second, it is a poor argument to suggest that light-skinned and dark-skinned blacks ought to go their separate ways just because whites have historically given special privileges to those blacks who more approximate white appearance. The fact is, the existence of a multiracial group would result in such a degree of ambiguity in the black community (regarding who is or is not black or multiracial) that colorism would actually be exacerbated rather than alleviated. So, contrary to Wardle's instigation of internal division within the black community, black people would tend to agree with sociologist F. James Davis. Davis says that even if black concern about conflicts over color differences were to grow more acute, it is doubtful that the remedies proposed would include doing away with the one-drop rule responsible for color variation in the black community.[126]

Thus, with multiracialists like Wardle in mind who are trying to fragment the black community and steal black history, we should take seriously the question of Ira Shaffer, a black resident of San Jose. Shaffer asked the readership of *Interrace* magazine: "What are your real motives? Is it to dilute or even eliminate the Black race altogether?"[127] The real motives of the multiracialists are difficult to discern, actually, because there are too many glaring contradictions.

Throughout this chapter I have drawn parallels between the racial classification system sought by the multiracialists and the classification system of the former white government of South Africa. Reginald Daniel, a multiracialist of black and white parentage, feels uncomfortable with this comparison. Suggesting that the recognition of a multiracial group in the United States would move toward the "inegalitarian pluralist model" of South Africa, Daniel says, "seems extreme."[128] Indirectly I received a similar response from the OMB administrator, Sally Katzen, with whom I shared a radio round table on the subject of multiracialism and the census. I had just expressed my opinion about a possible repetition of South African race relations, and Katzen said that she knows the decision of the OMB will have "implications" but not necessarily the ones voiced by the preceding speakers.[129] But this particular "extreme" and the possible apartheid implications that Katzen dismisses are exactly what remain possibilities, and I will detail the possible consequences in the next chapter. I will further examine the experience of coloured South Africans in order to determine what we might actually expect in this country were a similar group to emerge. Essentially, I will argue that a multiracial classification would create rather than alleviate problems as regards identity and self-esteem.

THREE

The Curses of the Amorphous Middle Status

In the last chapter I presented arguments against the creation of a multiracial classification by the federal government. In this chapter I will tease out the full possibilities—social, political, and economic—of the concerns expressed by the United States Commission on Civil Rights and the National Urban League when their representatives, Arthur Fletcher and Billy Tidwell, testified before the House subcommittee on the census. For instance, there is much that can be said about Fletcher's worry over the possible development of new "race behavior" among blacks. Fletcher told the census subcommittee that he fears a host of light-skinned blacks would "run for the door" the minute they have another choice in racial classification. They would run for the door not necessarily because their immediate parents are interracial, he fears, but because they sense that there would be some relief from the racism they generally face in this society. They might think, for instance, that economic opportunities would await them if they were classified as something other than black.[1] Fletcher concluded that, though he feared this, he did not know exactly what kinds of problems an "open door" of this kind might produce.[2]

In this chapter we hope to find out. As we proceed on this course, I will use the history of race relations between the coloured people of South Africa and their white and black reference groups as my principal source of data. I will do so because the episodes of that history become scenarios of possible race relations in the United States if a multiracial classification becomes a reality and takes root.

I do agree with one aspect of the multiracial movement: mixed-race people represent the need for a new social consciousness that would permit greater fluidity in people's racial identities and therefore more racial tolerance of those who wish to embrace multiple ethnicities. But I tend to diverge from many of the multiracialists in their belief that creating a new racial classification at the federal level will advance the cause of achieving greater fluidity in people's identities and greater racial tolerance of those who wish to embrace multiple ethnicities. The fact of the matter is that the census categories of race represent political, legal, and professional issues for the public. Therefore, any official racial classification is destined to create a sense of group membership and establish corollary social institutions, where neither had existed previously. This was suggested by Thomas Sawyer, chairman of the House subcommittee on the census, when he said at one of the congressional hearings on Directive No. 15 that the racial categories create "an illusion of specificity."[3]

Thus, while Francis Wardle says the struggle for a multiracial category is not divisive as long as multiracial people remember that the ultimate goal is to overcome racial classification,[4] there is some question as to whether this goal is even possible. How can the ideal of overcoming racial classification remain foremost when mixed-race people are expected to be loyal not only to the races of their parents but to the new multiracial "race" as well? The fact is, too, that solidifying a multiracial classification through federal legislation has the strong potential to undercut the loyalty that mixed-race people would otherwise have to the races of their parents. Additionally, a legislated classification has the strong potential to enhance the loyalty of mixed-race people to the multiracial group alone, as I will show to be the case in South Africa with the coloured people. Indeed, this was the fear of a young white (English) man of Cape Town, who is married to a young coloured woman. The young man informed me that he thought the addition of a multiracial classification in the United

States would add to racial polarization rather than alleviate the country's racial situation, since now there would be three rather than just two major racial groups. He also felt that mixed-race people might be pressured to associate only with other mixed-race people instead of with blacks or whites. A young coloured woman of Xhosa, English, and German background told me that, based on the behavior of South African coloureds toward blacks, she fears that the multiracial group in the United States would begin to see themselves as different and privileged, which would result in unfortunate divisions.

That racial categories create "illusions of specificity" and potentially solidify racial divisions can be easily illustrated. For instance, before the development of Directive No. 15, few people referred to themselves as Hispanic but rather went by their specific nationalities—Mexican, Dominican, and so forth. But the creation of the Hispanic identity, for the convenience of data collection (which is inconvenienced by smaller categories), resulted in this peculiarly American group which is found nowhere else in the world.[5] Similarly, the social construction of the white race, in essence a pan-ethnic group of Europeans, minimized ethnic differences among the European peoples that immigrated to the United States in the nineteenth and twentieth centuries. At the same time this white group solidified the division between itself and those who were not classified as white.[6] Thus, as mixed-race philosopher Naomi Zack says, without this illusion of specificity that results from social construction or external identification, there would not have been a white race, since race is not something that the body experiences psychologically or physically: "Racial identities must be based on racial identifications because the ordinary concept of race is a cultural artifact that varies from place to place and time to time. There is nothing in the nature of consciousness or the phenomenology of human bodily experience which, in the absence of external identification, can constitute a racial identity. Racial identities therefore come after racial identifications."[7] In turn, racial behavior comes after racial identities, which is the principal concern of this chapter.

My own behavior in Cape Town—where there are still white people, black people, and coloured people—vouched for this. I went to Cape Town thinking that I would be viewed as black there. I thought this not simply because I was black in the United States, but because in my previous trips to South Africa and other parts of the African continent, my acquaintances and newly acquired friends were all blacks. Moreover, in Cape Town I had inquired of three black women, African students at the University of the Western Cape, if they saw me as black or as coloured. They said that in appearance alone I looked black. In fact, I am the complexion of many black South Africans (especially the Xhosa people) and I have a particularly black phenotype. I do not look coloured, in the sense that most coloured people tend to look like light-skinned African Americans—which I do not. In addition, based on the way blacks and coloureds responded to me at the University of the Western Cape—black students noticing me and coloured students ignoring me—I felt that I was being identified as black. I felt that way to the extent that I subconsciously began to take on specific racial behavior. For instance, I felt comfortable smiling at black women and nodding "hello" to black men. On the other hand, I felt uncomfortable looking at coloured women and I did not nod to coloured men. So, when I walked across the center of campus with a coloured woman who was one of my acquaintances, I felt self-conscious about being with her. I felt as if we were an interracial pair, even though she looks like any number of light-skinned black Americans whom I would not have felt awkward to walk with on an American college campus.

But some of what I felt in South Africa in terms of my racial identification was but a delusion, on which I had subconsciously based my racial behavior. For I later came to realize that there were many coloured South Africans of my complexion and phenotype. I also came to learn from my coloured acquaintances that my black American history and culture suggested to them (and in many respects I concurred) that I had more in common with them than with black South Africans. Suddenly I started feeling coloured. I shed my sense of perceiving that I was crossing a racial boundary when I was with coloured people and began to accept that these are people who are very much like African Americans.

So, on a cultural and interpersonal level, where I fitted in in South Africa depended on whom I was with: I could be coloured or black. But even when I was feeling coloured, I could not escape the fact that on a political and philosophical level I was committed to being black in the sense of South Africa's black consciousness movement. It was this movement in South Africa that politicized our own one-drop rule in the United States and brought black and coloured South Africans together in the 1970s, 1980s, and early 1990s for their historical liberation struggle. For this reason the black consciousness movement is an important concept to understand as we proceed to analyze its antithesis. The antithesis is the idea that there exists or should exist a separate median group between whites and blacks, whether it be the coloured group in South Africa or the multiracial group in the United States.

It was the black consciousness movement, to define the concept by illustration, that brought together seventeen ministers of the coloured wing of the Dutch Reformed Church to sign on August 17, 1976, an unprecedented declaration condemning apartheid. In the document the signees proclaimed themselves to be in solidarity with all of the oppressed people in their country. In order to free themselves of the "divide and rule" politics of their country's white minority government, they announced that they would no longer accept privileges as so-called coloured people that were not also given to the rest of the black community.[8] Indeed, what better way to undermine racism and even racial classification than for all blacks of the "one drop" to say in a single voice that they are all black and the white government must break down the barrier for all of them together or none of them at all? What better way is there to undermine racism and racial classification than to say that they will not allow the white government to break off a piece of the disenfranchised community and accept it while leaving the rest behind? With this essentially said, the seventeen ministers called upon the "so-called Coloured people" to follow their clerical example so that as one community all dispossessed or "black" people in South Africa could struggle together to achieve their God-given humanity. "In all earnestness we call upon them to accept that the Black community is one inseparable entity," the document said of the coloured people, "that as one community they are deprived of all fundamental rights."[9] Among the seventeen signees was Allan Boesak, a 1967 graduate of the University of the Western Cape who did his doctoral work in theology at a seminary in the Netherlands. It was in the Netherlands that Boesak came into contact with the black theology of James H. Cone, a black American whose ideas he brought to bear on the black consciousness movement in South Africa.

Boesak, accompanied by the sixteen other coloured clergy, was one of those relatively few individuals around the world who rebuked the "divide and rule" strategy that had lured mixed-race people into a median or marginal group in which they were superior to blacks but inferior to whites. Such people, upon this kind of reconsideration of their status in society, tend to internalize the identity of "other" forced on them by the dominant group and thus come to reject the identity (coloured, mulatto, multiracial) that failed to gain them full acceptance in that dominant world. It is at this point that such people will seek to identify and align themselves with their subordinated compatriots, despite the social and cultural distance that had developed between them. In doing so, they sometimes use the advantages they have acquired in that median position (in Boesak's case his advanced theological training in the Netherlands) to become leaders of the lowest subordinate group and initiators of collective action among the two lower-subordinate strata. Thus we hear Boesak say in 1983 to a group of Indians, "We want *all* South Africans to have their rights; not just a select few, not just coloureds and Indians after they are made honorary whites."[10]

One of Boesak's struggles in the effort to effectuate "black consciousness" in the so-called black, coloured, and Indian communities of South Africa was to unite the segregated "black" churches of the Dutch Reformed denomination. Under apartheid the Dutch

Reformed Church in South Africa, the denomination of the majority of the country's white political hierarchy, was divided along racial lines into four segregated groups. The Dutch Reformed Church was the white wing, the Dutch Reformed Mission Church the coloured wing, the Reformed Church in Africa the Indian wing, and the Dutch Reformed Church in Africa the black wing. But Boesak, a minister in the Dutch Reformed Mission Church, saw the church as really comprised of only two parts—the ruling white church and the remaining ruled churches—and he wanted the churches suffering under white dominance to unite under the banner of blackness.[11]

At the turn of the 1980s, apartheid in the Dutch Reformed Church in South Africa was still holding firm, and Boesak would remark that "we still are a society where people are being judged by the colour of their skin rather than by the content of their character."[12] But around the turn of the 1990s, the political climate was beginning to warm. As of 1994, following the democratic elections, the black and coloured wings of the Dutch Reformed Church in South Africa united as the Uniting Reformed Church. Unfortunately the Indian group, comprised of that very group of South Africans to whom Boesak had appealed in 1983 and many times since, has not yet joined the Uniting Church. Also unfortunate is the fact that the black and coloured churches, albeit "united," still remain essentially segregated due to the fallout of apartheid. Although there are scattered Indian and white members in the coloured and black congregations of the Uniting Church, the apartheid legislation known as the Group Areas Act kept blacks and coloureds in segregated residential areas (separate areas for blacks, whites, coloureds, and Asians). In addition, during the apartheid era the Dutch Reformed congregations were neighborhood churches, and people were not encouraged to go to churches outside their neighborhoods.

To Boesak, a leading catalyst in actualizing the Uniting Church, black consciousness was the "positive corrective of and reaction to the negative existence of Black people in South Africa."[13] His important role in this corrective was the proliferation of black consciousness among the young coloured people of his genera-tion. For instance, coloured sociologist Jimmy Ellis told me that the black consciousness movement was for him and many others an emancipatory experience because it was striving to come to terms with the negative definition of coloured identity. Boesak's important role in the black consciousness movement also resulted in black consciousness being passed along to the succeeding gen-eration of coloured youths, many of whom went to the University of the Western Cape as he had from 1963 to 1967. One young coloured woman (the woman of Xhosa, English, and German ancestry), who was a student at the university during the 1970s when Boesak was student chaplain, told me, nearly repeating Boe-sak's words, that if you understand that whites have been conning you and that you actually have been treated as black, then you become black for political reasons.

Today black consciousness still exists among many coloured people, but it has also opened up to a new phase. It is a phase that has a longer history than black consciousness, as it does in the United States among black Americans. Some coloured people, who are either of the black consciousness mindset or influenced by it, are deciding to revisit their African roots, which have long been suppressed if not outright denied. This is a benchmark phe-nomenon, since, as I was told by a coloured woman, few coloureds ever stress their African roots. This evolution of a con-nection between black consciousness and African consciousness can be traced in a remark by coloured historian Roy du Pre:

> Despite their fear of the African, coloureds would have to consider the possibilities of throwing in their lot with the other victims of racism on the basis of common oppression, suffering and depriva-tion. . . . Thus, on the basis of common purpose (overthrowing a racist regime, destroying racism and creating a non-racist democra-tic society in which all are free and equal), coloureds ought logi-cally to abandon any desire to join with whites and throw in their lot with the rest of the oppressed. . . . After all, coloureds are also Africans, albeit of mixed ancestry. Their destiny lies with their fel-low-Africans.[14]

Some coloureds, such as the history professor with whom I spoke at the University of the Western Cape, actually call themselves African and reject the idea of being coloured, as du Pre does. Some coloureds, according to the three coloured nationalists I spoke with, are even willing to accuse black South Africans of being racists if they do not recognize the coloured people as indigenous Africans as well.

The idea of coloured people being considered a different ethnic group among such Africans as the Xhosa and Zulu would go a long way in contesting the claim from black nationalists that the coloureds are "settlers" like the whites. To the more politically minded coloured activist, taking on an African identity is also a way to prevent the wholesale assimilation of coloured people into the white Afrikaans culture and community. Among such persons is the secretary-general of the Pan-Africanist Congress (PAC), Benny Alexander, who changed his name to Khoisan X following the April 1994 elections. He said that the destruction of the indigenous Khoikhoi and Khoisan identity of the coloured people resulted in their assimilation into white culture and their inability to struggle against white domination. This, he argued, was seen by the fact that the coloured vote in the Western Cape went to the National Party, the party of the former white minority government. He continued, "When this happens you fail to vote away from the oppressive agent and you vote toward him."[15]

The point I am making by setting up this survey of a part of coloured history is that mixed-race Americans of black and white parentage should not need to wait for the creation of an American apartheid, and the resultant dashing of all hopes of acceptance by the majority community, to choose black consciousness (the black identity). That is, they should not need an explicit apartheid and white nonacceptance to choose black consciousness over the new multiracial ("coloured") identity during our continued struggle for liberation in the United States. Furthermore, as I will explore, the coloured classification in South Africa has resulted in an unsavory situation that could be reproduced in the United States: a whole group of mixed-race people being caught betwixt and between two major incompatible social groups and being politically manipulated by the propaganda of the group that is in power.

In sociological literature the betwixt position between two major incompatible social groups is called "marginal"—language popularized by sociologist Everett Stonequist, who first borrowed it from his professor, Robert E. Park. It is said that this "marginal situation," typically experienced by people of mixed racial ancestry, can result in individuals feeling isolation and uncertainty of belongingness. This feeling is often based on the marginal group existing at the outskirts of two reference groups while being a full member of neither.[16] Such groups may be marginal by virtue of the fact that the race that would accept them they despise, while the race they aspire to refuses them.[17] So, part of the marginality of coloured South Africans is that they are the "cultural equals" of whites but not their social equals.[18] Richard van der Ross recognized this marginality himself in 1963. He said, "The problem of the minority group is aggravated when the group is, in addition to being the numerical minority, also in a political minority, and is doubly aggravated when it is squeezed between other groups, to which it looks hesitantly, being uncertain of how it will be received by them. This is the ever-present problem of the Coloured people."[19]

H. F. Dickie-Clark, in a 1955-originated ten-year study of the coloured people of Durban, says that whites in South Africa have a certain unified identity based on the gains from their dominance and their guardianship of Western culture, and blacks have a unified identity based on their origin in Africa and their having maintained substantial parts of their indigenous culture. On the other hand, he says, coloureds have no culture of their own to champion: "The Whites can achieve a kind of unity of action on the basis of the gains from their dominance and their claim to represent and defend Western culture. Africans can draw politically on their African culture, their origin in Africa and on the obvious injustice of their complete social exclusion. . . . The Coloureds, however, have no distinctive Coloured culture of which they can claim to be exclusive champions, but are culturally tied to the

Whites."[20] This is essentially what South African scholar Z. J. De Beer means when he says coloured people live in the unfortunate position of being between "the hammer of white supremacy and the anvil of black nationalism."[21]

Part of the experience of marginality can also derive from the intermediary group being defined in an ambiguous way. With regard to coloured people, coloured historian Roy du Pre says the Population Registration Act of 1950, which required every South African to carry a racial identification card, simply defined a coloured person as someone who was neither a European nor an African. Thus, legally, coloured people were a non-group, says du Pre, a group created out of the left-overs of the other racial groups.[22] Similarly, van der Ross says that being coloured is to be "not anything which is not Coloured." He says that by defining himself in this way, we can see that it was easier for him to follow the lead of the apartheid government and say what he is not rather than say what he is.[23] Van der Ross continues with a point that would seem equally relevant to the American multiracials if the multiracialists were to succeed in their census movement: "Because we are the result of so much mixing, it is difficult, indeed impossible, to define our limits. . . . That is why, of all South Africans today, we have the least sense of identity."[24] Sociologist Jimmy Ellis added that the problem of coloured identity—the uncertainty of where they fit in since they are Western but kept out of mainstream Western (white) society—feeds directly into coloured "insecurity." This is not something that goes unnoticed by whites and blacks. Both a white Afrikaans woman in Cape Town (who is married to a coloured man) and a Zulu taxi driver in Johannesburg told me that coloured people are uncertain as to who they are and where they fit in. One coloured woman told me that she thought multiracials in the United States would fall into the very same trap as the coloured people did. She said they will be, as coloureds say, "orphans of the country"—that is, people who reject a black identity but are disallowed a white identity.

There are many mixed-race people on this side of the Atlantic Ocean who already understand the points being made by the coloured people. Like the seventeen coloured ministers who signed a declaration calling for black consciousness, these Americans are avoiding wholeheartedly the ever-present threat of the kind of racial behavior that would serve the whites in power. Heather Green, a Canadian of black and white parentage, captures the essence of that document signed by the coloured ministers on August 17, 1976. She says, "If I do anything short of vigilantly embracing my African identity—consciously, wholeheartedly and without illusions about African realities—then I may be swept away, co-opted, consumed and sucked into the European power structure, culture and mindset which preaches that because of my African blood, I am inferior." Green continues, "Identifying as an African woman, as a daughter of African people and African ancestors, I vow that I am not and will not become part of any value system which seeks to crush other races through its way of life."[25]

Green understands that if she does anything short of consciously and wholeheartedly embracing her black identity then she may be sucked into the European culture and power structure through a mindset that inferiorizes anyone with a "drop" of blackness. The black consciousness advocates aside, the history of South Africa shows us that when a median group of mixed-race people has privileges over a lower-strata group of blacks, that median group will become comfortable with its privileges and not easily relinquish them. They will not even relinquish them for the moral ideal of a nonracial society. So, we could presume that creating a median group in the United States, a group of mixed-race people like the coloureds in South Africa, would be retrogressive in terms of the historical progress of American race relations. For example, it is true that Sunday morning in the United States is still the most segregated time in American society, that black Christians tend to go to the institution whites know as the black church and white Christians tend to go to the institution blacks know as the white church. But who is to say that with the creation of a median group of mixed-race people that American Christian denominations would not end up like the principal church in South Africa.

Under apartheid the Dutch Reformed Church in South Africa had separate black and coloured wings, separate wings that joined hands in 1994 partly as a result of the black consciousness influence. Could such extremes in racial behavior occur in the United States once black consciousness is abandoned in favor of the creation of a multiracial group?

We know from historical experience in this country alone, as well as from our knowledge of the history of South Africa, that there is no end to the far-flung possibilities of racial behavior. So, in addition to the possibility that there could develop a multiracial church that is separate from the black church and the white church, there is also another possibility as mixed-race people move farther away from black consciousness. Whites, if they ever see themselves becoming a minority government in future generations (given the changing demographics), could do as the white minority government in South Africa did when they allowed some coloureds to reclassify as white. The white minority in Brazil does the same thing in admitting near-whites to their group. As I pointed out in chapter 1, with particular reference to Rev. David Botha, there are whites who would like to see white and coloured Afrikaans people assimilate. In this regard, what I did not say about the coloured professor whom I mentioned in chapter 1, the professor who said he would have no problem with a child of his being classified today as multiracial, is that he also said he would have no problem with whites and coloureds assimilating. He said that, since coloureds never had much political clout, having their numbers diminished by the assimilation that Botha desires is not a problem for him. My point is that we could expect similar attitudes in the United States. Since Arabs and Jews (both Semites) are presently classified as white in the United States, it would be a short step to mandate by law that all mixed-race people with a white parent be classified as white. This would mean that while "one drop" of black "blood" presently makes one black, the United States could end up like apartheid South Africa or present-day Brazil where a few drops of white "blood" could make one white. History bears this out.

On the other end of the spectrum of far-flung possibilities of racial behavior, we might even expect to see some mixed-race people within a new multiracial race calling for a multiracial homeland, like the more extreme coloured nationalists in South Africa. After all, reference to the multiracial community as "The Interrace Nation" is not too different from designations used by other nationalist groups that have called for separate homelands—the Nation of Islam, the Afrikaner Nation, and so forth. The several coloured nationalists I talked to in Cape Town told me that blacks from other areas of South Africa, especially the Transkei area, were "invading" the Cape area, squatting on the land and demanding housing and benefits. Because these coloured nationalists (or "Cape nationalists") fear that within a decade blacks could outnumber the coloured people in the Western and Northern Cape (where coloureds have staked their ancestral claims), they want an independent state in this dual region so they can control black immigration.

The African National Congress (ANC) has condemned such statements coming from coloured nationalists in Johannesburg and indicated that dividing South Africans based on their ethnicity is the last thing the country needs after all the years they fought against apartheid.[26] But the coloured nationalists I spoke with find such ANC statements to be mere hypocrisy since the ANC had supported a Palestinian homeland in the Middle East. Thus, it takes no prophecy, only a sense of humor for the absurd, to imagine what might come from the mouths of the multiracial nationalists of the United States if in future generations there exists this new race.

But with the seeming extremes and absurdity aside, the fact is that the coloured nationalists I met insisted (and I can hear some multiracial echoes in this) that to speak of pan-Africanism as black, as W. E. B. Du Bois did despite his own mixed heritage, is to forget that Africa is not only "black Africa" but is also "brown Africa." To speak of pan-Africanism as black is, they said, to forget that South Africa also has brown (coloured) people whose black ancestors, the Khoi peoples, were in the Cape area thousands of years before the other black ethnic groups. Yet despite their claims to being a part of what Du Bois called pan-Africanism, the Cape nationalists are in search of establishing a pan-coloured movement. This pan-coloured movement would include mixed-race people of various ethnicities throughout the world who would work together to obliterate their collective invisibility. By doing so, the forgotten brown race may be recognized worldwide alongside the black and white races. Although South African coloureds have their own unique ethnicity based on ancestral, historical, and cultural distinctions, the pan-colouredism that the Cape nationalists envision as linking the mixed-race people of South Africa and the United States would be based on the sociopolitical commonality of oppression. This oppression, they say, comes not only at the hands of the white race but the black race as well.

Whether or not a new race of American multiracials joins an international pan-coloured movement spearheaded by Cape nationalists in South Africa is not the point I am seeking to establish. The important point is that once a multiracial classification is established by the United States government, those Americans who are currently considered black might demonstrate the same kinds of racial behavior that coloured South Africans have demonstrated because of their marginal position in South African society. This is the reason Lisa Jones asks whether we might not be establishing a Cape Town, USA. Jones points out that Carlos Fernandez of the AMEA believes that a median racial category is not racist in itself since it is the way in which such a category is used that counts. However, she asks why we would not assume that such a median category would be equally manipulated in the United States. She says, "It's been asked before, and until I hear a good comeback, the question stands: Would 'multiracial' be akin to South Africa's 'colored' caste created under apartheid?"[27] Or we well might ask: Are we not establishing a Brazilia or Sao Paulo, USA? Although in Brazil the tradition of "whitening" (marrying lighter to whiten and socially heighten one's offspring) is not attributable to intentional white ideological manipulation,[28] it is still abused within the context of the institutional racism of whites.

All that I have just said intends to prepare the way for a question I think ought to be taken seriously with regard to the multiracial movement: Who is to say that the United States might not mock the "pigmentocracy" of South Africa or Brazil in an unsuspected swing toward radical conservatism? Pam Austin, a young adult American of white and black parentage, said in answer to this question:

> Considering who has been running this government lately, I look at that sometimes and I think, "You know, it's real possible for them to look down at this group [multiracials] and say, most of you are educated, most of you come from middle-class homes, okay, we could use those people, and you're not like those poor black folks over there, those folks down on the ground. You're different." I.e. better. And it's like creating that whole mulatto class that existed after the Civil War with everybody saying, "Well, you're a little bit better, a little bit different. Why don't you come over here with us?" Co-opting that whole group of people, using it as a buffer zone.[29]

Evidently Pam Austin's concerns have merit, for Paul Williams, Assistant Secretary of the Department of Housing and Urban Development (HUD), told the House subcommittee on the census that he believed that a person checking "multiracial" rather than "black" on a loan application for a new home would quite possibly benefit.[30]

Rainier Spencer, a young man of black and white parentage, understands that, given who is running this government and who is in the majority in this country, new categories end up being not progressive or subversive but a buffer between the white and black races. He says that regardless of the status of the mixed-race median group relative to the lowest subordinate group (blacks), the median group is still not permitted to be white. Spencer continues, "Society at large therefore performs no reassessment of its policies. It merely takes note of the fact that certain non-whites are creating classifications amongst themselves. What is truly quixotic is the idea that a mere amendment to the American system of racial categorization could possibly escape the structures of oppression and marginalization that support it."[31]

Spencer's point is backed by the research of Edward Reuter, as documented in his classic book, *The Mulatto in the United States* (1918). Reuter learned, for example, that the mulatto in Jamaica, when the island was a British colony, behaved in a way that benefited the white minority rulers. In hearing Reuter's comment about early-twentieth-century Jamaica, we can easily insert references to late-twentieth-century South Africa without disturbing the accuracy of his argument. Reuter wrote:

> The mulattoes are not a numerically important part of the Negro population, but the white rulers have realized their possibilities for harm as dissatisfied agitators among the blacks. They also have realized the possibilities of the group as a harmonizing factor in the racial situation. As a consequence, they have utilized the mixed-bloods as a means of control of the lower and more numerous group, and as a means of lessening the friction between extreme types of the population on the Island.

By catering to the mulattoes' desire for special recognition and by fostering their caste feeling of superiority to the blacks, the English have built up a middle-class group between the white aristocracy and the black peasantry. This group includes the educated and professional classes of the Negro group and the more successful colored individuals in all lines of human endeavor.

This mulatto class has been separated in sentiments and interests from the black group by a deliberate and thorough-going application of the "divide and rule" policy. By a judicious distribution of petty political offices and honors, the whites secure their loyalty and cooperation in the affairs of government in spite of the rigid color line which they draw against them in social affairs. Any Negro who shows ability or talent for leadership is diplomatically separated from the black group, and his or her loyalty to the government and to the ruling whites is assured by a political or other honor, proportional to his or her danger as a disgruntled agitator among the blacks.[32]

In Brazil, the process of "whitening" upholds white dominance in a similar fashion. Whitening is the process of darker-skinned people becoming increasingly white generation after generation by marrying lighter-skinned people. By adhering to the popular belief that this is the means of acquiring class elevation and greater economic and political participation, whitening has dampened polarities in race relations and defused potential explosions that may result from racial discrimination. Concurrently, by removing "qualified" people of color from the subordinate black group and encouraging their identification with the dominant whites, whitening prevents blacks and mulattoes from developing a connected sense of group identity arising from their shared subordination. This keeps at bay any united and powerful black opposition to whites.[33] Leslie Rout, Jr., a historian who traveled to Brazil several times, said he noticed that the animosity between blacks and mulattoes was very intense. As a result, he wondered which side the mulattoes would take if ever there were a race war. He answered his own question when he said that he recalled ever so clearly that mulattoes saw no relationship between themselves and darker-skinned people in Brazil or the United States.[34]

Similarly, the fact that a coloured South African who appeared white and was accepted as white could be reclassified as white under the apartheid policies resulted in many coloured people defending whites. According to van der Ross, this occurred if only for the reason that they too might one day become white. Van der Ross draws this illustration: "It is said that the English working classes will not do away with the aristocracy, as every working class mother hopes that one day *her* son or daughter may be a 'Sir' or a 'Lady'!"[35] In this regard, the worst part of the system of whitening is the etiquette of silence with regard to the issue of race. So strong is the desire of most whites and many black and mulatto Brazilians to adhere to the belief in racial democracy that a moratorium exists on the admission or discussion of racial discrimination. Anyone who raises the issue of racism or somehow expresses racial consciousness is seen as un-Brazilian and even as a threat to the unity and strength of the country.[36] Yet the etiquette of not discussing race and the resultant lack of racial consciousness prevents the possibility of identifying racist behavior and policies, and prevents organizing against racism for the protection and advancement of all Brazilians with African ancestry.

Indeed, similar analyses are revealed upon a careful scanning of the vast literature on mixed-race people in modern times. For instance, in his classic *Sex and Race: Negro-Caucasian Mixing in All Ages and All Lands* (1952), J. A. Rogers, the early twentieth-century black journalist, warns that whites practice "divide and conquer" by giving mulattoes certain privileges. History shows that the loyalty of mixed-race people as a group usually can be secured, Rogers says, if that group is granted a status higher than the minority-half of their mixed ancestry. He says of coloured South Africans that the little taste of freedom the white minority government gave them over blacks made them look more hungrily toward the whites and more disdainfully away from the blacks.[37] H. F. Dickie-Clark adds to this analysis in his book, *The Marginal Situation* (1966). He says that the creation of a median position in a society (an upper-subordinate group) tends to inhibit the political activity of that median group, whereas if there were no median group then the entire subordinate group, undivided, would use its numbers and energies to achieve equality with the dominant group. In other words, when there is a lower-subordinate group in a society (blacks), the upper subordinate group (mixed-race people) might be reluctant to risk losing its status through attempts to improve it. Therefore, the existence of a lower subordinate stratum is a constant reminder to mixed-race people, as it was to coloured South Africans under apartheid, that their position could easily worsen.[38]

In such a situation, only the lowest subordinate group is interested in overturning the status quo. Thus, prior to 1976, many coloureds stood with whites against blacks in the sense that they seemed to prefer rule by the white-minority National Party rather than risk a black government permitting blacks to compete equally for employment and to enter their residential areas and schools. As Z. J. De Beer wrote in 1961, this is the reason certain coloured intellectuals had little success in trying to lead their people into an alliance of protest with blacks. Instead, De Beer concluded, the coloured people stuck to the whites "as an ill-used wife will often stick to her husband."[39]

Richard van der Ross told me that he essentially agreed with this view. While he thought it would be presumptuous of him to say whether or not he approved of the multiracial movement in the United States, he did feel that he could describe the racial situation in his country and thereby issue a warning based on that experience. He said that a dominant white group could misuse the multiracial classification to divide the ranks of those trying to seek their rights—that is, that they could use this median group of "Europeanized hybrids" to co-opt the multiracials into the white ranks and thereby weaken blacks. It would not even be surprising, van der Ross said, if whites put their arms around the shoulders of multiracials without really embracing them, so that they could easily abandon them at some future point.

The most unfortunate part of the history of median (upper-subordinate) groups is that they are often molded into "white" racists, who Allan Boesak said are worse than whites. It is particularly unfortunate when in reality the white arm around their shoulders, the arm that has led them into racist behavior, does not really intend to embrace them. In this regard, apartheid succeeded in making racists out of the coloured people. In fact, this occurred to such a degree that van der Ross wrote in 1960 that it was nonsense for coloured people to think that their salvation lay with blacks:

> I call this last idea, the idea that the African will one day release us from our troubles, nonsense for a good reason. Why, in the first place, should he? Have the Coloured people ever shown any great love for the African? Haven't the Coloured people shared in the prosperity which both White and Coloured have gained from the African's labour? In the teaching profession, haven't our children been treated better . . . ? And haven't we accepted and shared in this differential treatment at his expense? In the trades, haven't we

benefited from the fact that we could become tradesmen, while he had to remain the labourer? And haven't we often heard the Coloured tradesman swear at his "boy" (b . . . . *kaffer!*) imitating and even bettering his White colleague? Why, then, should the African spare us?

So I think that many of the coloured people in the starry-eyed camp are being plain dishonest. They want to *use* the African. He must be the means to get us what we want, so we must now pat him on the back at every available opportunity. These very people must not underrate the African. He has seen through the White man—he can see through us.[40]

There was a time when any alliance with the lower-subordinate strata of society was unthinkable by the coloured people. But when the apartheid policies drastically reduced the advantages of being coloured, so that the disadvantages of the system outweighed the advantages, cooperation with all the government's opponents to abolish apartheid seemed to be the only reasonable strategy for procuring a viable future.[41] This feeling that the disadvantages of apartheid outweighed the advantages is what pushed blacks and coloureds together to fight side-by-side for a "new South Africa," which came to fruition in April 1994 when the country held its first democratic elections. But even after the apartheid system was dismantled and the country was moving toward the elections, the coloured people, still a median and marginal group, were yet to be manipulated by white politicians of the National Party.

During the 1994 election campaign, when President F. W. de Klerk of the National Party was running against Nelson Mandela of the ANC for the presidency, de Klerk's party strategized to convince the coloured people that, black consciousness notwithstanding, they were not black and in fact were deserving of the protection and privileges his party would give them if they won office. Van der Ross, though he turned down an offer to join the National Party, told me that the National Party was successful in their propaganda among the coloured people. "You are not black," they said to the coloured people. "You are like us"—even though the whites never before treated coloureds "like them," said van der Ross. The result of the coloured people being told that they are like the whites when they still were not treated like the whites is that they were pushed deeper into the marginality. As Arnold Green explains, even complete rejection is easier to bear than uncertain or grudging acceptance.[42]

This manipulation of the coloured people by the National Party was done solely by political maneuvering, the same kind that could convince a new race of multiracial Americans that new winds of political change are blowing in their favor. In South Africa this political maneuvering began in 1990 with President de Klerk's speech to Parliament on February 2, which political analysts have called the first campaign event of the 1994 election.[43] In that speech, in which de Klerk got a campaign jump on Mandela (whose freedom he was to announce), de Klerk spoke of a "new South Africa." He said the aim of necessary negotiations among representative leaders of the entire population was to ensure lasting peace. The Prohibition of Mixed Marriages Act and the Immorality Act, laws that had sometimes forced interracial couples to flee the country, had already been abolished in 1985.[44] But de Klerk said nothing explicit about the repeal of the staple laws of apartheid—the Population Registration Act and the Group Areas Act. He did not do that until his opening speech to the 1991 session of Parliament, on February 1. But in his famous 1990 address he did say of the "new South Africa": "The aim is a totally new and just constitutional dispensation in which every inhabitant will enjoy equal rights, treatment and opportunity in every sphere of endeavour—constitutional, social and economic."[45] He also said, "Our country and all its people have been embroiled in conflict, tension and violent struggle for decades. It is time for us to break out of the cycle of violence and break through to peace and reconciliation. The silent majority is yearning for this. The youth deserve it."[46] Ultimately the goal of the new "constitutional dispensation" was to create a democratic constitution and establish a universal franchise.[47]

The political jump that de Klerk got on Mandela with this speech of 1990, even before Mandela was released from prison shortly afterwards, was later helped by the country's religious establishment. This is illustrated in a small tract I picked up in an interracial church in Johannesburg in the summer of 1992. The tract was entitled "What Is the Answer?" and was published by the Gospel Publishing House in Roodepoort. Accompanying this question on the cover page is a photograph of Nelson Mandela (top left), Mikhail Gorbachev (top right), George Bush (bottom left) and John Major (bottom right). Inside the cover is a list of societal ills, among which is the statement "Racism divides our country." Ensuing is the statement that the answer to these problems cannot be found in politicians (no doubt those on the cover) but only in Christ. It should strike our attention that at that time Mandela was just out of prison and thus out of place in the group of national leaders, while it was the white minority government still in power at that time which escaped criticism. Mandela was imprisoned by the white South African government for twenty-seven years and yet, in a Christ-like spirit, he came out of prison calling for racial reconciliation, a new democracy that would be nonracial and nonsexist. Why was Mandela on the cover of this tract and not de Klerk?

During campaign speeches in coloured communities, de Klerk, in promoting a "new" National Party, made explicit apologies for the pain the apartheid policies of his party had caused the coloured people. Coloured voters outside the ANC seemed to accept the apology, particularly the older coloured people, one young coloured woman told me.[48] Additionally, the same coloured woman said that the National Party was successful in indoctrinating coloureds to believe that whites were the true authorities. The National Party was also successful in portraying the ANC as a party of blacks which would favor blacks over coloureds once Mandela was in power (electioneering not unfamiliar to American voters). In fact, the National Party even produced its own "Willie Horton" of the Republican campaign that helped get George Bush elected to the American presidency in 1988. The National Party produced a black (rather than "brown") image of the murderer known as the Station Strangler who had been terrorizing the coloured community for several years and was still at large. Evidently this propaganda was implying that without white rule and protection coloured people would be strangled to death under black majority rule.[49]

In a live televised campaign debate between the two leading presidential candidates, on April 14, 1994, Mandela confronted de Klerk on the racist electioneering of his party in the Western Cape.[50] But the National Party's campaign in the Cape continued to run on its strategy of instilling in the coloured community fear of being overrun by the black majority. Finally, the National Party never embraced the democratic ideal of nonracialism, because they wanted to maintain "minority rights" for whites and coloureds. This was a scenario that van der Ross had anticipated as early as 1961, since he knew even then that whites could not rule forever.[51]

In an essay analyzing the results of the election, Andrew Reynolds shares insights that could be a forecast of elections in the United States if a "coloured" or multiracial classification were to be created. Reynolds says that the success of the National Party in garnering the votes of the coloured people was a testament to a campaign that played on the fears coloureds have about their position in a democratic country where the overwhelming majority of people are black. The National Party played on these fears by using a "divide and rule" strategy that set disenfranchised coloureds against disenfranchised blacks, in part by instigating racist stereotypes within each community.[52] The successful portrayal of the ANC as a party of and for blacks is the reason that for many coloureds the only choice during the election was between voting for the National Party or sitting on the wall and not voting at all. H. F. Dickie-Clark terms this situation "political marginality," which he says results from conflicting pressures. Pushing the coloured people in one direction is their cultural whiteness, the recollection and remnants of their social equality with whites, and their intermediate status in the social hierarchy. The cross-pressures comprise the extensive social exclusion they share with blacks.[53]

In his analysis of the months leading up to the elections, Hermann Giliomee captured some of these conflicting pressures. He says that while the coloureds have not rushed to embrace the notions of a nonracial Afrikaans people, it is clear that they have little interest in the "nation" or "people" idea as defined by the ANC. It is also clear that they would prefer for the country to be built around the interests of whites (17 percent of the population) and themselves (10 percent of the population).[54] For his evidence Giliomee points to a February 1994 poll showing that 42 percent of coloureds favored the National Party, 17 percent the ANC, and that 38 percent were undecided or refused to say.[55]

The election was held April 26, 27, and 28, 1994, and as suspected the highest percentage of the coloured vote—30 percent (1.2 million)—went to the National Party. Only 4 percent of the coloured vote (0.5 million) went to the ANC.[56] The ANC won the presidency because the majority of the citizens of South Africa (70 percent) are black, but the National Party won the important Western Cape region, the only province to elect a white premier (governor). The coloured people, who comprise the largest voting block in the Cape, gave only a fourth of their vote in the race for premier (27 percent) to the ANC, even though the candidate the ANC had put up for the premiership was the coloured clergyman Allan Boesak. The coloured people gave two-thirds of their vote to the National Party, even though the candidate they had put up was none other than Hernus Kriel, the former Minister of Law and Order under the apartheid regime.[57] Now that the elections are over and the National Party holds regional power in the Western Cape, the Party's "divide and rule" tactics have left a legacy of tension between blacks and coloureds. Because so many coloureds voted for the National Party, many blacks consider them to be "sell-outs"—unreliable and inferior. Their vote just verifies for some of the more radical blacks their long-held belief that the coloureds, along with the whites, are "settlers" in South Africa.

As regards the political well-being of blacks in the United States, mixed-race blacks (those who wish to gather under a legislated category of "multiracial") could similarly choose to align themselves politically with whites. Or even if there were an inclination not to do so, such mixed-race blacks might be a minority among the entirety of multiracials and would lack influence in a group that would be as heterogeneous politically as it would be ethnically. Thus, only with their monoracial black kindred could mixed-race blacks have some degree of worthwhile political influence and protection. This should be understood in advance of any hasty decision to become "multiracial." For once a breach in kinship occurs between those who are black and those mixed-race blacks who defect to a more privileged racial classification, the breach would be difficult to heal, as we have learned from observing blacks and coloureds in South Africa.

Another possible concern is that mixed-race people with partial black ancestry could choose to align themselves culturally with whites. Carlos Fernandez of the AMEA says that racism and ethnocentrism would not flourish among multiracial people because they cannot hate the heritage of their parents without also disrespecting their parents and sacrificing their own integrity.[58] But just because someone is part black does not necessarily mean they would be in solidarity with the black struggle. One white American woman, who is married to a black man, says her father refused any relationship with her interracial family even though he was himself a mixture of white and Native American.[59] This behavior that contradicts Fernandez's claim would not be surprising to sociologist Everett Stonequist, for he believes that the reflex of mixed-race people is to identify with the dominant race, a reflex he acknowledges can create a gulf between mixed-race people and the subordinate race.[60] This is what Lisa Jones fears could happen in the United States. She says that if there is a goal in the quest to establish a multiracial category at the federal level, it appears to be an interest on the part of multiracials for assimilation into the white mainstream.[61] Linda James Myers, a clinical psychologist who works with mixed-race children, evidently fears the same. For she says that as these people aspire to associate with white privilege, black Americans would be pushed farther down the line.[62]

That the reflex of mixed-race people as a societal group is to identify with the dominant group, resulting in a gulf between mixed-race blacks and the subordinate black race, is also what South African history shows us. Through biological and cultural assimilation, coupled with a tendency toward social distinction based on color, the coloured population gradually assumed the social and cultural characteristics of white Western society. The church played a central role in the cultural acclimation of coloureds toward whiteness, insofar as most coloureds are Christians and follow the religious pattern found among whites.

Language has also played a role in shaping the shared worldview that coloureds have with the white Afrikaans people. More than four-fifths of the coloured population speak Afrikaans as their first language, a percentage that would have been higher were it not for those coloureds who taught their children English because they perceived Afrikaans to be the tongue of the ruling whites. To the coloured nationalists I spoke to, there is a nuance of difference in the way Afrikaans is spoken by whites and by coloureds, which results in a shade of dissemblance in the worlds of white and coloured Afrikaans speakers. On the other hand, Afrikaans is Afrikaans, and undoubtedly its coloured and white speakers share some good portion of a world. This same language that has helped shape a shared world between white and coloured Afrikaans people has also distanced coloureds from blacks, who speak their own ethnic languages. Regarding the cultural distance that differing languages can create, the young coloured woman of Xhosa, German, and English background told me that because she speaks no indigenous language of the blacks, theirs is "a world" that is closed to her.

In church, language, and politics, the assimilation of coloured people into the white Afrikaans culture has been thorough. It has been so thorough that coloureds enlisted and fought in all the wars waged by the South African government, serving "beyond the call of duty," according to van der Ross.[63] So, not only have the coloured people become full-fledged participants in the Western way of living, unlike the blacks due to their exclusion, but they have never known any other way of living. As a result, van der Ross says they have never had their own distinctive culture:

> If we examine the life-style of Coloured people . . . we shall find that the culture of the Coloured people is nothing other than the so-called Western or Western European culture, i.e., the culture of the people who come from Western Europe. We speak Afrikaans, English, or both, belong to Christian churches, wear Western clothing . . . , follow a legal system largely Roman-Dutch or Anglo-Saxon, have always followed a Western system of government, live in Western-style homes, prepare our food in the same manner as West Europeans, practise and enjoy Western European forms of music, art, dancing, sport, etc., etc. . . . They explain why Coloured people, who now travel abroad or beyond South Africa more and more, visit countries such as England, Holland, Germany, Canada, the United States and Australia more than others, and feel at home when they arrive there.[64]

Because coloured people have more in common with whites than with blacks,[65] van der Ross contests the notion that coloureds have a particular affinity for being around their "own kind." He says it is similar interests rather than color that is important to them.[66]

In addition to the cultural and political affinity that the multiracial Americans (as a legislated group) could have for whites, after the fashion of the affinity that many coloured South Africans have for the white Afrikaans people, there is the factor of colorism and racism that such an affinity could breed within an established multiracial community. In chapter 1 we heard a number of multiracialists argue that multiracial people would not be prejudiced but would be in solidarity with the black struggle. However, nowhere around the world where whites have created a median group, as they did in South Africa, do we see mixed-race people in any significant numbers reaching over the color line to intermingle with blacks. In Brazil the mulattoes, in their struggle to get on the white bandwagon, kick their darker kindred around even more severely than the whites.[67] Dickie-Clark, in explaining this, says that generally the closer an upper-subordinate group is to the despised lower-subordinate group, the harder the members of that upper group try to emphasize whatever differences they have with the less privileged and the more they tend to reject them.[68]

South Africa similarly suggests that the members of a new multiracial group in the United States would join whites in harboring racist attitudes against blacks. Coloured sociologist Jimmy Ellis told me that the creation of the coloured group led to racism against blacks because coloured people were raised to see themselves as more highly valued. This racism, he said, is one of the "major pitfalls" of the creation of a coloured group. Part of this racism that coloured people inherited from whites must naturally involve the very theological underpinnings of apartheid itself. Regarding the apartheid theology of the white Afrikaans people, Dutch Reformed minister J. A. Loubser contends in his book, *The Apartheid Bible* (1987), that the "curse of Ham" theory, the biblically-based notion that blacks are the "cursed sons of Ham," was once used to justify slavery but eventually became obsolete during the early part of the twentieth century.[69] However, elsewhere in his discussion of various myths that circulate among white South Africans about blacks Loubser implies that even the "curse of Ham" myth may lay latent in the subconscious of racists. He says, "Even among regular church members there are still individuals who almost seriously assure one that 'Blacks cannot go to heaven' and that 'it does not pay to do missionary work, because they fall back into sin the moment they are converted.' These are only some examples of the many myths in circulation."[70]

Whether or not it can be proven that the coloured people acquired from whites a belief that blacks are the "cursed sons of Ham" or that the blacks were perhaps more "cursed" than coloureds, it is the existence of coloured racism against blacks and the intensity of that racism which is at issue here.[71] One coloured woman (who is married to a coloured man) explained to me that because of their history of not knowing where they fit in, yet being told they should be like whites, coloured people end up being very racist. In the past, and to a smaller degree today, she continued, coloured women would be automatically attracted to white men, no matter how they looked. One of her sisters has been living with a white man for about fifteen years and her mother adores him.[72] Another sister is dating a Nigerian and her mother is unhappy because he is black. She also has a brother who is somewhat dark in complexion. Because he is coloured he would be accepted by a coloured woman, but if he turned out to be black he automatically would be unattractive. Likewise, her coloured husband is somewhat dark in complexion and her mother likes him, but if he were black (albeit the same complexion) her mother would again be unhappy with the relationship.

Another coloured woman (the one I have been describing as of Xhosa, English, and German background) told me that it was the coloured people who did not have contact with blacks during the liberation struggle who have maintained the old racial attitudes about blacks. These are older coloureds for whom the saying still rings true: "I'm poor but at least I'm not a kaffir [nigger]." The young black man who quoted this, the president of the Student Representative Council at the University of the Western Cape, also told me that some coloured parents have complained to the officials of the university because they do not want their children living in the hostels (dormatories) with blacks (who were first admitted to the university in 1978 under van der Ross). Perhaps the older coloured people have tended to maintain the old racial attitudes about blacks, but they evidently have been successful in passing some of those attitudes on to the younger generation. Even today on the campus of the University of the Western Cape, coloureds and blacks rarely mix. It is not simply because they speak different languages as their first tongue. After all, they can communicate to one another in English, the language in which most of the teaching is done at the university. This point was made by the General Secretary of the Student Representative Council, who is also a young black man. He told me that though there is some interracial dating between black and coloured students, there are still stereotypes working against such relationships.

While the administrators of the University of the Western Cape have been progressive in allowing integrated student hostels, there are other coloureds, including politicians, who have spoken of keeping the coloured people away from blacks and therefore "pure." In fact, there have been instances when coloured women who have married blacks have been ostracized by the coloured community.[73] One coloured woman likened this unspoken forbiddance within the coloured community to the restriction against bringing home a policeman (of any race) during the apartheid era. To this day, for example, such ostracism and maltreatment are experienced by the step-siblings of a young coloured woman who described herself as born to a coloured mother and an estranged white father. When this young woman's mother subsequently married a Malawian (a black), the children (her half-siblings) were dark in complexion and were called "kaffirs" both in the extended family and in the coloured community. This young coloured woman is now caring for the son of her sister. The boy is darker than the rest of the family (she, her husband, and their child) because the young woman's sister is of black (Malawian) and coloured parentage. She told me that the boy is regularly teased by coloureds in the neighborhood because of his darker color. She even told me that, because the boy is my complexion, I would experience the same racism if I were to walk through such a working-class coloured neighborhood. The young woman concluded, "It is in the coloured community that you find the worst racism."

There is another side to the equation in which coloured people have participated with whites in holding blacks down, which is that they have also held themselves down politically, economically, and ethically. Part of the strategy in the creation of a betwixt-and-between group of mixed-race people is permitting them some political privileges to placate their potential protests. Economically, as historian George Fredrickson says, the result of apartheid's racial stratification is that the coloured people accepted "the crumbs that fell from the white man's table."[74] In terms of the continued economic marginalization of the coloured community, some coloureds feel that while they helped the ANC to get where they are, they are now being betrayed by an affirmative action policy that benefits blacks. It was even reported in the American press that on September 15, 1994, coloureds had engaged in a protest, because after decades of inferior treatment by the white government they now feel they are victims of favoritism toward blacks in housing, services, and jobs.[75] A week later, in a letter to an editor of a South African newspaper, a coloured person wrote: "In years gone by South Africa was a white country. Today it is a black country. Where do the coloured(s) and Asian(s) fit in? Before we weren't white enough, today we aren't black enough." However, responds journalist Mike Siluma, blacks remember the days when coloureds and Indians were granted a better way of life by whites.[76]

In terms of the continued political marginalization of the coloured community, many coloureds feel that they are voiceless and powerless in the new political dispensation. This feeling of marginalization began emerging when negotiations during the elections were occurring between the ANC and the National Party, negotiations that were perceived as being about black and white interests alone. This is why coloured historian Roy du Pre commented on the fear the coloured people had that the new government under blacks might oppress the community. Du Pre warned blacks that the coloured people must not continue to be singled out for discrimination, for to do so would negate the principles of democracy that the liberators had long espoused. He says, "If a new government and sections of the electorate continue to single out people who were victims of the previous racist regime, what will have been the purpose of pressing for the removal of the National Party and the creation of a democratic, non-racist, 'new' South Africa? We will then merely have replaced one tyranny with another."[77] Even van der Ross, who always insisted that the coloured people were not a unique cultural group, has had second thoughts now that the elections are over. He told me that it is not that he supports the existence of a separate coloured group, it is simply that coloured people have no guarantee that they would be better off if they drop their group identity.

In the political and economic realm, then, coloured people paid a price in the past and may still have to pay a price in the future for accepting a median position in society that gave them privileges over blacks. But an even more exacting toll was paid in the past and may yet have to be paid by the coloured people in the ethical sphere, as Allan Boesak alluded to me, for their compliance or partial compliance in the racism whites dished out to blacks. Ethically, the in-between group opens itself up to what Frantz Fanon calls "the racial distribution of guilt."[78] Michele Paulse, a coloured South African raised in Canada, understands this. She comments that "ill-founded alliance with white people is part of the historical guilt of a people mixed with the white race."[79] It is bad enough to uphold values that discriminate against oneself and one's own people, but it is especially unethical to accept values that discriminate against one's neighbors: One may "turn the other cheek" for oneself, but not for one's neighbor. The acceptance by coloureds of a slot on the societal totem that was higher than the slot blacks held at the bottom helps justify the acceptance by whites of their place at the pinnacle of the racial totem. Whites could then ease their consciences by saying to themselves: "You found difference with your darker-skinned fellows and we find difference with you, our darker-skinned fellows. We are just doing unto you what you are doing unto others." Because individuals responding to subordination through passing, whitening, and participating in the upper-subordinate status can be viewed as accomplices in the continuing maintenance of subordinationist practices, it is understandable that they would be the source of scathing criticism from those left on the most subordinated side of the color line.

Part of the way in which coloured families have safeguarded for their descendants the achievement of passing, whitening, and participating in the upper-subordinate status is not only by discouraging their children from marrying blacks. They have also discouraged their children from marrying coloureds whose phenotype (skin and eye color, hair texture and color, and facial features) are more black than white. The coloured woman of Xhosa,

English, and German background told me that it is true that coloured mothers tend to want their daughters to marry men who have fair skin, straight hair, and blue eyes. Of this, van der Ross says:

> Having learnt as much as we have from the White South Africans . . . we have not been slow to acquire their vices, too. One of the chief of these is colour prejudice. In physical appearance the Coloured people range from those indistinguishable from Africans on the one hand, to those indistinguishable from Europeans on the other. Being White in South Africa qualifies one for numerous privileges, and it is therefore understandable that to some people, who have the necessary physical qualifications in regard to pigmentation, features, hair form and texture, etc., being white represents the epitome of achievement. And once one has gained acceptance (however precarious) into the ranks of the whites, one regards it as one's first duty to safeguard this achievement for one's self and one's children.[80]

With regard to hair texture and color, van der Ross says he once received a letter from a coloured man who said coloured people were divided into four groups. There were those with light straight-hair, those with dark straight-hair, those with light woolly-hair, and those with dark woolly hair.[81] According to the interpretation of one white Afrikaans woman I spoke to, the latter group, those with dark woolly hair, are "Bushmen" (a derogatory term used by whites). In South Africa, she told me with a smirk, I would be a Bushman.

The concern over the particulars of phenotype may not be as extreme among the coloured people as it is among the mulattoes in Brazil, where it has been said that there are at least forty racial classifications depending on people's skin tone, shade, hair texture, and lip width.[82] But there is a greater misfortune that coloured South Africans share, perhaps equally, with the mulattoes of Brazil—the practice of "whitening."[83] Brazilians prescriptively engage in transforming black into white through this conscious or unconscious practice of intermarriage and miscegention so that their offspring become lighter and lighter and are eventually able to escape identification with the lowest subordinate group of society—blacks. They do this also by abandoning the identifiable cultural traits of black people. Historian Leo Spitzer says that the impetus behind whitening derives from the promise of future status improvement for their children and grandchildren.[84] Dickie-Clark says that some coloured South Africans similarly maintained a belief that they would be absorbed by whites as the color bar came down, or at least their offspring if they themselves (as parents) "breeded white."[85]

So, the scholarly portrayal and even the self-portrayal of the coloured people as a community caught up in internal prejudices based on phenotype, contradicts the storybook portrayal of the coloured community in a tour booklet compiled by the South African Geographical Society in 1979. The booklet, titled *The Cape Town of the Coloured People*, said that coloured people were "the only fully integrated group" in a society that maintains strict segregation laws, and that not even the American "melting pot" had produced such visible proof of integration.[86] This misinformed portrayal of the coloured community should suggest to us that the American multiracialists, who are portraying in storybook fashion the emerging mixed-race "community" in the United States, are equally misinformed. If coloured South Africans teach us anything, it is that a multiracial group would have its own internal prejudices to contend with. Some of the tension could result from an unspoken policy of whitening and the resultant internal color hierarchy.

Through my references to the practice of "whitening" I have been suggesting that South Africa is not the only place where we can learn needed lessons about the pitfalls of a middle-ranked mixed-race classification. We can learn lessons from Brazil as well, particularly since Brazil was once viewed by whites and blacks alike as a racial paradise whose system of race relations might be applied in the United States to the solving of its racial dilemma. In fact, some blacks during the early twentieth century felt so hopeless with regard to race relations in the United States and were so enamoured by Brazil's society that they looked proudly to Brazil rather than to Africa as a black homeland and potential place of refuge. By the mid-twentieth century, however, a number of prominent black Americans had visited Brazil and had begun to question its image as a colorblind utopia. By the mid-1960s the utopian image had disintegrated. Black Americans had awakened to the fact that, despite the lack of overt racial discrimination based on genotype (invisible heritage) and phenotype (visible physical characteristics), and despite the acceptance of intermarriage, black and mulatto Brazilians lacked office, power, and wealth in every sphere of their society. In fact, black Americans began to fear that as the United States brought down the curtains of racial segregation and white attitudes began to change, the United States might actually become more like Brazil. Historian Cleveland Donald, Jr., writing in the early 1970s, is one who warned of the possibility. He warned that American racial attitudes, given the thrust of integration and "other forces" disintegrating the black community, could shift toward the traditional Brazilian attitudes on race.[87]

Topping off the fact that black and mulatto Brazilians are subordinate in every sphere of society is that they lack pride in their Africanness, much like most coloured South Africans lack pride in their African roots. In Brazil this has occurred by no accident, given the undermining of pride in blackness and the concurrent emphasis on improving one's social status through "whitening." This is why "whitening" is also called "ethnic lynching" in other parts of Latin America. Its purpose is to weed out African culture, to deny blacks their black identity, and to force blacks to assimilate into whiteness in succeeding generations. Frantz Fanon, the black intellectual from Martinique who played a key role in the Algerian revolution against French colonialism, complained that "from black to white is the course of mutation. One is white as one is rich, as one is beautiful, as one is intelligent."[88] He further remarks that "the black man should no longer be confronted by the dilemma, *turn white or disappear*."[89] Fanon was frustrated by the fact that his West Indian compatriots who studied, lived, and sought to marry in Paris, adhered to this ideology of whitening.

For instance, he takes issue with a memoir by a woman named Mayotte Capecia, titled *Je suis martiniquaise*, published in Paris in 1948. Capecia said that she learned her grandmother was white and had married a black man of Martinique and that she was proud of the fact that her mother was mixed and that she herself somewhat approximated whiteness.[90] Fanon's response is that Capecia wanted a kind of "lactification." He states, "For, in a word, the race must be whitened. . . . Whiten the race, save the race, but not in the sense that one might think; not 'preserve the uniqueness of that part of the world in which they grew up,' but make sure that it will be white."[91] This is the reason W. E. B. Du Bois felt that racial mixing in Brazil had not elevated blacks in society or given any value to their Africanness, and that it would not do so in other parts of the world.[92]

This "ethnic lynching" has been evidenced in South Africa where the white Afrikaans people, particularly the politicians of the National Party, have told the coloured people, despite their partial black roots in the Khoi people: "You are not black" and "You are like us." As Rainier Spencer remarked earlier, given who is running our own government and given who is in the majority in this country, who is to say that a new middle-ranked mixed-race classification would not end up being abused as a buffer between whites and blacks?[93] All of the foregoing discussion—about phenotypal discrimination among the "brown" peoples of South Africa and Brazil and the racism that results against blacks—suggests to us this important point: not only would there likely be new racial behavior among a new American people classified as multiracial, but there would likely be, in this racist society of ours, a new layer of racism imposed on those who occupy the lowest stratum of society—blacks.

Already cultural critic Lisa Jones claims to recognize among the multiracialists a certain extremist group that is claiming a unique status for mixed-race people, a unique status because their mixed heritage and consequential experiences allegedly free them from racial bias.[94] Some multiracialists are also claiming that mixed-race people are the most beautiful people on earth, and these assertions are being made with little modesty and some intended racial animosity. Edwin Darden, president of the Interracial Family Circle in Washington, D.C., published an article entitled "Being Perfect," in which he claims that his biracial children are "as close to perfection as a human being can get." He continues on to say that some day the world will realize that his children, indeed all mixed-race children, are "the best."[95] Likewise, an anonymous multiracialist from Overland Park, Kansas, says that he finds the kind of beauty and near-perfection of mixed-race people to be uncanny. He also says that he senses some fear and resentment from both whites and blacks that mixed-race people will prove themselves to be not the small and misunderstood population they were once thought to be, not a "subrace" of people, but a "superrace" as they are destined to become.[96]

Additionally, as some multiracialists begin down the road of racial bigotry by cock-a-doodling about their alleged specialness, certainly in part to bolster the identity and self-esteem of themselves or that of their mixed-race children, they subtly assault the identity and self-esteem of black Americans. For instance, Candace Mills, the editor of *Interrace* magazine, commented on the fact that actress Halle Berry (who considers herself black) was voted "most beautiful black woman in America" by the readership of *Ebony* magazine. Mills wrote, "Yes, Berry is beautiful. But *Black?*" She went on to say that it is likely that Berry's European features (her white mother's contribution) are what the readers of *Ebony* found "most beautiful."[97] Mills could say the same about actresses Dorothy Dandridge, Lena Horne, Jasmine Guy, and many others: "Yes, beautiful; but black?" Where might this usurping of black achievement end? Moreover, when it does end, what will be left for those whom the multiracialists consider the "truly" black?

Once such racism among multiracialists begins—boasting about the specialness of mixed-race people and assaulting those who choose to identify as black—there may be no turning back if and when a multiracial classification is legislated. Once the people of such a legislated classification fall into all the social, political, and ethical traps that await peoples of the median track, the classifications will take on a life of their own. Then the multiracials will essentially be stuck with their legislated identity and the consequential marginality, just as coloured South Africans are, now that white minority rule is done with and nonracialism is the official policy.

It is a fact that many coloured people now wish to shed their coloured identity and social marginality. For while others can speak pridefully of being of Zulu or Xhosa ethnicity, standing up to say "I'm coloured" is not so politically correct right now. For instance, coloured sociologist Jimmy Ellis told me that in terms of political categories he would prefer just to call himself a South African and thereby associate with the broader ideals and values of the nation under the new constitution. Ellis is old enough to recall the year 1950 when he was defined as coloured by the Population Registration Act—that is, defined as neither white nor black. He said that the category "coloured" was not of his making but imposed on him and others who resented it. Coloured historian Roy du Pre, of a similar belief, wrote just before the 1994 election that, "Apartheid is dead, the 'Coloured' label has been abolished; the 'Coloured' people are no more."[98] However, the coloured identity cannot be gotten rid of so easily. This is what the president of the Student Representative Council at the University of the Western Cape was getting at when he told me that the racial ideology of apartheid has "mutated into a life of its own" now that apartheid is officially over. So, the relinquishment of a racial identity does not come so easily. H. F. Dickie-Clark was therefore correct in his prediction that, "whatever the future shape of South African society, it is not likely that the Coloured's marginal situation will entirely disappear until colour and 'race' lose their social significance altogether."[99] Unfortunately, that day when color and race lose their social significance in South Africa is still a long way off, even though the democratically elected government is trying to push the country toward nonracialism.

So, apartheid was introduced in 1948; in 1950 the Population Registration Act, the cornerstone of the National Party's apartheid policy, placed every South African within a racial classification; in June 1991 apartheid and racial classification were abolished; but the political, social, and economic consequences continue. This is the history of which the United States must take heed, particularly since Allan Boesak was right in his comment to me that the United States is digressing with regard to race relations. Just as Dickie-Clark has predicted that the marginal situation of the coloured people of South Africa will not entirely disappear until color and race lose their social significance altogether,[100] so have I predicted that a multiracial classification in the United States will result not in the transcending of the race problem but in the emergence of the same kind of intermediary caste system that the former white government of South Africa used to shore up their political, economic, and racial supremacy. I also predict that a racial label will be easier to procure than to eliminate.

FOUR

Thou Shalt Not
Racially Classify

At the turn of the twentieth century, W. E. B. Du Bois said that the problem of the century would be the problem of the color line. Indeed, that has been true, and it appears likely to remain so as the century comes nearer to a close. This is something that even South Africans notice when they come to this country. For instance, South African writer Mark Mathabane said, "One of the things I quickly learned after arriving in America in 1978 was that this nation—despite its freedom, democracy, and claims of being a melting pot where differences are not only tolerated but celebrated—was far from the racial utopia I had imagined it to be while I groaned under apartheid oppression. This shocked and disappointed me."[1]

I have found that most South Africans view the racial situation in the United States from one of two perspectives. Some see the racial problem as resolved and American society as the exemplar of democracy. Others who have visited the United States, or have learned about American society from someone who has visited, see our society for what it is—a place in which black Americans are still "kaffirs." A Zulu taxi driver from Soweto, who works in Johannesburg, told me that he thought the racial situation was actually better in South Africa than in the United States, because in American society, he had learned from a New Yorker, racism is "hidden." Allan Boesak said the same thing to me. He believes South Africa has a better chance than the United States in solving its historical race problem.

However, most South Africans I spoke to—coloured, black, and white—were surprised to learn that racial classification and discrimination still existed in the United States. One white man, who described himself in the politically incorrect way as an Afrikaner, said that he thought democracy was the "password" of Americans and that democracy was so strong that black Americans were no longer discriminated against. The Reverend David Botha, the retired Afrikaans minister of the Dutch Reformed Mission Church, said that when he visited the United States in 1964 the push was toward trying to create one integrated society. Thus he is surprised that some Americans are trying to create a new racial classification. The word "surprised" was also used by the president of the Student Representative Council at the University of the Western Cape as he expressed his reaction to my news about the multiracial movement in the United States. A young coloured woman (who is married to a white man of English ethnicity) essentially thought the same thing. She found it to be "very strange" that Americans would want to start a new racial group when South Africans are trying to get away from racial classification. Boesak said the whole thing was "crazy."

So, the American dilemma of the twentieth century indeed has been the problem of the color line, a line that has been so tenacious that it has convinced some mixed-race Americans that they would prefer to straddle the line if they cannot fully cross it. But what does the multiracial movement suggest to us about the problem of the twenty-first century? If we listen to the multiracialists, we might think that the blessing of the twenty-first century, as a result of their doings, will be the blurring of the color line. I have argued in the last two chapters that I do not believe there will be any such blurring. Rather, I believe that the problem of the twenty-first century will be the predicament of the readjustment of the color line. If we do not take heed of what South Africa has to teach us of race relations, the color line will be adjusted not toward any real improvement in the subordinate status of mixed-race people, but just enough for there to be a fresh disbursement of the guilt of the white majority—what Frantz Fanon calls "the racial distribution of guilt."

To be sure, a multiracial classification in the United States would not move the country away from race consciousness. For such a classification would require a firming of the color line in order for the heterogeneous group of mixed-race people to be encapsulated into the "community" that multiracialists say will come to fruition. The fact is, Americans of interracial parentage are people of multiple ethnicities, indeed they are often unsure of their choice of ethnicity because of their multifarious ancestry. In ethnicity, culture, color, class, and so forth, mixed-race people cannot be comfortably grouped. They are only an emerging "community" if they are made so by legislation, but to try and legislate them into a racial group would be as racist in the United States as it was in apartheid South Africa.

In ethnicity, culture, color, class, and so forth, the mixed-race people of South Africa were heterogeneous. Thus, they were only fashioned into the "coloured community" by means of legislation. In Richard van der Ross's words, therefore, strictly speaking there is no coloured group. Rather, the most that can be said is that there is a large number of heterogeneous people whom apartheid law grouped together and regarded as "coloured."[2] Clearly, heterogeneity exists in the coloured group, and it is extensive. As put in a 1979 brochure for an excursion into the coloured community by members of the South African Geographical Society, "From a purely racial point of view . . . there is no such thing as a 'typical coloured.' Skin colour ranges widely from white to black and cannot be used as a significant criterion for classification. There are no physical traits that are characteristic of this population group."[3] In addition, there are Christian coloureds and Muslim coloureds, Afrikaans-speaking coloureds and English-speaking coloureds. There are coloureds who want to be white and coloureds who want to remain coloured, coloureds who want to be black and coloureds who want to be African.

This boundless heterogeneity in the coloured community would only be reproduced in the sought-after multiracial community in the United States, according to the two mixed-race Americans with whom I spoke together in Cape Town. The young woman, who is from the state of Washington, has a white mother and a black (mixed-race) father. The young man, who is from Colorado, has a Chinese mother (from Taiwan) and a black father. The young man was raised primarily in Asia—six years in Japan, five years in Thailand, and three years in Taiwan. But after that he spent sixteen years in the United States, where people presumed he was black and most of his friends in fact were black. Though these two young adults have some things in common—both are mixed-race Americans, both were living temporarily in Cape Town—neither of them sees how their own experiences, let alone the experiences of all mixed-race people, could possibly be considered alike. The young woman feels that the multiracial classification being promoted is too broad, and she does not see how creating a legal race of multiracials would bring together people of vastly different experiences and ethnicities. Thus, she feels that putting a multiracial category on the United States census would be simplistic and artificial.

Shanti Thakur, a Canadian filmmaker of East Indian and Danish parentage who produced a film about multiracial people, came to a similar conclusion about the heterogeneity of mixed-race people. After her experience interviewing myriad mixed-race people, she does not feel comfortable with grouping such a wide assortment of people and experiences under the rubric of a multiracial community. The experiences she heard about were so different from one another, she discovered, because some mixed-race people identify with one culture, some with both cultures, and some with neither culture.[4] Likewise, Henry Der, of the National Coalition for an Accurate Count of Asians and Pacific Islanders, says there are so many combinations of multiraciality that we must wonder what can be said about the common experiences they are alleged to share. For instance, Der wants to know what commonalities people of white and black parentage share with people of Korean and Hawaiian parentage. He says that this is a question that needs to be answered by the multiracialists. Before a decision to establish a multiracial category would be appropriate, Der believes that the multiracialists must have the burden of documenting what distinct experiences or disadvantages they have in common in contrast to people of the protected monoracial groups.[5]

Der is echoed by Michael Thornton, a sociologist of black and Japanese parentage. Thornton says that if all multiracial people share some common background, then we should be told what it is and how it binds them more closely together than to their parents' racial groups, for it appears that there is little basis for the alleged commonalities other than some superficial factors. "Do multiracials have a core (cultural) heritage, or are they viewed as alike by others in society?" Thornton asks. "Are multiracials seen as a different (racial/ethnic) group from, say, Blacks?" Thornton answers his rhetorical questions by insisting that mixed-race people are too biologically and ancestrally diverse to constitute a community. What really seems to bind them together, he continues, is not race or culture but living with "an ambiguous status." But even this is an experience shared by all oppressed peoples, Thornton says.[6] Such a community, we should point out, is exactly what coloured South Africans comprise. In this regard, W. H. Thomas states in an essay on the coloured people that it is often claimed that the coloured community is more appropriately defined in a negative way because it is a group that is discriminated against. He agrees that indeed a major characteristic of the coloured community is the particular kind of discrimination relevant to its members.[7] At any rate, Michael Thornton believes that facing a different set of problems resulting from being oppressed is not a sufficient basis to constitute a racial group or culture.[8] Gitanjali Saxena, a Canadian of East Indian and German parentage, agrees that mixed-race people may constitute a "situational community" but not a cultural or racial one: all come from completely different racial groups whose identities are generally traceable to their ancestors.[9]

Thus by ethnicity, culture, color, class, region, and so forth, mixed-race people cannot be comfortably grouped, but are only an emerging "community" if they are made so by legislation that would be as racist in the United States as it was in apartheid South Africa. But the census movement of the multiracialists has served a valuable purpose nonetheless, for extremes always frighten people into more moderate and reasonable action that we would not have executed if the extreme position had not been taken in the first place. To be sure, establishing another racial classification is extreme when the acknowledged ideal of the multiracialists themselves is nonracialism. Moreover, as I illustrated in the last chapter, a new racial classification is sure to be followed with new forms of unbecoming racial behavior.

Now that we have been duly warned of the possible extremes of a new race in the United States, the question to answer is: What is the compromise, the midway point between the past invisibility of mixed-race Americans and the legislating of a new racial classification? That is the question I want to answer in this chapter while keeping in mind van der Ross's final comment to me when we met. He remarked that his gut reaction to the multiracial movement is that neither I nor anyone else could put the brakes on it. The best thing anyone could hope to do, he said, is to determine how the movement could be nudged in a direction that would suit the plight of black Americans and the goals of the nation as a whole. As we try to determine what direction would best serve black Americans and the country, we should understand what (after all that has been said thus far) the core concern is. Congressman Thomas Petri of Wisconsin, a member of the House subcommittee on the census, articulated this core concern at one of the 1993 hearings after hearing Susan Graham and Carlos Fernandez testify. He said that he thought the resistance to a new multiracial category resulted from people worrying that an additional category would create more divisions rather than move the country in a unifying direction.[10]

Indeed, a wide range of people, including black and mixed-race people, share this core concern. Shaun Shields, an adult of black, white, and Chinese ancestry, comments: "No one wants to have a situation like that of South Africa, where people are labeled and classified according to fine distinctions between color differences."[11] Michele Paulse, a coloured South African who was raised in Canada, claims that because artificial separation between coloureds and blacks in South Africa upheld apartheid, she could not support the movement for a separate category for mixed-race Americans.[12] Simone Brooks, a teenager of black and white parentage, says the country has enough racial separation as it is. Brooks also says she herself has had enough separation without having to be split into another group: "I'm separated enough as it is. I'm separated as a woman; I'm separated from Whites because I'm black; I'm separated from Blacks because I'm part white. I don't need any more separation in my life."[13] Moreover, if Brooks were an only child in an interracial family, she would also be separated as a family member, since first generation mixed-race children have no mixed-race family members with whom they can identify.

Rainier Spencer, a young man of black and white parentage, is also critical of the introduction of a new racial category, because it is based and dependent on the corrupt concept of race. He argues that though it is nearly impossible to talk about social issues without making reference to race, we should avoid making the waters of race any murkier than they already are. "While all racial talk is ultimately nonsense, the biracial movement merely shifts the terminology while establishing a tripartite racial division in place of the old bifurcated one," says Spencer. "The answer for us lies in tearing down false racial categories, not in erecting new ones that are just as erroneous."[14] In a letter to the editor of *Interrace* magazine, Ira Shaffer, who identified himself as a black resident of San Jose, made a similar comment: "If the goal of *Interrace* readers is to overcome racial prejudice, or even racial groups, then why create another racial group or classification—that is, 'biracial' or 'multiracial'? If race doesn't matter, then why make such a big deal about biracial or multiracial people?"[15] Candace Mills, the magazine editor to whom Shaffer wrote, in fact agrees. Indeed she agrees without contradicting the fact that she still wants her daughter to grow up with a strong identity as a mixed-race person.[16] Mills writes, "Is the fight for a multiracial category in the best interest of our children? Not if a 'multiracial' category will lead to the division of peoples of color as it has in countries like Brazil and South Africa." She continues, "Multiracial should be acknowledged but do we really *need* a 'multiracial' category to legitimize their existence?" She concludes, "Are we so blinded by our *need* for a label that we have lost sight of what we are *really* doing—further separating the human race?"[17]

Mills's point is essentially agreed to by the two mixed-race Americans, the black woman from Washington and the black man from Colorado, who had been living temporarily in Cape Town when I met them. The young man, of black and Chinese parentage, said that what his year-long experience of living in South Africa suggests to him is that legislating a multiracial category in the United States would result more in "an opening of Pandora's box" than in solving the problem multiracialists are trying to address. Using the idea of multiracialism to bring about awareness is acceptable, he asserted, but to push it further than that will lead to divisiveness, of which American society has plenty already. The young woman of black and white parentage similarly remarked that no one seeing South Africa for the extended nine-month period that she had would want to replicate a situation where differences were seized on by the white government in order to "divide and rule" the peoples of color (a point also made by Boesak). She concluded that the movement to have a multiracial classification legislated would end up forcing an apartheid-like recognition of mixed-race people down the throats of the country's citizens and thus move the country away from its previous goal of integration.

The young interracial couple—she coloured and he white (English)—whom I met in Cape Town when they had been married only six months, concurred with the foregoing views. The couple suspected that the way in which their future children might be classified would not matter to them because they feel that their identities as Christians and as South Africans would override external identification by race and color. The husband did admit, however, that from a secular perspective he would not be troubled by their future children being classified as coloured because that is what coloured is—mixed. For that matter, he said, he would not be troubled by their future children being classified as multiracial.

If a child of theirs ever came home from school and asked "Who am I?" then the multiracial identification would seem sufficient. It would especially be appropriate if it made their child feel more secure in terms of identity and if the races were equal and not hierarchical. Despite this openness to racial identification, however, the couple were against the idea of the United States or South Africa legislating an identity that automatically throws all mixed-race people together. The young woman felt that South Africans need to move completely away from race, since they had fought so hard and long not to be classified. Since South Africa is moving away from racial classification, she concluded, so should the United States.

Another coloured woman, also married to a white Englishman (a second-generation South African) whom she met in the anti-apartheid struggle, was apprehensive about the multiracial movement from the start. "It makes me scared," she told me. She felt that being coloured has been "destructive" for coloured people in South Africa. "Stay away from it as far as possible," she warned. "I don't think it's a solution at all."

A man of English and Afrikaans parentage, who is married to an Indian woman (Muslim) whom he met during the "struggle," finds many of the arguments for multiracialism (as I described them from the perspective of chapter 1) to be valid. He particularly likes the idea of society acknowledging the existence of a vast pool of people who are multiracial. However, he insisted that any multiracial identity must be voluntary or people's freedoms would be limited. Apartheid had been so devastating in locking people out from one another and one another's cultures, he said, that it is liberating to be free just to be who you are—no longer just a definition. "It's nice to be in South Africa at this time," he concluded.

Another coloured woman, the young woman of Xhosa, English, and German ancestry, told me that as long as people have eyes they will perceive differences, but that she considers it a bad idea for the United States to legislate those differences. She even feels that it would be acceptable for mixed-race people to identify themselves as multiracial but that making a "big thing" of an entire middle group would create problems in the long run. It would be "foolish," she said with carefully chosen words, given the evidence of South African history where classifications have been exploited once they were created.

This young woman's views were corroborated by a coloured friend of hers, also a graduate of the University of the Western Cape (in sociology). He felt that the Americans pushing for the governmental legislation of a multiracial classification were going to open up the possibility of all sorts of unforeseen problems, since such legislation would deepen racial consciousness rather than alleviate it. Although he was sensitive to the issue of identity, he felt that mixed-race people should be able to identify themselves as they wished, without an "artificial" category. Such a category would be "artificial," he explained, because it would lump together so many different ethnic groups under a single name, as happened to the coloured people of his country. At the same time he recognized the need of black Americans to be able to rally behind their existing racial designation for the sake of assuring affirmative action and ensuring that there is no repeat of past discrimination.

The present generation of students at the University of the Western Cape evidently seems to agree. The General Secretary of the Students Representative Council at the University, a black African National Congress (ANC) member, said that the general mood among students is to work to dismantle racial divisions. They want to press toward nonracialism and unity in the university community, he said, while also recognizing ethnic differences, and the challenge in the United States should be to determine how to harmonize society rather than how to digress into new divisions. The president of the Student Representative Council, also a black ANC member, agreed, given that he strongly affirmed the nonracial policy of the ANC.

Coloured sociologist Jimmy Ellis told me that he was skeptical about the multiracial movement, given that it reminds him of the old apartheid system that drew distinctions between groups. To solidify a mixed-race identity through legislating a multiracial classification, he figured, would force Americans deeper into racial groups, racial thinking, and racial behavior. For to be put in a category is to be able to be identified specifically and thus responded to in a certain way. Ellis concluded that American society needs to mature by moving toward the ideals propagated by such great American leaders as Martin Luther King, Jr. He feels that King's ideal of people being judged by the content of their character rather than the color of their skin is still achievable.

The coloured professor whom I mentioned in chapter 1 who said he would have no problem identifying his own child as multiracial added a remark that I did not include at that time. He concluded that theoretically he had no difficulty with the legislation of a multiracial category in the United States, but that in reality "danger lurks there." The danger, he explained, results from the potential abuse of that middle group by the government.

The Reverend David Botha, the retired Afrikaans clergyman whose congregation included Jimmy Ellis for seventeen years, felt the same way. He said that while he felt that a multiracial movement could not occur in South Africa at this time, he understood that perhaps now there were currents in the United States that could sustain such a movement. However, to be consistent with his long-held views about coloured South Africans, he would prefer for mixed-race Americans to go with their cultural affinity—whether it be white or black—rather than to go with a new, legal, middle group. After all, he concluded, once black and white Americans are reconciled, this problem of what to do with mixed-race people will likely vanish.

My own view is the result of having used the University of the Western Cape as a microcosm for the study of race relations among peoples of color in South Africa. I feel that the racial clannishness that apartheid has left in its wake is not something that black and mixed-race black Americans would find at all attractive in America. Yet this racial clannishness, or some semblance of it, is what could and likely would develop if this country were to pursue the course of action promoted by multiracialists.

But if we believe (as I do) that mixed-race people represent the need for a new social consciousness that would permit greater fluidity in people's racial identities and therefore more racial tolerance for those who wish to embrace multiple ethnicities, then what alternatives are there for mixed-race people in terms of their racial identification? If the ultimate goal of the multiracialists is really to undermine race, then perhaps they should not seek a legislated classification but should encourage mixed-race people to elude classification by checking the "other" category on the United States census. Or perhaps the multiracialists should encourage mixed-race people to check "other" and write in the identification of "American." This is in keeping with the statement Carlos Fernandez made before the House subcommittee on the census that it should be the United States, which has drawn on the peoples of the world for its citizenry, that should set the example for multiracial living.[18] Yes, then mixed-race people should be called "Americans," not "multiracials."

Naturally, to premise this identification on the statement that mixed-race people are the epitome of the American citizen, because they embody the "melting pot" ideal, will only anger a lot of Americans. It would make people angry just as it probably makes a lot of black South Africans angry to hear some coloured people claim that they are the only true South Africans because their Khoi ancestors resided in the Western Cape before the other African ethnic groups came into the area. But unattached to such antagonistic claims, the word "American" is the only classification that cannot have a racial meaning because it is overshadowed by national meaning. Jimmy Ellis made the point when he said that he prefers to call himself a South African and thereby associate with the broader ideals and values of the nation under the new interim constitution.

Mixed-race Americans could therefore follow the lead of South Africa, whose open-minded citizens now just want to be known as South Africans—no racial classification attached. In this respect, the aforementioned coloured woman (who is married to a second-generation South African of English ethnicity) said that although her children look white, she and her husband would never permit them to be classified under any racial category. If the government insisted that they must choose, she told me passionately, then they would defy the government and not choose—unless one of the categories is "South African" or simply "African." Immediately she asked me with regard to the multiracials in the United States, "What about an American identity?" She felt that pursuing an American identity, rather than going deeper into race consciousness with a multiracial identity, would be more in tune with occurrences in today's world. Other coloureds have said the same thing, but a third-year coloured student at the University of the Western Cape made the point with an interesting twist. After I explained the multiracial movement to her in the way that I presented it in chapter 1, she said that she found the whole matter to be funny because she had been under the impression that all Americans were proud just to be Americans.

An American identity for mixed-race people is certainly one possibility, then. However, there is one problem, essentially connected to an inconsistency in the multiracialists' claim that mixed-race people are the epitome of the American "melting pot" idea. The problem is that mixed-race people do not feel like full American citizens because of the discrimination they have historically faced as a result of the persistent old-fashioned ideas about miscegenation. Perhaps this is why the multiracialists are pushing for a multiracial identity rather than for the right to call themselves Americans.

There is also the question of simply abolishing racial classification altogether. The Office of Management and Budget (OMB) has received suggestions that classifications by race and ethnicity be eliminated because they continue the overemphasis on race, which results in societal divisions.[19] "That is a suggestion that has been made," says Sally Katzen, the administrator of the OMB, "that it is only by getting rid of categories that we will be able to stop focusing, some would say, on that which divides us, and allow us to look at that which brings us together."[20]

One of the people Katzen was probably thinking about when she made this remark is John Cougill, an African American who gave a testimony before the OMB in his own behalf. Cougill said he would like to see the term "race" removed from the definition of "black" in Directive No. 15 since "black" is the only category specifically mentioning the term: "*Black*. A person having origins in any of the black racial groups of Africa." But even this is but an intermediate step, Cougill explains, for it is the collection of racial data itself that perpetuates racism since there is no such thing as race. Cougill even went so far as to state that he believes the National Association for the Advancement of Colored People (NAACP) and Denny's restaurant chain (which was sued by the NAACP for racial discrimination) have good reason to sue the OMB and the Census Bureau for damages resulting from their administration of racial categorization (hence racial discrimination) as a harmless way of life.[21]

Black sociologist Yehudi Webster backed up Cougill's perspective about abolishing racial classification altogether when he shared a radio talk show with Sally Katzen. Believing that the use of "race" language helps perpetuate racial division, Webster said: "If we say we want harmony and peace and justice in the society, why do we continue to classify people in this polarized, binary fashion? Isn't it obvious that as long as we maintain the classifications we are intensifying an awareness of differences? We are actually making people see one another or see each other as belonging to different camps. And that means they will increase their discrimination against one another."[22] Webster writes elsewhere that part of the means by which we intensify racial awareness of divisions through the use of the idea of race is by trying to create racial solutions: "Racial solutions are developed for racial problems; these solutions, however, generate more racial problems. Jim crowism produced the civil rights movement, which called for affirmative action, black power, and multiculturalism, which foster tensions between nonwhites and whites."[23]

Sally Katzen's response to the idea that racial categories ought to be abolished altogether is based on the requirements of law. She said on the radio talk show, "That is, I think, a great inspirational thought and I would hope our country could be there at some point. But the existing laws to be enforced do require the basic data on various components of our population."[24] Carlos Fernandez agreed, on the occasion of his representation of the Association of Multi-Ethnic Americans (AMEA) before the House subcommittee on the census. He said, "It might be argued that racial and ethnic classifications should be done away with entirely. But such a view is utopian and also distorts the reality of continuing divisions based on race and ethnicity."[25] Susan Graham essentially said the same: that doing away with racial categories is not realistic, while what her organization proposes is realistic.[26] Nathan Lynch, of Columbus, Ohio, framed the point in an interesting way in a response to remarks about race being unscientific, illogical, fictitious, and a tool of oppression. He said, "On such a basis, one might also try to abolish religion."[27]

This is in fact the polarity we are dealing with when we speak of race—religion versus rationality. Trying to abolish race is like trying to abolish religion. To put it differently, until religion is abolished, race will not be. For both are rooted in people's belief in the unseen and the unprovable. With faith, on which religion and race depend, rationality and evidence pale and cannot disprove anything. Despite the fact that most Americans (indeed most human beings) live by "faith" rather than rationality, Yehudi Webster insists that racial classifications must be abolished because they have little to do with rational thinking.[28] He said on the radio talk show we shared with Sally Katzen, "It seems to me that we really don't have a racial problem. . . . I think what we have is a lack of respect for reasoning and standards for how we think and argue." Webster went on to complain that people ignore arguments by anthropologists, biologists, and other scholars who contest the concept of race, which leads him to believe that Americans really have a thinking problem. "Society is badly educated in the sense that there's an absence of logic, an absence of courses in reasoning and critical thinking," he continued. "And as a result, people, . . . instead of recognizing that you are a human being, . . . simply allocate you to a racial group . . . and then discriminate against you."[29]

In this regard, Webster sounds much like Kwame Anthony Appiah, the philosopher of Ghanaian and English parentage who also considers race an outmoded idea and believes black people should therefore no longer build alliances based on the concept of race.[30] But for whom has the idea of building black "racial" alliances become an outmoded idea? If we read Appiah and Webster carefully, the idea has become outmoded for intellectuals for whom inconsistency in belief is a sign of irrationality. That is to say, the idea has become outmoded for intellectuals who hold up Rationality as the object of requisite faith. In this respect, Appiah says: "Rationality is best conceived of as an ideal, both in the sense that it is something worth aiming for and in the sense that it is something we are incapable of realizing. It is an ideal that bears an important internal relation to that other great cognitive ideal, Truth."[31] Appiah concludes that while we cannot change the world by evidence and reasoning alone, we certainly cannot expect to change the world without these things.[32]

It may be, however, that the idea of Rationality and Truth completely replacing the irrationality of racial identity is an idea whose time has not yet come, particularly for the oppressed who require their own irrationalities to fend off the irrationalities of the powerful. Appiah's reaction to such a response immediately proceeds into the sphere in which philosophers (privileged intellectuals) think—he edifies the ideals of Truth and Rationality and says that he believes people who do not hold to this Enlightenment faith have given in to temptation and fallen into intellectual apostasy: "One temptation . . . , for those who see the centrality of these fictions in our lives, is to leave reason behind: to celebrate and endorse those identities that seem at the moment to offer the best hope of advancing our other goals, and to keep silence about the lies and the myths. But . . . intellectuals do not easily neglect the truth."[33] Actually, history shows that white intellectuals often reveal only a part of truth, often only enough to camouflage the irrationalities of race that stabilize their own privilege. The reality regarding Appiah's assumption that truth predicated in the academy trickles down in the form of national policy to fashion increasing quality of life for the masses, is that only some of the truth trickles down. Perhaps the most important truths are guarded by white intellectuals who have ideological agendas to protect, a point I will reinforce momentarily by pointing to white intellectuals in South Africa.

Certainly Appiah is correct that societies profit from the academic institutionalization of the imperative that truth not be neglected. But this quest for truth has only left us with the question: Whose truth? In the meantime, while the powerful and privileged maintain their favored truths that are undergirded with deeply set irrationalities regarding race, we cannot expect the unprivileged and oppressed to unbridle themselves of their irrationalities regarding race in favor of these so-called "truths" that belong to other groups. Many coloured South Africans feel this way as well—for instance, that it is not yet time for them to "throw their identities to the wind," even though those created identities were based on racist irrationalities. Webster would lead black Americans in the opposite direction, however. For he believes that if we simply stop using racial classification, we will come to the conclusion that human beings, not white people per se, committed atrocities against other human beings—just other human beings and not black, brown, red, or yellow human beings per se.[34] Are women to presume, then, that generic human beings, not men per se, have committed rape against other human beings—just other human beings and not women per se? This question is the strange product of Webster's "reasoning and critical thinking."

We cannot expect the unprivileged and oppressed to discard their irrationalities regarding race and the essential blessings of their particular race until the privileged and powerful discard their irrationalities regarding race. This is a point made by Nathan Lynch in response to Rainier Spencer's article entitled "False Categories." Spencer had suggested that multiracial people reject racial classification because it is racist, and that they respond to questions of identity by saying they do not believe in race. Lynch responds by saying that race may be a biological myth but it is a sociopolitical reality. He says further that he believes that a frank assessment of race, rather than a quixotic rejection of the concept, is the most promising way to an eventual breakdown of racial classification and the conflicts that ensue.[35]

This is my point: We need a frank assessment of race, indeed an obliteration of racism, before the people at the bottom of the social and economic totem of American society abandon the unity and protective barrier that race has brought them so far. As van der Ross said to me about coloured people, it is not that black people support a black race above higher ideals of nonracialism. The problem is that black people have no promise that they would be better off if they drop their group identity. In any case, we are all stuck with the current racial classifications until we can make them do the opposite of what they originally were intended to do—liberate us rather than keep us in captivity. In other words, we need the current racial classifications in order to fight racism, because as soon as we discard the racial classifications black people are still going to be discriminated against. As I suggested in chapter 2, we must be careful not to abandon the idea of race too hastily and not to let those groups that have been history's oppressors forget their behavior too soon. Otherwise these behaviors may slip up on us once again when our backs are turned because they have not been properly acknowledged and addressed. In this regard, we must scrutinize the efforts of various white organizations who argued before the OMB that the classification of "white" should be replaced with "European American" because the term "white" cannot escape being tainted by the history of racism in this country. We can see the same eager jostling of many whites in South Africa who, formerly known as "Afrikaners," now want to be known in the politically correct way as "Afrikaans people."

Societies need a frank assessment of race and an obliteration of racism before the peoples at the bottom of societal totems abandon the unity and protective barrier of race, as argued by Desiree Lewis with regard to South African society. In her article entitled "'Race': South Africa's Censored Four-Letter Word," Lewis says that today prospects are not good for reassessing race in post-liberation South Africa. This is due to the heavy suspicion South Africans have about racial consciousness and to the fact that whites are dependent on a commitment to nonracialism for the sake of their future interests as a minority group.[36] Much of this suspicion has been instigated by white intellectuals who have insisted on the analysis of class over race, as well as by political philosophies propagated in the media, in the academy, and in publications. These forces have evoked a certain blindness toward racialism (racial categorization) in the name of nonracialism and have thus sidelined the discourse on race over the last decade.[37] Lewis says: "Racialism, we have been encouraged to feel, is the problem. Why reinforce this oppressive way of thinking? Why submit to the categorisations of the rulers by affirming your racial consciousness?" She continues, "Insisting on race as a legitimate and necessary category of analysis is automatically equated with primordialism, futile extremism, irrationality, violence and impractical politics. We see this, for example, in the pained and knowing expression that many (progressive) White academicians suddenly assume when any Black person brings up the subject of race."[38] Lewis says of blacks needing to draw attention to reality and the affects of white supremacy for the sake of redressing racialism: "If this is not done, non-racialism simply renders racialism invisible, since racialism cannot be wished away, and non-racialism will not merely disappear when hegemonic philosophies say so."[39] Coloured historian Roy du Pre concurs with Lewis, adding:

> Many well-meaning South Africans may advance the view that publicising atrocities, wrongs and grievances may retard progress to reconciliation and a non-racial democratic society. Those who constantly remind the people of the actions of the government and its agents may even be singled out as stumbling blocks and traitors to the cause of a "New" South Africa. However, it is not the historians who are the danger to a new South Africa but those who wish to cover up the crimes of the past. The fact is that it is hard to build a new society on ground that has unpunished crimes buried just beneath the surface. Is it not imperative to get the matter out

into the open, get it out of our system so that we never have to look back, wondering if the ghosts of the past will come back to haunt us?[40]

In this regard, Jimmy Ellis told me that the University of the Western Cape was also well meaning in its longtime resolve not to teach a sociology course on race relations, which it has not done since the mid-1970s. The argument supporting the suspension of that course, he explained, is that to teach it would reinforce a false construct, an idea (race) that does not exist and which some scholars did not want to acknowledge as existing. But this attitude, continued Ellis, has prevented giving critical attention to what has been occurring racially in the country. Thus sums black South African journalist Mike Siluma: "In our new, democratic, nonracial and still evolving society we do tend to avoid dealing with the awkward, embarrassing issue of race."[41]

As Siluma points out in another newspaper article, whether or not there is an explicit discussion of race, racial tensions and racism itself still exist in President Mandela's South Africa. For instance, Siluma criticizes the belief among some black nationalists that blacks should build their own competitive schools in the townships because sending their children to white schools shows a lack of self-awareness on the part of the black parents. In terms of the attitudes of whites, Siluma criticizes a well-established South African journalist who claimed that black journalists are overstepping their bounds in demanding a voice in the traditionally white-controlled media. This white journalist also said blacks should start their own media empires to reflect their own views, since the white-dominated media is not ready for an unlimited influx of blacks. Siluma concludes that the attitudes of both the black and white nationalists suggest that race relations will continue on its past course and that there will be death for affirmative action and continued white domination. Thus, Siluma asks whether South Africa wants real unity as "one nation" or whether it wants the antithesis: "Or do we want to be a mixture of tribal and racial groups, reluctantly held together by force of circumstance? A country where blacks are banished to the disillusioned periphery of national life to nurse an abiding national grievance, while whites hold on to power and privilege, hoping the blacks will one day spontaneously cease to exist."[42]

As we consider Yehudi Webster's proposal that the United States government cease racial classification altogether, it should be obvious now that societies need frank assessments of race and the obliteration of racism before the peoples at the bottom of societal totems abandon the unity and protective barrier of race. That such frank assessments, as we hear from Siluma, may appear to retard progress toward racial reconciliation and nonracial democratic societies, whether in the United States or South Africa, was understood by Allan Boesak. In a 1977 lecture to a coloured political organization, Boesak said that "we live in this country, black and white, and ultimately we belong together. And we must learn, as Martin Luther King has said, to live together as brothers, or we shall perish together as fools."[43] Boesak truly believes that black and white belong together in peaceful co-existence, that reconciliation and nonracialism are the highest societal ideals to be sought. But he also considered it foolish for the divided ranks of peoples of color to continue to perpetuate white control and for those divided ranks not to galvanize around the racial idea of blackness.[44] He explained: "It is no longer possible, nor wise, to ignore or try to avoid the fact that Black Consciousness and Black Power have come to stay—at least for the forseeable future, and I am convinced that history shall reveal their decisive influence on South African politics."[45] These were the mid-1970s, the years when Boesak was the student chaplain at the University of the Western Cape and coloured students were joining the black consciousness movement. Whether or not the older coloured people were galvanized in great numbers, these coloured students were rejecting coloured identity as the construct of the white supremacist government. They were all becoming black.

Nelson Mandela, despite the fact that he had before, during, and after his twenty-seven years of imprisonment argued in favor of a nonracial society, has never been blind to Boesak's balancing act—the denunciation of race but the dependency on race until the vestiges of racism are obliterated. For example, in his presidential inauguration address, "A Time to Build," delivered in Pretoria upon the opening of Parliament on May 10, 1994, President Mandela said to the representatives of the international community that he trusted that they would continue to stand by South Africa as its citizens tackle the challenges of building a nonracial democracy. "The time for the healing of the wounds has come," he said. "The moment to bridge the chasms that divide us has come. The time to build is upon us." But despite this policy of nonracialism, the country's supreme law at the time of that 1994 speech, the interim *Constitution of the Republic of South Africa* (1993), which the ANC helped shape, still found it necessary to acknowledge the existence of race while it also sought to establish the fundamental rights of dignity, equality, and freedom for every South African. Located in the most important part of the interim Constitution, the Bill of Rights, under the heading "Equality," one of the critical passages read: "No person shall be unfairly discriminated against, directly or indirectly, . . . on one or more of the following grounds in particular: race, gender, sex, ethnic or social origin, colour, sexual orientation, age, disability, religion, conscience, belief, culture or language."

The Mandela government intends to put the Bill of Rights into practical action through the Reconstruction and Development Programme (RDP). This is the policy framework of the ANC which it released before the elections and uses as its social welfare or affirmative action plan. The document says of itself: "The RDP is an integrated, coherent socio-economic policy framework. It seeks to mobilise all our people and our country's resources toward the final eradication of apartheid and the building of a democratic, non-racial and non-sexist future."[46] According to the document, this last vestige of apartheid is the economic inequality derived from a history of colonialism, racism, apartheid, sexism, and so forth.[47] One of the six basic principles of the RDP is "Nation-building," which reads in part: "Central to the crisis in our country are the massive divisions and inequalities left behind by apartheid. We must not perpetuate the separation of our society into a 'first world' and 'third world'—another disguised way of preserving apartheid."[48]

South Africa is a society that is divided into two worlds—first world and third world—in that whites own 98 percent of the wealth, which they acquired under white minority rule. Under white rule, whites took all the best land and are the ones who live in the plush homes of such well-to-do areas of Cape Town as Somerset West (mixture of Afrikaans and English whites) and Stellenbosch (strongly a white Afrikaans area). One old coloured woman at the first church Allan Boesak administered before the area was taken over by whites said to the young pastor: "They said we would never have to move. This small piece of earth is mine, my tears, my sorrow. This week I want you to preach about the commandment Thou shalt not steal."[49] The places that the whites took over in Cape Town stand in stark contrast with the depressed areas to which blacks and coloureds were moved, which are sprawled along the flat lands known as the Cape Flats—black townships like Khayalitsha (the largest black township) and Guguletu (the township where white American Amy Beale was killed), coloured townships like Blue Downs, and squatter areas like the Cross-Roads (which has the largest squatter population). To this effect, editor Jon Qwelane wrote in *Tribute*, the popular black South African magazine: "As far as white South Africa is concerned very little has changed since the elections: they still enjoy the trappings of power and privilege, and the same opulent lifestyles of old; they have the security and comfort of homes and jobs, and they rate on a par with the well-off worldwide." Qwelane continues, "Flip the coin over and notice the contrast: even though blacks have won the political kingdom, the cold truth is that for many of our people the new South Africa is still only a rumour."[50]

In contrast to the balancing act that is required to bring the third world up to par—denouncing race but depending on it until the vestiges of racism are obliterated—the view of affirmative action by the National Party, as articulated when it was running toward the April 1994 election, was that it does nothing more than replace the old racism with a new racism. "Racist affirmative action whereby people are appointed not according to merit, qualifications, experience or talent, but on racial or ethnic preference, is unacceptable," the National Party said. "Because, if the objective is simply to rectify past discrimination against that group, it is just apartheid in reverse. Or plainly put, one cannot replace racism with racism."[51]

So, no rationally thinking, nonracist person in South Africa really believes racial discrimination will cease with the end of racial classification or that racial classification is not needed to help rectify past discrimination. It just happens that there are conditions in South Africa that facilitate the balancing act of denouncing race but depending on it until the vestiges of racism are obliterated. While it is politically incorrect to use the old racial identities from the apartheid epoch, there are ways by which government and other institutional officials can identify the ethnicity of South Africans without having to ask for racial identification on applications, school forms, birth certificates, and the like. Jimmy Ellis explained to me, for instance, that official racial designations are not used for applications to the University of the Western Cape, but for purposes of affirmative action, black students can be identified by their geographical locations (certain townships), their languages (ethnic tongues other than English or Afrikaans), and their last names (which generally are not Anglicized like coloured names). So a parallel exists between the governments in South Africa and the United States in understanding that racial classification is needed in order to identify "protected" groups. The difference between the two countries, however, is that in South Africa there are ways of determining who is who, while in the United States blacks generally speak English, have English last names, and have increasingly migrated out of known segregated black neighborhoods or have been pushed out by "urban renewal."

My point is that the desire of Yehudi Webster, Kwame Anthony Appiah, and others simply to abandon the idea of race, and to do so immediately, is politically naive. Indeed, it is suicidal. We need racial classifications in order to undermine race, because white racism has long surpassed the point where it is perpetuated merely by racial classification itself. In other words, even if the OMB were to discard Directive No. 15 and the Census Bureau were to cease its collection of racial data, black people would still be discriminated against. The difference would be that they would be discriminated against without federal protection, the same and only protection that got black people out of slavery in the 1860s.

While it is not wise to abandon the current racial classifications just yet, neither should we go any deeper into racial classification by adding a multiracial category. After all, the acknowledged goal of the multiracial movement itself is to escape race altogether. Thus, the United States needs the same balancing act that has been necessary in South Africa, where there is a denouncing of race but a dependency on it until the vestiges of racism are obliterated.

With South Africa as a reminder of this balancing act, the United States should be carrying the responsibility of setting the standard by which colorblind democracies should work. Historian Arthur Schlesinger, Jr. lays this burden at our doorstep. He says that in a world replete with ethnic and racial antagonisms, it is especially essential that the United States serve as an example of how a highly variegated society maintains its unity.[52] But with the addition of a multiracial classification to its rostrum of races, the United States would be led further into race consciousness, thus enhancing the "cult of ethnicity" and the resulting "tribalization of American life" that Schlesinger says threatens the unity of the country.[53] Thus, we must face the stark reality that nowhere in the modern world has the recognition of a race of mixed-race peoples resolved the racial problems of that society. Rather, splintering coloured peoples into such classifications of "race" and "mixed race" has aggravated race relations from the perspective of society's oppressed peoples. It may be, then, that the undoing of racial classification will come not by initiating a new classification, which will only give Americans the impression that mixed-race people can be neatly classified, but by our increased recognition that there are millions of people who cannot be put into neat categories.

One thing is certain, the "tribalization of American life" is not going to be prevented by multiracialists creating a formula by which they narrowly define who can or cannot be multiracial. For the multiracial ideal to work in the most theoretically suitable situation, it must be open for all mixed people—anyone at all who owns up to being racially mixed (which everyone is). It is only with the broadest definition of multiracial that the multiracialists could possibly meet their own ideal of everyone recognizing their multiraciality, their human oneness. This was clearly understood by the coloured nationalists I spoke to in Cape Town—evidently better than it is understood by the American multiracialists. One of the coloured nationalists told me that the face of the future is coloured (mixed-race) people, who can only increase in numbers as racial barriers are increasingly crossed. Even white Afrikaans people can be considered coloured, they added, since they have 6 to 8 percent mixed ancestry. According to the nationalists, whether or not white Afrikaans people choose to join the coloured (mixed) race is up to them but they must not be excluded, and the same should be true in the United States if the ideal of multiracialists is to work: the multiracialists cannot exclude blacks or whites from the category since both have some mixed ancestry somewhere in their lineage.

It is obvious that approximately 70 percent of African Americans have some mixed-race lineage that goes back several generations. Additionally, all Latinos and Filipinos are so-called multiracial, and most Native Americans and Native Hawaiians are too. Notwithstanding the obvious, however, the theoretical answer to the question of how many multiracial people there are in the United States must be this: there are approximately 250 million American citizens and there are approximately 250 million multiracial people. Given this premise, the only thing a modified Directive No. 15 could do for the census is tell us how many of the 250 million Americans choose to see themselves as multiracial or wish to be classified as that. But even if all Americans were to come to recognize their multiraciality, which is the stated ideal of many multiracialists, society still would have made little progress. This is because society still would be split along lines of phenotype, ethnicity, and class, as we see among the "multiracial" coloured people in South Africa. Additionally, once a racial classification were created it would be difficult to repeal it, as I argued in the previous chapter.

Thus, we seem to be left with fewer choices in our attempt to answer the question of what to do about the classification of mixed-race people, since both the elimination of current racial classifications and the creation of a new classification leave us with deeper dilemmas. Perhaps Rainier Spencer, of mixed parentage himself, is correct in his belief that the ideal should be to identify as not both black and white but as neither black nor white, since the principal tenet of the multiracial movement is that they do not believe in racial categories.[54] That would certainly be the higher moral ground to take for those who wish to make a statement of protest. But for those who wish to identify themselves racially, for the sake of self-esteem and so forth, the answer for them should be to identify with either or both of the races that comprise their mixed background.

While the multiracial category that Susan Graham wants so much would essentially establish a new race, other people have in fact suggested that mixed-race people simply check more than one category among the existing racial classifications. For example, the two mixed-race Americans who had been living in Cape Town for extended periods when I met them felt that it would be ideal for them to be able to choose more than one racial category on the United States census and other applications and school forms. Lise Funderburg, the mixed-race author of *Black, White, Other* (1994), also believes that on the census and other forms mixed-race people should just check off every category that applies to their background rather than reducing their identity to a single multiracial category.[55] George Dailey, former coordinator of the elementary and secondary education program for the Census

Bureau, told the OMB that the teachers and administrators he worked with actually were not asking for a "multiracial" category but for the ability to identify multiple racial backgrounds.[56]

How should mixed-race people be identified, then? On the census, application, and school forms they should be able to check the categories that apply to their racial background, which would permit the government to provide data on the number of mixed-race people in the country. This would help meet one of the important goals of the multiracialists: bringing to the attention of the American citizenry a part of the nation's family that has been invisible.

How should mixed-race people be primarily counted? I agree with Arthur Fletcher, chairperson of the United States Commission on Civil Rights, that mixed-race blacks should be counted wholly (not partly) as black. Fletcher told the House subcommittee that the eight civil rights commissioners he represents would not like to see the addition of a multiracial classification, which would result in dividing into parts a person's racial mix or in the removal of members from existing minority groups. Both of these outcomes could undermine civil rights enforcement and deny certain minorities full political representation and their fair share of federally funded programs.[57] Some multiracialists themselves understand this. I pointed out in chapter 1, for instance, that mixed-race sociologist Reginald Daniel feels that some form of disaggregation of the multiracial category is not only justifiable but necessary so that the measuring of African American demographics is not negatively affected in a way that could undermine policies designed to redress racial inequities.[58]

Aside from the coloured nationalists, most of the coloured and white South Africans I have mentioned, including the interracial couples, liked the idea of mixed-race people being able to check all of the categories that identify their racial background. This would not prevent the recognition of mixed-race people, but would rather approximate the South African situation before apartheid and its legislation of a coloured group, when it was common knowledge that there were people of mixed background but the authorities never got around to recognizing mixed-race people officially. Coloured people therefore emerged almost imperceptibly and peaceably. After slavery ended in 1834 this group of mixed-race people became citizens and people began to speak of the "coloured people," not as a legal category but as a demographic group. During the early twentieth century, before the beginning of the apartheid regime in 1948, color discrimination was on the increase among whites, even though the name "coloured" was not legislated and coloured people themselves used the designation positively and pridefully. Neither was there any restriction on intermarriage, so the numbers of coloured people grew. It was only after 1948, with the ascendancy of the Afrikaner's National Party, that coloureds were put in a racial pigeonhole. Indeed, President P. W. Botha, during his racist reign of terror, used to speak of the coloured people as a nation in the process of becoming. Yet this history of becoming a people is a history that most coloured people would undo if they had the power. Thus the idea of mixed-race people checking all of the categories that identify their racial background is as close as they can get to nonracialism while still claiming a racial identity.

A situation where mixed-race blacks are able to select multiple identities will no doubt require an adjustment on the part of monoracial blacks. But African Americans must open up new space for mixed-race blacks to be biracially black. That is, African Americans must not place membership restrictions on mixed-race people who say they are half black and half whatever else, or both black and something else. Journalist Itabari Njeri agrees that if African Americans continue to abuse mixed-race people who have black ancestry but who do not identify solely as black, then they are simply forcing the creation of a multiracial classification by forcing the exodus of mixed-race blacks from even a partial black identity.[59] Indeed, the black community cannot hold certain of its members in limbo, feeling uneasy with their interracial marriages or their biracialness, and expect them to wait for acceptance.

Moreover, in the previous chapter we saw what happened when coloured South Africans felt they were being held in limbo by the ANC as it was seeking to win the country's first democratic election. The coloured people gave their block vote to the National Party, which won that party the governorship of the Western Cape. So, considering what Jimmy Ellis told me about nonracialism being a position that can be embraced by many more people than black consciousness, African Americans can at least compromise with regard to their previous stance of suspicion as regards mixed-race people. The only way to bring mixed-race blacks back within the fold is to open up the category of black, making it an acceptable rubric for everyone with the "one drop." Only black people can impart the values of blackness to those who are uncertain about blackness, for example that the black community is a "steady home." But an appreciation for blackness will not happen if we perpetuate a narrow definition of what blackness is.

An important and (perhaps for some) uncomfortable requirement for opening up the category of black and bringing mixed-race people back into the fold is that the black community relax its rather tight-fisted position on interracial marriage. After all, the parents of mixed-race people are intermarried, so that intermarriage cannot be denounced or belittled without also insulting the mixed-race blacks we want to keep in the black community. In other words, we have to respect the position of someone like the young South African black woman I spoke to in Cape Town, who is dating a South African Englishman with the idea of possible marriage. We cannot pin her in a corner by questioning her like some of her black kindred have: "Why after all these years of apartheid are you taking a white man?" We must accept her answer that some whites are not so bad and are in fact nice and friendly, and that she and her white male companion see each other as individuals rather than colors. In this regard, the belief of Yvette and Daniel Hollis, the interracial couple who are the co-editors of *New People*, should be understood. They believe that the racial attitudes of most people are still stuck in the 1970s while the attitudes of others, such as themselves, have crossed the racial chasm and set an example by not allowing race to prevent them from having a full life.[60]

The black community must therefore accept mixed-race blacks who choose white spouses, even though we may wonder if this reflects their primary racial identification. The black community must also accept the fact that some of these white spouses in interracial marriages will not want to be black even in the symbolic sense, even while they may disassociate themselves from white racism. For instance, a mixed-race woman named Rosa Warder said that her white mother did not like being considered an "honorary" black person by blacks just because she was married to a black man, but rather wanted to be recognized as a white person who was just a decent human being.[61] Finally, and certainly not least, the black community must accept as black those of mixed race who want to be black-identified, even though they may not look black and may not know what it feels like to be discriminated against on a daily basis like darker-skinned people.[62]

That it may be ideal for mixed-race people to be permitted to identify themselves by checking two or more categories on the census, on applications, and on school forms was borne out to me when I analyzed the way I myself felt in South Africa. I mentioned in chapter 3 that when I first went to Cape Town I felt certain that I would be viewed as black and that three black students at the University of the Western Cape told me that in appearance alone I looked black. I also explained in that chapter that some of what I felt was but a delusion, for I later came to realize that there were many coloured people of my complexion and phenotype and that I had as much or more in common with them than with blacks. So, finally I realized that on a cultural and interpersonal level, where I fit in depended on who I was with: I could be black or coloured. I have made good acquaintances among the coloured people in Cape Town and I feel a true kinship, not to mention that they look like my own African American people at home. I have also made many good acquaintances among blacks in Johannesburg and I feel a true kinship. In Soweto, a suburb of Johannesburg, I have two old friends, a Xhosa woman whom I met in the United States in 1988 and her Zulu husband, whom I met in South Africa in 1992. They look like my own African American people at home. In Cape Town I saw a little coloured girl who looks just like the daughter of my best friend in the United States when she was three years old. In Johannesburg I saw a black child who looks just like my own daughter. So, just as mixed-race people in the United States are said to exist between (and even link) the communities of their parents, in South Africa I feel that I am somewhat a part of both the coloured and black communities—that I am a part of neither completely but of both partly.

So, here is the parallel question, resulting from my South African panorama, as regards mixed-race Americans checking categories on the United States census, on applications, and on school forms: in South Africa, how am I to choose which group I should identify with when I really identify with both coloureds or blacks? How am I to choose sides between the "race" of Desmond Tutu (who is black) and the "race" of Allan Boesak (who is coloured)? In fact, why would I even want to be apart from both groups in some separate classification? It is a privilege to be a part of both groups, particularly when I am free of the history of separation and feelings of dissension that still plague the two groups in their feelings toward one another. Even though I know that in the Cape Province, coloured people were given more privileges than blacks by the white minority government and were (and often still are) racist in their attitudes toward blacks, I do not wish to be forced away from coloured people on some ethical grounds, because I feel a kinship with them despite the troubles of history. Neither do I wish to be squeezed between blacks and coloureds in some third, median group. That will only distinguish me from both, when what I prefer is to be a part of both.

Is it good that in South Africa, African Americans are considered a people betwixt and between the coloureds and blacks? It could be if African Americans were a community there. For recognizing our connection with both communities, we could serve as a bridge toward reconciliation. But if we were to form our own middle group and declare "We are the African Americans!" then we would be just that—another group, nothing more. So, were I among a group of, say, African American expatriates living in

South Africa with citizenship, I would prefer to be able to check on a South African census both "black" and "coloured." If I were to marry, it could be either to a coloured woman or a black woman without it being deemed an interracial marriage, and our children would be both coloured and black and, as far as I am concerned, would have the freedom to identify with either or both. If I were a person of hope, then, given South Africa's push for a nonracial society, I would prefer to check "South African." Then I could marry anyone I wished without the marriage being deemed interracial, and my so-called "mixed" children would not be "multiracial" but simply South African—citizens ideally judged by the content of their character rather than by the race of their parents.

This is the South African ideal, of which Nelson Mandela is the ultimate symbol. If it can be the South African ideal, promoted by a black man imprisoned for twenty-seven years and due every right to be bitter toward his unjust captors, then it should also be the American ideal, for which Martin Luther King, Jr., is the ultimate symbol. If the King national holiday, held in January each year, is to mean anything to us at all, it ought to mean nonracialism. As I said in chapter 2, how can we venerate King (the American Mandela)—or for that matter Mandela (the South African King)—and with a clear conscience move deeper into racial classification, given the models of morality these two men have become? What the United States needs is not a multiracial "race" but a multiracial coalition to work to overcome the obstacles impeding nonracialism. No matter how long it takes, we can only walk the moral ground if we expend our energies to push ever so intently (albeit slowly) away from racial classification. Then and only then will we be able to say we are a people judged by the content of our character rather than by the color of our skin.

If the citizens within our society cannot manage to grasp this ideal, then it is the responsibility of the United States government, which looks upon the nation from a broader perspective, to make a decision that moves the nation in the direction of the nation's ideals—one people under God "indivisible." For the government to add a multiracial classification to the rostrum of races, lumping together a heterogeneous group of mixed-race people for administrative purposes (as was done to the coloured South Africans by an apartheid government), is for that government to move the nation into a direction opposite to that of post-apartheid South Africa.

[POSTSCRIPT]

I ended the last chapter saying that it is the responsibility of the United States government to move the nation in the direction of the ideal of Americans being one "indivisible" people. We must admit, however, that the United States has never had a Nelson Mandela for president, a man novelist Susan Sontag says was president even before he was released from prison. Writing several years before Mandela's release, Sontag declared that Mandela was "de facto head of state, the president of a democratic country that does not yet exist but will exist."[1] Sontag also said of Mandela, the world's longest-held political prisoner: "This man is exemplary. Because of who he is, how he has behaved, what he has said (and goes on saying); because the cause of which he has been for decades a preeminent leader is just; and because his version of it is the most mature, politically and morally, the most realistic, the one most likely to lead to reconciliation and to avoid the otherwise inevitable carnage."[2] When in prison, as Sontag says, Mandela was a symbol, living in what was (given the realities of the country at the time) a symbolic place—a prison. Today he is equally symbolic: a resurrection of Martin Luther King (a greater King), emerging from prison at age seventy-two, February 11, 1990. He alone stands as the ultimate symbol of racial reconciliation, so much so, as French philosopher Jacques Derrida says, that even his enemies admire him without admitting it.[3] If anyone in the mid-1990s is going to claim the moral high ground with regard to race, then they must reflect on it through the example of this great man: What would Mandela say?

Nonracialism has been Mandela's ideal as far back as we can remember. In concluding his speech to the South African people on the day of his release in Cape Town, Mandela quoted words he had read during his trial in 1964. In doing so, he showed that those words are as true today as they were twenty-seven years earlier: "I have fought against White domination and I have fought against Black domination. I have carried the ideal of a democratic and free society in which all persons live together in harmony and with equal opportunity. It is an ideal which I hope to live for and to achieve. But, if needs be, it is an ideal for which I am prepared to die." Words such as these continued to characterize Mandela's election campaign for South Africa's presidency. Consequently, the image of South Africa as once torn by racial hatred but now coming to terms with itself as a multiracial society pervaded the American media as the election was growing near. Then, after the elections, came President-elect Mandela's rekindled appeal for national reconciliation, which intrigued Americans of all colors. In this speech, Mandela declared South Africa "free at last," borrowing from the words made famous by King, whose widow, Coretta Scott King, stood at his side. That speech was replayed on the American public affairs network, C-SPAN, for nearly two days, and excerpts were printed in newspapers around the United States. Paul Taylor, writing for the *Washington Post* on May 3, 1994, said: "For the past half-century, South Africa has been the most preached-at country in the world. Now it is preaching to the world."[4] Stephen Rosenfeld, writing for the *Washington Post* on May 13, 1994, wondered if what was unfolding in South Africa could not be bottled and injected elsewhere in the world to calm disputes that burden American foreign policy.[5]

But what about injecting the South African magic into our own society? The question is particularly relevant since South African novelist Mark Mathabane and his wife Gail are correct that, while a new epoch of racial reconciliation has dawned in South Africa, many in the United States believe the sun is setting on their best days of racial peace.[6] So, what about injecting the South African magic into American society? We have had ample opportunity to hear the man who carries that magic in his heart, such as on October 3, 1994, when President Mandela was in the United States and gave the United Nations a message that resounded throughout the country. Mandela declared that racism could "stubbornly . . . cling to the mind and deeply inflict the human soul. And where it is sustained by the racial ordering of the material world, as is the case in our country, that stubbornness can multiply a hundredfold. And yet however hard the battle will be, we will not surrender. Whatever the time it will take, we will not tire." He added, "It will perhaps come to be that we who have harboured in our country the worst example of racism since the defeat of Nazism, will make a contribution to human civilisation by ordering our affairs in such a manner that we strike an effective and lasting blow against racism everywhere."[7]

President Bill Clinton felt the magic spreading on that occasion, and responded with inspiration in his welcome of Mandela to the White House. This was the first time a South African president had been received by the United States with full honors, and President Clinton said on this distinctive occasion: "The struggle in South Africa has always had a special place in the heart of America. For after all, we fought our own most terrible war here in our own land over slavery. And our own civil rights movement has taken strength and inspiration from, and given aid to, your fight for liberty."[8] Clinton, mindful of civil wars in Rwanda and Bosnia, said about Mandela's promotion of reconciliation in his racially divided country: "Now all over the world there are three words which spoken together express the triumph of freedom, democracy and hope for the future. They are, 'President Nelson Mandela.'"[9] Clinton also said, "In you, sir, we see proof that the human spirit can never be crushed. For twenty-seven years we watched you from your prison cell inspire millions of your people with your spirit and your words. You are living proof that the forces of justice and reconciliation can bridge any divide." Clinton continued, "Americans take great pride in the role we played in helping to overcome apartheid and in support for free elections which led to your presidency. Now we are working with you to build a new South Africa. And most important in this age of ethnic, religious, and racial strife the world over, you can be our partner and together our two nations can show the world that true strength is found when we come together despite our differences."[10]

Afterwards, Marian Wright Edelman, director of the Children's Defense Fund, remarked to a journalist: "It just tells you that anything is possible. And that you just have to hang in there and speak for what is right. . . . How can you look at this man and not be hopeful?"[11] Similarly, Africare founder C. Payne Lucas said, "He's an inspiration to everyone, and it transcends color. There was nothing worse than South Africa. It was a living hell, and he put it all together."[12]

Because of these very qualities that Edelman and Lucas speak of, the Clinton administration urged President Mandela, during his visit to the United States, to meet the ousted president of Haiti, Bertrand Aristide. They were hoping that Mandela's promotion of reconciliation in South Africa would serve as an example for Aristide when he was restored to power. About this Clinton said, "The most important thing South Africa can do for Haiti has been accomplished by President Mandela coming to the United States at this historic moment, and then on top of that agreeing to meet with President Aristide. The Haitian people will see that you can bring a country where there have been deep, even bloody divisions together and work together in a spirit of freedom, reconciliation, democracy and mutual respect."[13] Indeed, the Mandela magic might have been part of what was behind Aristide returning to his country on October 15 and saying to his friends and foes alike: "No to violence, no to vengeance, yes to reconciliation."[14] The rest has been history in Haiti.

But before we take President Mandela and South Africa as the great example for us to follow, we might be inclined to ask that question of questions: If they are to be the divine example, then why did God—who is unendingly knowledgable, powerful, present, and good—prolong the suffering of the oppressed peoples of South Africa under tyrannical white rule? If we are to believe that God had a plan all along, then it must be that God saved the liberation of this African land for last, so the world would pay attention to the slow but steady, magical unwinding of a profound destiny: the release of The Captive (the one who rose from prisoner to president) and the release of the captives (the dispossessed masses of South Africa) so the world could see the true spirit of human reconciliation shine. We can no more ignore the meaning of his "coming" than we could a "second coming." Thus, all of the religious arguments made by the laypeople and intellectuals of the multiracial movement pale in the light of the man who adds a new commandment for the world's faithful to follow: Thou shalt not racially classify.

[NOTES]

Notes to the Preface

1. Heather Green, "This Piece Done, I Shall Be Renamed," in Carol Camper, *Miscegenation Blues: Voices of Mixed Race Women* (Toronto: Sister Vision Press), 301.

2. Hanna Rosin, "Boxed In," *New Republic*, January 3, 1994, 14.

3. Joel Williamson, *New People: Miscegenation and Mulattoes in the United States* (New York: Free Press, 1980), 187.

4. Williamson, *New People*, 195.

5. Roy H. Du Pre, *Separate but Unequal: The "Coloured" People of South Africa—A Political History* (Johannesburg: Jonathan Ball Publishers, 1994), 10.

6. See the entirety of Camper, *Miscegenation Blues*, and specifically the comment of Gitanjali Saxena, in Carol Camper, host, "Mixed Race Women's Group—Dialogue One," in Camper, *Miscegenation Blues*, 40.

7. See Sharon Begley, "Three Is Not Enough: Surprising New Lessons from the Controversial Science of Race," *Newsweek*, February 13, 1995, 67–69.

8. Yehudi Webster, on Wayne Olney, host, "Racial Categories on the Next Census: Should They Be Changed or Should They Be Eliminated Altogether," *Which Way L.A.?* KCRW Radio, Santa Monica College, California.

9. W. E. B. Du Bois, *Dusk of Dawn: An Essay Toward an Autobiography of a Race Concept* (New York: Harcourt Brace, 1940), 153.

10. Richard E. van der Ross, "Taking a Look at the Whites," *Cape Times*, December 15, 1960, in Richard E. van der Ross, *Coloured Viewpoint: A Series of Articles in the Cape Times, 1958–1965 by R. E. van der Ross*, ed. J. L. Hattingh and H. C. Bredekamp (Bellville, South Africa: The Western Cape Institute for Historical Research/University of the Western Cape, 1984), 143.

Notes to the Introduction

1. Katherine Wallman, Office of Management and Budget, Public Hearing(s) on Standards for the Classification of Federal Data on Race and Ethnicity, July 11, 1994, 4–5.

2. Carlos A. Fernandez, Review of Federal Measurements of Race and Ethnicity, Hearings before the Subcommittee on Census, Statistics and Postal Personnel of the Committee on Post Office and Civil Office and Civil Service, House of Representatives, 103rd Congress, June 30, 1993 (Washington, D.C.: U.S. Government Printing Office, 1994), 134.

3. Harry A. Scarr (Acting Director of the Bureau of the Census), Review of Federal Measurements of Race and Ethnicity, April 14, 1993, 10. See also Christine C. Iijima Hall, "Coloring Outside the Lines," in Maria P. P. Root, ed., *Racially Mixed People in America* (Newbury Park, Calif.: Sage, 1992), 327.

4. Scarr, Review of Federal Measurements of Race and Ethnicity, 10.

5. Scarr, Review of Federal Measurements of Race and Ethnicity; Katherine Wallman, Office of Management and Budget, Public Hearing(s), 2.

6. Dale Warner, Office of Management and Budget, Public Hearing(s), July 14, 1994, 78.

7. Louis Massery, Office of Management and Budget, Public Hearing(s), July 7, 1994, 51, 57.

8. Hamzi Moghrabi, Office of Management and Budget, Public Hearing(s), July 11, 1994, 9, 51. See also Beesan Barghouti (representing the Arab-American Institute in Washington), Office of Management and Budget, Public Hearing(s), July 11, 1994, 16–17.

9. Joseph E. Fallon, Office of Management and Budget, Public Hearing(s), July 7, 1994, 14.

10. Warner, Office of Management and Budget, Public Hearing(s), 78.

11. Fallon, Office of Management and Budget, Public Hearing(s), 15.

12. Fallon, Office of Management and Budget, Public Hearing(s), 16–17.

13. Gerhard Holford, Office of Management and Budget, Public Hearing(s), July 14, 1994, 81.

14. Holford, Office of Management and Budget, Public Hearing(s), 82.

15. Donald H. Freiberg, Office of Management and Budget, Public Hearing(s), July 14, 1994, n.p.

16. Letter to the Editor, *Interrace*, May/June 1992, 7.

17. Thomas Sawyer, on Wayne Olney, host, "Racial Categories on the Next Census: Should They Be Changed or Should They Be Eliminated Altogether," on *Which Way L. A.?* KCRW Radio, Santa Monica College, California.

18. F. James Davis, *Who Is Black?: One Nation's Definition* (University Park: Pennsylvania State University Press, 1991), 181.

19. Davis, *Who Is Black?* 184.

20. Roy Harrison, Office of Management and Budget, Public Hearing(s), July 14, 1994, 133.

21. Roy H. Du Pre, *Separate but Unequal: The "Coloured" People of South Africa—A Political History* (Johannesburg: Jonathan Ball Publishers, 1994), 9.

22. Richard E. van der Ross, "Group Identity and the Coloured People," MS, lecture at the Abe Bailey Institute of Interracial Studies, June 17, 1994, from the files of Jimmy Ellis, University of the Western Cape, Cape Town.

23. George M. Fredrickson, *White Supremacy: A Comparative Study in American and South African History* (New York: Oxford University Press, 1981), xviii. See also George M. Fredrickson, *Black Liberation: Comparative History of Black Ideologies* (New York: Oxford University Press, 1995).

24. "The Minister Who Learnt to Hate, and Love," *Sunday Times* (South Africa) March 9, 1980, 5.

25. Dion Basson, *South Africa's Interim Constitution: Text and Notes* (Kenwyn, South Africa: Juta, 1994), xix.

26. Fredrickson, *White Supremacy*, xix, 94.

27. Also see Ralph J. Bunche, *An African American in South Africa: The Travel Notes of Ralph J. Bunche, 28 September 1937–1 January 1938*, ed. Robert R. Edgar (Johannesburg: Witwatersrand University Press, 1992), 28.

28. Everett V. Stonequist, *The Marginal Man: A Study in Personality and Culture Conflict* (New York: Russell and Russell, 1961 [1937]), 106–7.

Notes to Chapter 1

1. Richard E. van der Ross, *100 Questions about Coloured South Africans* (Cape Town: University of the Western Cape Printing Department, 1993), 5.

2. Van der Ross, *100 Questions about Coloured South Africans*, 32.

3. Teja Arboleda, Office of Management and Budget, Public Hearing(s) on Standards for the Classification of Federal Data on Race and Ethnicity, July 14, 1994, n.p.

4. Arboleda, Office of Management and Budget, Public Hearing(s), July 14, 1994, n.p.

5. F. James Davis, *Who Is Black?: One Nation's Definition* (University Park: Pennsylvania State University Press, 1991), 181.

6. Francis Wardle, "Tomorrow's Children," *New People*, September/October 1991, 5.

7. "The Case against Mixed Marriage," *Ebony* 6, no 1 (November 1950): 50, 51, 54.

8. "The Case against Mixed Marriage," 55.

9. *Interracial Classified* (newsletter), August 1992, 3.

10. Susan Fister [Assistant Professor, Eastern Kentucky University] to Jon Michael Spencer, September 27, 1994.

11. Susan Graham, Review of Federal Measurements of Race and Ethnicity, Hearings before the Subcommittee on Census, Statistics and Postal Personnel of the Committee on Post Office and Civil Office and Civil Service, House of Representatives, 103rd Congress, First Session, June 30, 1993 (Washington, D.C.: U.S. Government Printing Office, 1994), 113, 115.

12. Carlos A. Fernandez, Review of Federal Measurements of Race and Ethnicity, 127, 134.

13. Fernandez, Review of Federal Measurements of Race and Ethnicity, 134.

14. G. Reginald Daniel, "Beyond Black and White: The New Multiracial Consciousness," in Maria P. P. Root, ed., *Racially Mixed People in America* (Newbury Park, Calif.: Sage, 1992), 340.

15. Sally Katzen, on Wayne Olney, host, "Racial Categories on the Next Census: Should They Be Changed or Should They Be Eliminated Altogether," on *Which Way L.A.?* KCRW Radio, Santa Monica College, California.

16. Fernandez, Review of Federal Measurements of Race and Ethnicity, 126, 128.

17. Susan Graham, on Olney, "Racial Categories on the Next Census."

18. Cited in Candace Mills, "'Multiracial': Worth Fighting For?" *Interrace*, November 1993, 27.

19. Cited in Janita Poe, "Multiracial People Want a Single Name That Fits," *Chicago Tribune*, May 3, 1993, 13.

20. Roy Harrison, Office of Management and Budget, Public Hearing(s), July 14, 1994, 134.

21. Davis, *Who Is Black?*, 144.

22. Lora Pierce, "Double Standard?" *Interrace*, May/June 1992, 22.

23. Graham, Review of Federal Measurements of Race and Ethnicity, 105–6.

24. Graham, Review of Federal Measurements on Race and Ethnicity, 108.

25. William Keating, Office of Management and Budget, Public Hearing(s), July 7, 1994, 20.

26. Ruth Provost (legislative chairperson of the Massachusetts Parent Teacher Student Association), Office of Management and Budget, Public Hearing(s), July 7, 1994, 21.

27. Mark Mathabane and Gail Mathabane, *Love in Black and White* (New York: HarperCollins, 1992), 217.

28. Graham, Review of Federal Measurements of Race and Ethnicity, 125.

29. Jan Haley, Office of Management and Budget, Public Hearing(s), July 11, 1994, 13.

30. George Daily, Office of Management and Budget, Public Hearing(s), July 11, 1994, 44, 48.

31. Daily, Office of Management and Budget, Public Hearing(s), July 11, 1944, 44.

32. Senator Ralph David Abernathy III, Senate Bill 149 (as passed), Georgia Act No. 1193, signed for April 14, 1994, the General Assembly of Georgia, section 1, p. 2.

33. *A Rainbow of Color*, September/October 1994, 3.

34. Graham, Review of Federal Measurements of Race and Ethnicity, 120.

35. Graham, Review of Federal Measurements of Race and Ethnicity, 119.

36. Graham, Review of Federal Measurements of Race and Ethnicity, 109.

37. Susan Graham, "I'm Not an 'Other,'" *New People*, March/April 1992, 9.

38. Graham, Review of Federal Measurements of Race and Ethnicity, 119.

39. Fernandez, Review of Federal Measurements of Race and Ethnicity, 127.

40. Cynthia Chamble to the Editor, *Interrace*, September/October 1993, 5.

41. Cited in "I Don't Know Who I Am," *Sally Jessy Raphael Show*, November 16, 1993.

42. Cited in Lise Funderburg, *Black, White, Other: Biracial Americans Talk about Race and Identity* (New York: William Morrow, 1994), 41, 42, 43, 45, 47.

43. Cited in Funderburg, *Black, White, Other*, 44.

44. Cited in Funderburg, *Black, White, Other*, 48, 49.

45. Teresa Kay Williams, "Prism Lives: Identity of Binational Americans," in Root, *Racially Mixed People in America*, 286.

46. Christine C. Iijima Hall, "Please Choose One: Ethnic Identity Choices for Biracial Individuals," in Root, *Racially Mixed People in America*, 254.

47. Hall, "Please Choose One," 255.

48. Roy H. Du Pre, *Separate but Unequal: The "Coloured" People of South Africa—A Political History* (Johannesburg: Jonathan Ball Publishers, 1994), xvi, 5.

49. Du Pre, *Separate but Unequal*, 223.

50. E. Franklin Frazier, *The Negro Church in America* (New York: Schocken, 1974), 83.

51. Booker T. Washington, cited in John M. Burgess, "Opening Presentation" (Convocation of Black Theologians, April 1978), *Saint Luke's Journal of Theology* 22, no. 4 (September 1979): 245.

52. Molefi Kete Asante, "Racing to Leave the Race: Black Postmodernists Off-Track," *Black Scholar* 23, nos. 3 and 4 (Spring/Fall 1993): 50.

53. Cited in Elizabeth Atkins, "Parents of Biracial Children Debate the Wisdom of Afrocentric Education," *New People*, May/June 1993, 7.

54. G. Reginald Daniel, "Eurocentrism, Afrocentrism, or 'Holocentrism'?" *Interrace*, May/June 1992, 33.

55. Francis Wardle, "Hindsight Doesn't Count in Racial War," *New People*, July/August 1994, 6.

56. Rainier Spencer, "The Melanin Myth," *Interrace*, April 1994, 24.

57. Spencer, "The Melanin Myth," 25.

58. Cited in Funderburg, *Black, White, Other*, 123.

59. Cited in Funderburg, *Black, White, Other*, 123, 127, 132.

60. Cited in Funderburg, *Black, White, Other*, 273–74.

61. Cited in Funderburg, *Black, White, Other*, 288.

62. Anne Vespry, in Carol Camper, host, "Mixed Race Women's Group—Dialogue Two," in Carol Camper, *Miscegenation Blues: Voices of Mixed Race Women* (Toronto: Sister Vision Press, 1994), 277.

63. Cited in Funderburg, *Black, White, Other*, 136.

64. Letter to the Editor, *Interrace*, May/June 1992, 7.

65. Graham, Review of Federal Measurements of Race and Ethnicity, 170.

66. Graham, Review of Federal Measurements of Race and Ethnicity, 119.

67. Hall, "Please Choose One," 256, 263.

68. Jamoo to the Editor, *Interrace*, May/June 1992, 6.

69. Cited in Funderburg, *Black, White, Other*, 34.

70. Cited in Funderburg, *Black, White, Other*, 34.

71. Cited in Funderburg, *Black, White, Other*, 85.

72. Cited in Funderburg, *Black, White, Other*, 28.

73. Nila Gupta, in Camper, "Mixed Race Women's Group—Dialogue Two," in Camper, *Miscegenation Blues*, 288–89.

74. Juanita Tamayo Lott (President of Tamayo Lott Associates), Review of Federal Measurements of Race and Ethnicity, April 14, 1993, 69.

75. Cited in Poe, "Multiracial People Want a Single Name That Fits," 13.

76. Carlos A. Fernandez, "Justice in Alabama?" *New People*, July/August 1994, 8.

77. Elroy Stock to the Editor, *Interrace*, March 1994, 2.

78. Edward Byron Reuter, *The Mulatto in the United States: Including a Study of the Role of Mixed Races throughout the World* (Boston: Richard G. Badger/Gorham Press, 1918), 373.

79. Joel Williamson, *New People: Miscegenation and Mulattoes in the United States* (New York: Free Press, 1980), 109.

80. David C. Kaufman, "Biracial Experiences in the United States," *Interrace*, April 1994, 19.

81. Francis Wardle, "Are Biracial Children and Interracial Families a Threat to the Progress of Blacks in the U.S.?" *Interrace*, September/October 1992, 44.

82. Wardle, "Are Biracial Children and Interracial Families a Threat to the Progress of Blacks in the U.S.?" 44.

83. Gabriela, "What It Means to Be Bi-Racial," *Interrace*, September/October 1992, 24.

84. Fernandez, Review of Federal Measurements of Race and Ethnicity, 132.

85. Fernandez, Review of Federal Measurements of Race and Ethnicity, 168.

86. Wardle, "Are Biracial Children and Interracial Families a Threat to the Progress of Blacks in the U.S.?" 43.

87. Sandy Cirillo, "Beautiful People without a Name," *Interrace*, January/February 1991, 23.

88. Cited in Poe, "Multiracial People Want a Single Name That Fits," 13.

89. Arthur M. Schlesinger, Jr., *The Disuniting of America: Reflections on a Multicultural Society* (New York: Norton, 1992), 15, 16.

90. Wardle, "Are Biracial Children and Interracial Families a Threat to the Progress of Blacks in the U.S.?" 44.

91. Kathlyn Gay, *The Rainbow Effect: Interracial Families* (New York: Franklin Watts, 1987), 130.

92. Gregory Stephens, "Mixed-Race Children Put Equality Issues in Focus," *Oakland Tribune*, July 2, 1994.

93. Fernandez, Review of Federal Measurements of Race and Ethnicity, 128.

94. Cited in Funderburg, *Black, White, Other*, 166.

95. Mathabane and Mathabane, *Love in Black and White*, 217

96. Cited in Lawrence Wright, "One Drop of Blood," *The New Yorker*, July 25, 1994; G. Reginald Daniel, on Olney, "Racial Categories on the Next Census."

97. Daniel, on Olney, "Racial Categories on the Next Census."

98. Daniel, on Olney, "Racial Categories on the Next Census."

99. Fernandez, Review of Federal Measurements of Race and Ethnicity, 127, 131.

100. Fernandez, Review of Federal Measurements of Race and Ethnicity, 171.

101. Naomi Zack, *Race and Mixed Race* (Philadelphia: Temple University Press, 1993), 164.

102. Fernandez, Review of Federal Measurements of Race and Ethnicity, 130.

103. Paul Lample and Marcia Lample, "The Baha'i Faith and the Oneness of Humanity," *Interrace*, July/August 1992, 16, 17, 18.

104. *The Vision of Race Unity: America's Most Challenging Issue* (Wilmette, Ill.: Baha'i Publishing Trust, 1991), 10.

105. *The Vision of Race Unity*, 1, 3.

106. Lample and Lample, "The Baha'i Faith and the Oneness of Humanity," 18.

107. Sally Katzen, Review of Federal Measurements of Race and Ethnicity, 215.

108. Jon Michael Spencer, on Olney, "Racial Categories on the Next Census"; see Verna Arvey, *In One Lifetime* (Fayetteville: University of Arkansas Press, 1984), 163.

109. Romona Douglass, Review of Federal Measurements of Race and Ethnicity, 152.

110. Kendra Wallace, Office of Management and Budget, Public Hearing(s), July 14, 1994, 16–17, 19.

Notes to Chapter 2

1. Cited in Lise Funderburg, *Black, White, Other: Biracial Americans Talk about Race and Identity* (New York: William Morrow, 1994), 22, 228.

2. Cited in Funderburg, *Black, White, Other*, 229, 233, 235.

3. Cited in Funderburg, *Black, White, Other*, 310.

4. Cited in Funderburg, *Black, White, Other*, 207.

5. Camille Hernandez-Ramdwar, "Ms. Edge Innate," in Carol Camper, ed., *Miscegenation Blues: Voices of Mixed Race Women* (Toronto: Sister Vision Press, 1994), 3, 5.

6. Cited in Funderburg, *Black, White, Other*, 250, 254.

7. Nannie H. Burroughs, "Church Leader Argues against Mixed Marriage," *Ebony* 6, no. 1 (November 1950): 50.

8. Hettie Jones, "Mama's White," *Essence*, May 1994, 152.

9. Lisa Jones, *Bulletproof Diva: Tales of Race, Sex, and Hair* (New York: Doubleday, 1994), 204–5.

10. Hettie Jones, "Mama's White," 79, 151.

11. Hettie Jones, "Mama's White," 151.

12. Jones, *Bulletproof Diva*, 32.

13. Cited in Funderburg, *Black, White, Other*, 350.

14. Cited in Funderburg, *Black, White, Other*, 56, 57, 58, 59.

15. James H. Cone, *Black Theology and Black Power* (New York: Harper Collins, 1989 [1969]), 152.

16. Candy Mills, "'Multiracial': Worth Fighting For?" *Interrace*, November 1993, 25.

17. See, for example, the stories of Seth Price and Sallyann Hobson, in Funderburg, *Black, White, Other*, 52, 60, 66. Also see Jonathan Brower,

"The Doctor Is In," *Interrace*, November/December 1992, 31; Kathlyn Gay, *The Rainbow Effect: Interracial Families* (New York: Franklin Watts, 1987), 71–72.

18. Everett V. Stonequist, *The Marginal Man: A Study in Personality and Culture Conflict* (New York: Russell and Russell, 1961 [1937]), 10.

19. Cited in Funderburg, *Black, White, Other*, 85.

20. Jones, *Bulletproof Diva*, 32.

21. Cited in Teresa Kay Williams, "Prism Lives: Identity of Binational Amerasians," in Maria P. P. Root, ed., *Racially Mixed People in America* (Newbury Park, Calif.: Sage, 1992), 287.

22. Angelo Ragaza, "All of the Above: Mixed Race Asian Americans Are Changing the Look and Meaning of Asian America," *A. Magazine* 3, no. 1 (n.d.): 76.

23. Cynthia L. Nakashima, "An Invisible Monster: The Creation and Denial of Mixed-Race People in America," in Root, *Racially Mixed People in America*, 176.

24. Christine C. Iijima Hall, "Please Choose One: Ethnic Identity Choices for Biracial Individuals," in Root, *Racially Mixed People in America*, 259.

25. Williams, "Prism Lives," 299–300.

26. Williams, "Prism Lives," 283.

27. Williams, "Prism Lives," 296.

28. F. James Davis, *Who Is Black?: One Nation's Definition* (University Park: Pennsylvania State University Press, 1991), 178.

29. Davis, *Who Is Black?* 180.

30. Frantz Fanon, *Black Skin, White Masks*, trans. Charles Lam Markmann (New York: Grove, 1967), 10.

31. Alton B. Pollard III, "The Last Great Battle of the West: W. E. B. Du Bois and the Struggle for African America's Soul," in Gerald Early, ed., *Lure and Loathing: Essays on Race, Identity, and the Ambivalence of Assimilation* (New York: Penguin, 1993), 47.

32. Kwame Anthony Appiah, *In My Father's House: Africa in the Philosophy of Culture* (New York: Oxford University Press, 1992), 176.

33. Houston A. Baker, Jr., "Caliban's Triple Play," in Henry Louis Gates, Jr., ed., *"Race," Writing, and Difference* (Chicago: University of Chicago Press, 1986), 384–85.

34. Wayne Olney, host, "Racial Categories on the Next Census: Should They Be Changed or Should They Be Eliminated Altogether," on *Which Way L.A.?* KCRW Radio, Santa Monica College, California, August 4, 1994.

35. Beverly Smythe to the Editor, *Interrace*, March 1994, 2.

36. Wayne Olney and Susan Graham, on Olney, "Racial Categories on the Next Census."

37. See the entirety of Camper, *Miscegenation Blues*, and specifically the comment of Gitanjali Saxena, in Carol Camper, host, "Mixed Race Women's Group—Dialogue One," in Camper, *Miscegenation Blues*, 40.

38. Susan Graham, on Olney, "Racial Categories on the Next Census."

39. William O. Brown, *Race Relations in the American South and in South Africa: A Comparison of Backgrounds, Realities, and Trends* (Boston: Boston University Press, 1959), 6; H. F. Dickie-Clark, *The Marginal Situation: A Sociological Study of a Coloured Group* (London: Routledge and Kegan Paul; New York: Humanities Press, 1966), 113, n3; George M. Fredrickson, *White Supremacy: A Comparative Study in American and South African History* (New York: Oxford University Press, 1981), 255–56.

40. Hanna Rosin, "Boxed In," *The New Republic*, January 3, 1994, 14.

41. Carlos A. Fernandez, in Review of Federal Measurements of Race and Ethnicity, Hearings before the Subcommittee on Census, Statistics and Postal Personnel of the Committee on Post Office and Civil Office and Civil Service, House of Representatives, 103rd Congress, First Session, June 30, 1993 (Washington, D.C.: U.S. Government Printing Office, 1994), 133.

42. Graham, on Olney, "Racial Categories on the Next Census."

43. Susan Graham, Review of Federal Measurements of Race and Ethnicity, 166.

44. Candy Mills, Editorial, *Interrace*, November/December 1992, 8.

45. Mills, "'Multiracial,'" 25.

46. Jamoo, "Where Are All the Dark-skinned Black Women?" *Interrace*, May/June 1992, 14, 15.

47. Cited in Lisa Jones, "The Blacker the Berry," *Essence*, June 1994, 62.

48. Francis Wardle, "Hindsight Doesn't Count in Racial War," *New People*, July/August 1994, 17.

49. Francis Wardle, "Lani Guinier's Real Confirmation: She's Biracial," *New People*, September/October 1993, 7.

50. Wardle, "Lani Guinier's Real Confirmation," 7.

51. Francis Wardle, "It's Open Season on Race and Identity," *New People*, May/June 1993, 13.

52. Ramona E. Douglass, "A Multiracial's Dissent," *New People*, July/August 1994, 4.

53. Lois Melina, "Advice for Parents of Children of Mixed Racial Heritage," *Adopted Child* (newsletter) 9, no. 5 (May 1990), n.p.

54. R. E. van der Ross, *100 Questions about Coloured South Africans* (Cape Town: University of the Western Cape Printing Department, 1993), 14.

55. Arthur A. Fletcher, Review of Federal Measurements of Race and Ethnicity, 252.

56. Fletcher, Review of Federal Measurements of Race and Ethnicity, 273.

57. Mike Siluma, "Divisions Wrought by Apartheid Are Still Intact," *The Star International Weekly* (Johannesburg), September 22, 1994, 14. Also see Ralph J. Bunche, *An African American in South Africa: The Travel Notes of Ralph J. Bunche, 28 September 1937–1 January 1938*, ed. Robert R. Edgar (Johannesburg: Witwatersrand University Press, 1992), 160.

58. Roy H. Du Pre, *Separate but Unequal: The "Coloured" People of South Africa—Political History* (Johannesburg: Jonathan Ball Publishers, 1994), 269.

59. Jones, *Bulletproof Diva*, 61.

60. Naomi Zack, *Race and Mixed Race* (Philadelphia: Temple University Press, 1993), 165.

61. Cited in Rosin, "Boxed In," 14.

62. Roi Ottley, "5 Million U.S. White Negroes," *Ebony* 3, no. 5 (March 1948): 24.

63. Cited in Funderburg, *Black, White, Other*, 343.

64. Cited in Funderburg, *Black, White, Other*, 235.

65. Michele Paulse, "Commingled," in Camper, *Micegenation Blues*, 46.

66. Carol Camper, "Into the Mix," in Camper, *Miscegenation Blues*, xxiii.

67. Heather Green, "This Piece Done, I Shall Be Renamed," in Camper, *Miscegenation Blues*, 298–99.

68. Gavin Lewis, *Between the Wire and the Wall: A History of South African "Coloured" People* (Cape Town: David Philip, 1987), 3.

69. Cleveland Donald, Jr., "Equality in Brazil: Confronting Reality," *Black World* 22 (November 1972), in David J. Hellwig, ed., *African-American Reflections on Brazil's Racial Paradise* (Philadelphia: Temple University Press, 1992), 210–11.

70. Angela M. Gilliam, "From Roxbury to Rio—and Back in a Hurry" (1970), in Hellwig, *African-American Reflections on Brazil's Racial Paradise*, 178.

71. Fletcher, Review of Federal Measurements of Race and Ethnicity, 252, 257.

72. Billy J. Tidwell, Review of Federal Measurement of Race and Ethnicity, 234.

73. Paul Williams, Review of Federal Measurements of Race and Ethnicity, 281.

74. Lawrence Wright, "One Drop of Blood," *New Yorker*, July 25, 1994, 47.

75. The Case against Mixed Marriage," *Ebony* 6, no. 1 (November 1950): 55.

76. Hettie Jones, "Mama's White," 152.

77. Mark Mathabane and Gail Mathabane, *Love in Black and White* (New York: HarperCollins, 1992), 144.

78. Themba Sono, *Reflections on the Origin of Black Consciousness in South Africa* (Pretoria: Human Sciences Research Council Publishers, 1993), 34.

79. Richard E. van der Ross, "Coloured People's Dilemma," *Cape Times*, January 25, 1963, in Richard E. van der Ross, *Coloured Viewpoint: A Series of Articles in the Cape Times, 1958–1965, by R. E. van der Ross*, ed. J. L. Hattingh and H. C. Bredekamp (Bellville, South Africa: The Western Cape Institute for Historical Research/University of the Western Cape, 1984), 219.

80. Cited in Mary Ann French, "The Triumph of Nelson Mandela," *Washington Post*, October 5, 1994, C-11.

81. Davis, *Who Is Black?* 11.

82. Gilliam, "From Roxbury to Rio—and Back in a Hurry," 177–78.

83. Fernandez, Review of Federal Measurements of Race and Ethnicity, 127, 134.

84. Heather Green, in Carol Camper, host, "Claiming Identity: Mixed Race Black Women Speak," in Camper, *Miscegenation Blues*, 208.

85. Melina, "Advice for Parents of Children of Mixed Racial Heritage," n.p.

86. Davis, *Who Is Black?* 144.

87. Melina, "Advice for Parents of Children of Mixed Racial Heritage," n.p.

88. Carol Camper, "Genetic Appropriation: A Response to a White Liberal Fad," in Camper, *Miscegenation Blues*, 163.

89. Camper, "Genetic Appropriation," 165.

90. Camper, "Genetic Appropriation," 165–66.

91. Camper, "Genetic Appropriation," 167.

92. Camper, "Genetic Appropriation," 164.

93. Camper, "Genetic Appropriation," 168.

94. Graham, Review of Federal Measurements of Race and Ethnicity, 120.

95. Graham, on Olney, "Racial Categories on the Next Census."

96. Cited in Graham, Review of Federal Measurements of Race and Ethnicity, 121.

97. Cited in Funderburg, Black, White, Other, 245.

98. "Back to School Editorial," Insight: The Official Voice of the Interracial Family Connection 7, no. 9 (September 1994): 1.

99. Lawrence Tenzer, "The Census—A Target for Recognition," Interrace, July/August 1992, 33.

100. Michael Moore D'Annunzio, "Reflections of a Biracial Man," Interrace, November/December 1992, 20.

101. See Jamoo, "Interrace People," Interrace, September/October 1992, 20; Gregory Stephens, "Mixed-Race Children Put Equality Issues in Focus," Oakland Tribune, July 2, 1994; Candy Mills, "In the News: Interracial News from Around the World," Interrace, November 1993, 10; D'Annunzio, "Reflections of a Biracial Man," 20.

102. Edwidge Danticat, "History? Herstory? Our Story," New People, September/October 1993, 18; Daniel Hollis, "Just What Does Afrocentrism Mean?" New People, September/October 1993, 17.

103. Stephens, "Mixed-Race Children Put Equality Issues in Focus."

104. Zack, Race and Mixed Race, 144.

105. William Grant Still, "A Symphony of Dark Voices," Opera, Concert and Symphony, May 1947, 38; "The Negro and His Music," War Worker, October 1943, 15; "The Men behind American Music," Crisis, January 1944, 12.

106. Yvette Walker Hollis, "Shades of Jazz," New People, September/October 1991, 14.

107. "Jimi Hendrix Ignited Rock for '60s Minorities," New People, November/December 1992, 11.

108. Novella Ann Hickman, "Biracial Parenting," Interrace, January/February 1993, 29.

109. Jones, Bulletproof Diva, 61.

110. Jones, Bulletproof Diva, 61–62.

111. Frederickson, White Supremacy, 133.

112. See "Reforming the Dutch Reformed Church," Challenge (Johannesburg), December/January 1994/95, 10.

113. Edward Byron Reuter, *The Mulatto in the United States: Including a Study of the Role of Mixed-Blood Races throughout the World* (Boston: Richard G. Badger/Gorham Press, 1918), 104.

114. Graham, Review of Federal Measurements of Race and Ethnicity, 108, 110.

115. Mills, "'Multiracial,'" 26.

116. Jon Brower, "Your Questions Answered," *Interrace*, September/October 1993, 14.

117. Nila Gupta, in Carol Camper, host, "Mixed Race Women's Group—Dialogue Two," in Camper, *Miscegenation Blues*, 277.

118. Cited in Funderburg, *Black, White, Other*, 112.

119. Jones, *Bulletproof Diva*, 31.

120. Mills, "'Multiracial,'" 23.

121. Francis Wardle, "Are Biracial Children and Interracial Families a Threat to the Progress of Blacks in the U.S.?" *Interrace*, September/October 1992, 44.

122. Fernandez, Review of Federal Measurements of Race and Ethnicity, 131.

123. Kathy Russell, Midge Wilson, and Ronald Hall, *The Color Complex: The Politics of Skin Color among African Americans* (New York: Harcourt Brace Jovanovich, 1992), 3.

124. Wardle, "Lani Guinier's Real Confirmation," 7.

125. Russell, Wilson, and Hall, *The Color Complex*, 5.

126. Davis, *Who Is Black?* 178.

127. Ira Shaffer to the Editor, *Interrace*, August/September 1994, 4.

128. G. Reginald Daniel, "Beyond Black and White: The New Multiracial Consciousness," in Root, *Racially Mixed People in America*, 399.

129. Sally Katzen, on Olney, "Racial Categories on the Next Census."

Notes to Chapter 3

1. Arthur A. Fletcher, Review of Federal Measurements of Race and Ethnicity, Hearings before the Subcommittee on Census, Statistics and Postal Personnel of the Committee on Post Office and Civil Office and Civil Service, House of Representatives, 103rd Congress, First Session, November 3, 1993 (Washington, D.C.: U.S. Government Printing Office, 1994), 273.

2. Fletcher, Review of Federal Measurements of Race and Ethnicity, 273.

3. Thomas C. Sawyer, Review of Federal Measurements of Race and Ethnicity, June 30, 1993, 92.

4. Cited in Candance Mills, "'Multiracial': Worth Fighting For?" *Interrace*, November 1993, 27.

5. Lawrence Wright, "One Drop of Blood," *New Yorker*, July 25, 1994, 53.

6. Sharon M. Lee, "Racial Classifications in the US Census: 1890–1990," *Ethnic and Racial Studies* 16, no. 1 (January 1993): 85.

7. Naomi Zack, *Race and Mixed Race* (Philadelphia: Temple University Press, 1993), 143.

8. "NGK Clerics Sign Statement," *Cape Times*, August 18, 1976.

9. "NGK Clerics Sign Statement."

10. Allan Boesak, *Black and Reformed: Apartheid, Liberation, and the Calvinist Tradition*, ed. Leonard Sweetman (Maryknoll, N.Y.: Orbis, 1986), 121.

11. Allan Boesak, "The Sins of the Church Are the Sins of the Whites," *Sunday Times* (South Africa), April 23, 1978; Mark August, "Re-unification of NGK Churches Is Chaplain's Aim," *Cape Times*, November 19, 1976, 13.

12. Allan Boesak, "Race Relations and the Challenge of the Eighties," MS, Allan Boesak Papers, Institute for Historical Research, University of the Western Cape, Cape Town.

13. "Black Power Here to Stay—Chaplain," *Cape Times*, January 4, 1977.

14. Roy H. du Pre, *Separate but Unequal: The "Coloured" People of South Africa—A Political History* (Johannesburg: Jonathan Ball Publishers, 1994), 233–34.

15. Khoisan X, "Why I Changed My Name," *IMVO* (King Williams Town, South Africa), September 29, 1994, 8.

16. Everett V. Stonequist, *The Marginal Man: A Study in Personality and Culture Conflict* (New York: Russell and Russell, 1961 [1937]), 3, 21.

17. Stonequist, *The Marginal Man*, 21.

18. H. F. Dickie-Clark, *The Marginal Man: A Sociological Study of a Coloured Group* (London: Routledge and Kegan Paul; New York: Humanities Press, 1966), 105, 128.

19. Richard E. van der Ross, "The Coloured Dilemma," *Cape Times*, January 25, 1963, in Richard E. van der Ross, *Coloured Viewpoint: A*

Series of Articles in the Cape Times, 1958–1965, by R. E. van der Ross, ed. J. L. Hattingh and H. C. Bredekamp (Bellville, South Africa: The Western Cape Institute for Historical Research/University of the Western Cape, 1984), 218.

20. Dickie-Clark, *The Marginal Situation,* 113.

21. Z. J. De Beer, *Multi-Racial South Africa: The Reconciliation of Forces* (London: Oxford University Press, 1961), 20.

22. Du Pre, *Separate but Unequal,* 3–4.

23. Richard E. van der Ross, "The Coloured People," MS, talk broadcast over the BCC in 1957, 1, Richard E. van der Ross Papers, Institute of Historical Research, University of the Western Cape.

24. Richard E. van der Ross, *100 Questions about Coloured South Africans* (Cape Town: University of the Western Cape Printing Department, 1993), 5.

25. Heather Green, "This Piece Done, I shall Be Renamed," in Carol Camper, ed., *Miscegenation Blues: Voices of Mixed Race Women* (Toronto: Sister Vision Press, 1994), 300–301.

26. "Coloured Ethnicity Gets Support," *Cape Times,* October 4, 1994, 2.

27. Lisa Jones, *Bulletproof Diva: Tales of Race, Sex, and Hair* (New York: Doubleday, 1994), 58.

28. Leo Spitzer, *Lives in Between: Assimilation and Marginality in Austria, Brazil, and West Africa, 1780–1945* (Cambridge, U.K.: Cambridge University Press, 1989), 126.

29. Cited in Lise Funderburg, *Black, White, Other: Biracial Americans Talk about Race and Identity* (New York: William Morrow, 1994), 321.

30. Paul Williams, Review of Federal Measurements of Race and Ethnicity, November 3, 1993, 273.

31. Rainier H. Spencer to the Editor, *Interrace,* November 1993, 8.

32. Edward Byron Reuter, *The Mulatto in the United States: Including a Study of the Role of Mixed-Blood Races throughout the World* (Boston: Richard G. Badger/Gorham Press, 1918), 331–33.

33. Spitzer, *Lives in Between,* 125–26.

34. Leslie B. Rout, Jr., "Brazil: Study in Black, Brown and Beige," *Negro Digest* 19 (February 1970), in David J. Hellwig, ed., *African-American Reflections on Brazil's Racial Paradise* (Philadelphia: Temple University Press, 1992), 195, 197.

35. Richard E. van der Ross, "Group Identity and the Coloured People," paper given at Abe Bailey Institute of Interracial Studies, June 17, 1971, 5, from the files of Jimmy Ellis, University of the Western Cape, Cape Town.

36. David J. Hellwig, Introduction, in Hellwig, *African-American Reflections on Brazil's Racial Paradise*, 6.

37. J. A. Rogers, *Sex and Race: Negro-Caucasian Mixing in All Ages and All Lands*, vol. 1 (St. Petersburg, Fla.: Helga M. Rogers, 1952), 131, 132.

38. Dickie-Clark, *The Marginal Situation*, 115.

39. De Beer, *Multi-Racial South Africa*, 20.

40. Richard E. van der Ross, "Gaining Trust of the African," *Cape Times*, November 17, 1960, in van der Ross, *Coloured Viewpoint*, 139–40.

41. Dickie-Clark, *The Marginal Situation*, 68.

42. Cited in Dickie-Clark, *The Marginal Situation*, 12.

43. Robert Mattes, "The Road to Democracy: From 2 February 1990 to 27 April 1994," in Andrew Reynolds, ed., *Election '94 South Africa: The Campaigns, Results and Future Prospects* (Cape Town: David Philip, 1994), 2–3.

44. Mark Mathabane and Gail Mathabane, *Love in Black and White* (New York: HarperCollins, 1992), 247, 255.

45. Complete speech in Hari Sharan Chhabra, *New South Africa: Problems of Democratic Transition* (New Delhi, India: Africa Publications, 1994), 172.

46. Cited in Chhabra, *New South Africa*, 183–84.

47. Cited in Chhabra, *New South Africa*, 184.

48. See Hermann Giliomee, "The National Party's Campaign for a Liberation Election," in Reynolds, *Election '94 South Africa*, 56–57.

49. Daniel Silke and Robert Schrire, "The Mass Media and the South African Election," in Reynolds, *Election '94 South Africa*, 137.

50. Silke and Schrire, "The Mass Media and the South African Election," 129.

51. Richard E. van der Ross, "Common Cause with Africans," *Cape Times*, June 1, 1961, in van der Ross, *Coloured Viewpoint*, 170.

52. Andrew Reynolds, "The Results," in Reynolds, *Election '94 South Africa*, 193.

53. Dickie-Clark, *The Marginal Situation*, 118.

54. Giliomee, "The National Party's Campaign for a Liberation Election," 52, 53.

55. Giliomee, "The National Party's Campaign for a Liberation Election," 54.

56. Reynolds, "The Results," 191, 192.

57. For percentages see Reynolds, "The Results," 201.

58. Carlos A. Fernandez, "La Raza and the Melting Pot: A Comparative Look at Multiethnicity," in Maria P. P. Root, ed., *Racially Mixed People in America* (Newbury Park, Calif.: Sage, 1992), 140–41.

59. Kathlyn Gay, *The Rainbow Effect: Interracial Families* (New York: Franklin Watts, 1987), 72.

60. Stonequist, *The Marginal Man*, 50–51.

61. Jones, *Bulletproof Diva*, 57.

62. Cited in Rogers Worthington, "Black-and-White Question: Mixed-Race Families Push for New Race Classifications," *News and Observer* (Raleigh), July 10, 1994, 5-E.

63. Richard E. van der Ross, "The Contribution of the Coloured People, 1652–1971," MS, Richard E. van der Ross Papers.

64. R. E. van der Ross, *Myths and Attitudes: An Inside Look at the Coloured People* (Cape Town: Tafelberg Publishers, 1979), 8–9.

65. Van der Ross, "Common Cause with Africans," 169.

66. Van der Ross, *Myths and Attitudes*, 13.

67. Ollie Stewart, "In U.S.A. It's Jim Crow, in Brazil, 'Run Around,'" *Baltimore Afro-American*, June 29, 1940. In Hellwig, *African-American Reflections on Brazil's Racial Paradise*, 98.

68. Dickie-Clark, *The Marginal Situation*, 150.

69. J. A. Loubser, *The Apartheid Bible: A Critical Review of Racial Theology in South Africa* (Cape Town: Maskew Miller Longman, 1987), 7–8.

70. Loubser, *The Apartheid Bible*, 133.

71. Also see Ralph J. Bunche, *An African American in South Africa: The Travel Notes of Ralph J. Bunche, 28 September 1937–1 January 1938*, ed. Robert R. Edgar (Johannesburg: Witwatersrand University Press, 1992), 186–87.

72. See Bunche, *An African American in South Africa*, 72.

73. Van der Ross, "Group Identity and the Coloured People," 21.

74. George M. Fredrickson, *White Supremacy: A Comparative Study in American and South African History* (New York: Oxford University Press, 1981), 263.

75. Bill Keller, "Mixed-Race S. Africans Riot Over 'Favoritism,'" *The News and Observer* (Raleigh), September 16, 1994.

76. Mike Siluma, "Divisions Wrought by Apartheid Are Still Intact," *The Star International Weekly* (Johannesburg), September 22, 1994, 14.

77. Du Pre, *Separate but Unequal*, xv–xvi.

78. Frantz Fanon, *Black Skin, White Masks*, trans. Charles Lam Markmann (New York: Grove, 1967 [1952]), 103.

79. Michele Paulse, "Commingled," in Camper, *Miscegenation Blues*, 46.

80. Van der Ross, "The Coloured People," 3.

81. Richard E. van der Ross, "Colour-in-Colour Divisions," *Cape Times*, February 9, 1961, in van der Ross, *Coloured Viewpoint*, 152.

82. Deloris A. Brown, "Black Consciousness vs. Racism in Brazil," *The Black Scholar* 11 (January/February 1980), in Hellwig, *African American Reflections on Brazil's Racial Paradise*, 228.

83. See Bunche, *An African American in South Africa*, 75.

84. Spitzer, *Lives in Between*, 37.

85. Dickie-Clark, *The Marginal Situation*, 158.

86. *The Cape Town of the Coloured People* (An excursion organized for the Congress of the South African Geographical Society held at the University of Cape Town, June 29–July 3, 1979), [1].

87. Cleveland Donald, Jr., "Equality in Brazil: Confronting Reality," *Black World* 22 (November 1972), in Hellwig, *African-American Reflections on Brazil's Racial Paradise*, 214.

88. Fanon, *Black Skin, White Masks*, 51–52.

89. Fanon, *Black Skin, White Masks*, 100.

90. Cited in Fanon, *Black Skin, White Masks*, 46–47.

91. Fanon, *Black Skin, White Masks*, 47.

92. W. E. B. Du Bois to Edward Weeks, October 2, 1941, in Hellwig, *African-American Reflections on Brazil's Racial Paradise*, 119.

93. Spencer to the Editor, 8.

94. Jones, *Bulletproof Diva*, 58, 59.

95. Edwin Darden, "Being Perfect," *Interrace*, January/February 1991, 3.

96. Letter to the Editor, *Interrace*, May/June 1992, 7.

97. Mills, "'Multiracial,'" 25.

98. Du Pre, *Separate but Unequal*, 254.

99. Dickie-Clark, *The Marginal Situation*, 130.

100. Dickie-Clark, *The Marginal Situation*, 130.

Notes to Chapter 4

1. Mark Mathabane and Gail Mathabane, *Love in Black and White* (New York: HarperCollins, 1992), 216.

2. Richard E. van der Ross, "Group Identity and the Coloured People," MS, lecture given at Abe Bailey Institute of Interracial Studies, June

17, 1971, from the files of Jimmy Ellis, University of the Western Cape, Cape Town.

3. *The Cape Town of the Coloured People* (an excursion organized by the Congress of the South African Geographical Society held at the University of Cape Town, June 29–July 3, 1979), 1.

4. Shanti Thakur, "Domino: Filming Stories of Interracial People," in Carol Camper, ed., *Miscegenation Blues: Voices of Mixed Race Women* (Toronto: Sister Vision Press, 1994), 349.

5. Henry Der, Review of Federal Measurements of Race and Ethnicity, Hearings before the Subcommittee on Census Statistics and Postal Personnel of the Committee on Post Office and Civil Office and Civil Service, House of Representatives, 103rd Congress, First Session, June 30, 1993 (Washington, D.C.: U.S. Government Printing Office, 1994), 96.

6. Michael C. Thornton, "Is Multiracial Status Unique?: The Personal and Social Experience," in Maria P. P. Root, ed., *Racially Mixed People in America* (Newbury Park, Calif.: Sage, 1992), 324–25.

7. W. H. Thomas, "Socio-Economic Development of the Coloured Community," in Hendrik W. van der Merwe and C. J. Groenewald, eds., *Occupational and Social Change among Coloured People in South Africa: Proceedings of a Workshop of the Centre for Intergroup Studies at the University of Cape Town* (Cape Town: Juta, 1976), 68.

8. Thornton, "Is Multiracial Status Unique?" 325.

9. Gitanjali Saxena, in Carol Camper, host, "Mixed Race Women's Group—Dialogue One," in Camper, *Miscegenation Blues*, 40.

10. Thomas E. Petri, Review of Federal Measurements of Race and Ethnicity, June 30, 1993, 169.

11. Kathlyn Gay, *The Rainbow Effect: Interracial Families* (New York: Franklin Watts, 1987), 24.

12. Michele Paulse, "Commingled," in Camper, *Miscegenation Blues*, 43–44.

13. Cited in Lise Funderburg, *Black, White, Other: Biracial Americans Talk about Race and Identity* (New York: William Morrow, 1994), 320–21.

14. Rainier H. Spencer, "False Categories: Old and New," *Interrace*, Spring/Summer 1993, 8.

15. Ira Shaffer to the Editor, *Interrace*, August/September 1994, 4.

16. Candace Mills, "Editor's Memo," *Interrace*, July/August 1992, 6.

17. Candy Mills, "'Multiracial': Worth Fighting For?" *Interrace*, November 1993, 27, 28.

18. Carlos A. Fernandez, Review of Federal Measurements of Race and Ethnicity, June 30, 1993, 132.

19. Katherine Wallman, Office of Management and Budget, Public Hearing(s) on Standards for the Classification of Federal Data on Race and Ethnicity, July 11, 1994, 3–4.

20. Sally Katzen, on Wayne Olney, host, "Racial Categories on the Next Census: Should They Be Changed or Should They Be Eliminated Altogether," on *Which Way L.A.?* KCRW Radio, Santa Monica College, California, August 4, 1994.

21. John Cougill, Office of Management and Budget, Public Hearing(s), July 14, 1994, 10, 11, 13.

22. Yehudi Webster, on Olney, "Racial Categories on the Next Census."

23. Yehudi Webster, *The Racialization of America* (New York: St. Martin's Press, 1992), 7. See also Lawrence Wright, "One Drop of Blood," *New Yorker*, July 25, 1994, 54.

24. Katzen, on Olney, "Racial Categories on the Next Census."

25. Fernandez, Review of Federal Measurements of Race and Ethnicity, 127 and 131.

26. Cited in Mills, "'Multiracial,'" 26.

27. Nathan D. Lynch to the Editor, *Interrace*, March 1994, 2.

28. Webster, *The Racialization of America*, 8.

29. Webster, on Olney, "Racial Categories on the Next Census."

30. Kwame Anthony Appiah, *In My Father's House: Africa in the Philosophy of Culture* (New York: Oxford University Press, 1992), 176.

31. Appiah, *In My Father's House*, 116.

32. Appiah, *In My Father's House*, 179.

33. Appiah, *In My Father's House*, 179.

34. Webster, *The Racialization of America*, 55.

35. Nathan D. Lynch to the Editor, *Interrace*, September/October 1993, 7.

36. Desiree Lewis, "'Race': South Africa's Censored Four-Letter Word," *Political and Economic Monthly* (Harare) 7, no. 7 (April 1994): 39.

37. Lewis, "'Race,'" 39.

38. Lewis, "'Race,'" 39.

39. Lewis, "'Race,'" 39.

40. Roy H. Du Pre, *Separate but Unequal: The "Coloured" People of South Africa—A Political History* (Johannesburg: Jonathan Ball Publishers, 1994), xv.

41. Mike Siluma, "Divisions Wrought by Apartheid Are Still Intact," *Star International Weekly* (Johannesburg), September 22, 1994, 14.

42. Nike Siluma, "Are We Going Back to an Apartheid Future?" *Star* (Johannesburg), October 13, 1994, 16.

43. Allan Boesak, "Black Consciousness, Black Power and 'Coloured Politics'" (lecture to the Labour Party), MS, January 3, 1977, 11, Allan Boesak Papers, Institute for Historical Research, University of the Western Cape, Cape Town.

44. Boesak, "Black Consciousness, Black Power and 'Coloured Politics,'" 11.

45. Boesak, "Black Consciousness, Black Power and 'Coloured Politics,'" 1.

46. *The Reconstruction and Development Programme: A Policy Framework* (Johannesburg: African National Congress, 1994), 1.

47. *The Reconstruction and Development Programme*, 2.

48. *The Reconstruction and Development Programme*, 5.

49. "The Minister Who Learnt to Hate and Love," *Sunday Times* (South Africa), March 9, 1980, 5.

50. Jon Qwelane, Editorial, *Tribute*, February 1995, 5.

51. "Affirmative Action: Apartheid in Reverse," *Sunday Times* (South Africa), January 16, 1994, 7.

52. Arthur M. Schlesinger, Jr., *The Disuniting of America: Reflections on a Multicultural Society* (New York: Norton, 1992), 20.

53. Schlesinger, *The Disuniting of America*, 18, 43, 133.

54. Spencer, "False Categories," 8.

55. Cited in Edwidge Danticat, "An Interview with Author Lise Funderburg," *New People*, July/August 1994, 23.

56. George Dailey, Office of Management and Budget, Public Hearing(s), July 11, 1994, 45–46.

57. Fletcher, Review of Federal Measurements of Race and Ethnicity, 252, 257.

58. G. Reginald Daniel, "Beyond Black and White: The New Multiracial Consciousness," in Root, *Racially Mixed People in America*, 340.

59. Itabari Njeri, "Who Is Black?" *Essence*, September 1991, 117.

60. Yvette Hollis and Daniel Hollis, "Editor's Corner," *New People*, July/August 1994, 2

61. Cited in Funderburg, *Black, White, Other*, 30.

62. See, for example, Paul Whitaker, cited in Funderburg, *Black, White, Other*, 219.

Notes to the Postscript

1. Susan Sontag, "This Man, This Country," in Jacques Derrida and Mustapha Tlili, eds., *For Nelson Mandela* (New York: Seaver/Henry Holt, 1987), 50.
2. Sontag, "This Man, This Country," 49.
3. Jacques Derrida, "The Laws of Reflection: Nelson Mandela, in Admiration," in Derrida and Tlili, *For Nelson Mandela*, 13.
4. Cited in Timothy D. Sisk, "A US Perspective of South Africa's 1994 Election," in Andrew Reynolds, ed., *Election '94 South Africa: The Campaigns, Results and Future Prospects* (Cape Town: David Philip, 1994), 156.
5. Cited in Sisk, "A US Perspective of South Africa's 1994 Election," 156.
6. Mark Mathabane and Gail Mathabane, *Love in Black and White* (New York: HarperCollins, 1992), 260.
7. Cited in Peter Fabricius and Chris Whitfield, "Rapturous Reception for Mandela Speech at United Nations," *The Argus* (Cape Town), October 4, 1994, 11.
8. Cited in Mary Ann French, "The Triumph of Nelson Mandela," *The Washington Post*, October 5, 1994, C-11.
9. Steven Greenhouse, "Mandela Asks U.S. to Help in the Rebirth of His Nation," *New York Times*, October 5, 1994, A9.
10. Cited in Peter Fabricius and Chris Whitfield, "You'll Never Walk Alone: Clinton's Pledge to S.A.," *Angus* (Cape Town), October 5, 1994, 17.
11. Cited in French, "The Triumph of Nelson Mandela," C-11.
12. Cited in French, "The Triumph of Nelson Mandela," C-11.
13. Cited in Steven Greenhouse, "Mandela Says U.S. Must Aid World's Poor," *New York Times*, October 7, 1994, A-3.
14. Cited in John Kifner, "'No to Vengeance,'" *New York Times*, October 16, 1994, 1.

[BIBLIOGRAPHY]

Abernathy, (Senator) Ralph David III. Senate Bill 149, Georgia Act No. 1193. Signed for April 14, 1994, the General Assembly of Georgia.

"Affirmative Action: Apartheid in Reverse." *Sunday Times* (South Africa), January 16, 1994, 7.

Appiah, Kwame Anthony. "The Uncompleted Argument: Du Bois and the Illusion of Race." In Henry Louis Gates, Jr., *"Race," Writing, and Difference*. Chicago: University of Chicago Press, 1986.

———. *In My Father's House: Africa in the Philosophy of Culture*. New York: Oxford University Press, 1992.

Arvey, Verna. *In One Lifetime*. Fayetteville: University of Arkansas Press, 1984.

Asante, Molefi Kete. "Racing to Leave the Race: Black Postmodernists Off-Track." *Black Scholar* 23, nos. 3 and 4 (Spring/Fall 1993): 50–51.

Atkins, Elizabeth. "Parents of Biracial Children Debate the Wisdom of Afrocentric Education." *New People*, May/June 1993, 6–7.

August, Mark. "Re-unification of NGK Churches Is Chaplain's Aim." *Cape Times* (Cape Town), November 19, 1976, 13.

"Back to School Editorial." *Insight: The Official Voice of the Interracial Family Connection* 7, no. 9 (September 1994): 1.

Baker, Houston A., Jr. "Caliban's Triple Play." In Henry Louis Gates, Jr., *"Race," Writing, and Difference*. Chicago: University of Chicago Press, 1986.

Basson, Dion. *South Africa's Interim Constitution: Text and Notes*. Kewyn, South Africa: Juta, 1994.

Begley, Sharon. "Three Is Not Enough: Surprising New Lessons from the Controversial Science of Race." *Newsweek*, February 13, 1995, 67–69.

"Black Power Here to Stay—Chaplain." *Cape Times* (Cape Town), January 4, 1977.

Boesak, Allan. "Black Consciousness, Black Power and 'Coloured Politics,'" MS. Lecture to the Labour Party, January 3, 1977. Allan Boesak Papers, Institute for Historical Research, University of the Western Cape, Cape Town.

———. "The Sins of the Church Are the Sins of the Whites." *Sunday Times* (South Africa), April 23, 1978.

———. *Black and Reformed: Apartheid, Liberation, and the Calvinist Tradition*. Ed. Leonard Sweetman. Maryknoll, N.Y.: Orbis, 1986.

———. "Race Relations and the Challenge of the Eighties," MS. Allan Boesak Papers, Institute for Historical Research, University of the Western Cape, Cape Town.

Bradshaw, Carla K. "Beauty and the Beast: On Racial Ambiguity." In Maria P. P. Root, ed., *Racially Mixed People in America*. Newbury Park, Calif.: Sage, 1992.

Brower, Jonathan. "The Doctor Is In." *Interrace*, November/December 1992, 31.

———. "Your Questions Answered." *Interrace*, September/October 1993, 14.

Brown, Deloris A. "Black Consciousness vs. Racism in Brazil." *Black Scholar* 11 (January/February 1980). In David J. Hellwig, ed., *African-American Reflections on Brazil's Racial Paradise*. Philadelphia: Temple University Press, 1992.

Brown, William O. *Race Relations in the American South and in South Africa: A Comparison of Backgrounds, Realities, and Trends*. Boston: Boston University Press, 1959.

Bulbring, Edyth. "Whitney Lined Up for SA after Wowing Mandela." *Sunday Times* (South Africa), October 9, 1994, 1.

Bunche, Ralph J. *An African American in South Africa: The Travel Notes of Ralph J. Bunche, 28 September 1937–1 January 1938*. Ed. Robert R. Edgar. Johannesburg: Witwatersrand University Press, 1992.

Burgess, John M. "Opening Presentation" (Convocation of Black Theologians, April 1978). *Saint Luke's Journal of Theology* 22, no. 4 (September 1979): 245.

Burroughs, Nannie H. "Church Leader Argues against Mixed Marriage." *Ebony* 6, no. 1 (November 1950): 50.

Camper, Carol, host. "Claiming Identity: Mixed Race Black Women Speak." In Carol Camper, ed., *Miscegenation Blues: Voices of Mixed Race Women*. Toronto: Sister Vision Press, 1994.

————. "Genetic Appropriation: A Response to a White Liberal Fad." In Carol Camper, ed., *Miscegenation Blues: Voices of Mixed Race Women*. Toronto: Sister Vision Press, 1994.

————. "Into the Mix." In Carol Camper, ed., *Miscegenation Blues: Voices of Mixed Race Women*. Toronto: Sister Vision Press, 1994.

————, ed. *Miscegenation Blues: Voices of Mixed Race Women*. Toronto: Sister Vision Press, 1994.

————, host. "Mixed Race Women's Group—Dialogue One." In Carol Camper, ed., *Miscegenation Blues: Voices of Mixed Race Women*. Toronto: Sister Vision Press, 1994.

————, host. "Mixed Race Women's Group—Dialogue Two." In Carol Camper, ed., *Miscegenation Blues: Voices of Mixed Race Women*. Toronto: Sister Vision Press, 1994.

The Cape Town of the Coloured People. An excursion organized for the Congress of the South African Geographical Society held at the University of Cape Town, June 29–July 3, 1979.

"The Case against Mixed Marriage." *Ebony* 6, no. 1 (November 1950): 50–57.

Chhabra, Hari Sharan. *New South Africa: Problems of Democratic Transition*. New Delhi: Africa Publications, 1994.

Cilliers, S. P. *The Coloureds of South Africa: A Factual Survey*. Cape Town: Banier Publishers, 1963.

Cirillo, Sandy. "Beautiful People without a Name." *Interrace*, January/February 1991, 23.

"Coloured Ethnicity Gets Support." *Cape Times* (Cape Town), October 4, 1994, 2.

Cone, James H. *Black Theology and Black Power*. New York: Harper-Collins, 1989 [1969].

Cose, Ellis. "One Drop of Bloody History: Americans Have Always Defined Themselves on the Basis of Race." *Newsweek*, February 13, 1995, 70–72.

Courtney, Brian A. "Freedom from Choice: Being Biracial Has Meant Denying Half of My Identity." *Newsweek*, February 13, 1995, 16.

Daniel, G. Reginald. "Beyond Black and White: The New Multiracial Consciousness." In Maria P. P. Root, ed., *Racially Mixed People in America*. Newbury Park, Calif.: Sage, 1992.

————. "Eurocentrism, Afrocentrism, or 'Holocentrism'?" *Interrace*, May/June 1992, 33.

D'Annunzio, Michael Moore. "Reflections of a Biracial Man." *Interrace*, November/December 1992, 18–20.

Danticat, Edwidge. "An Interview with Author Lise Funderburg." *New People*, July/August 1994, 22–24.

Darden, Edwin. "Being Perfect." *Interrace*, January/February 1991, 3.

———. "The Lovings vs. Virginia." *Interrace*, May/June 1991, 16.

Davis, F. James. *Who Is Black?: One Nation's Definition*. University Park: Pennsylvania State University Press, 1991.

De Beer, Z. J. *Multi-Racial South Africa: The Reconciliation of Forces*. London: Oxford University Press, 1961.

Derrida, Jacques. "The Laws of Reflection: Nelson Mandela, in Admiration." In Jacques Derrida and Mustapha Tlili, eds., *For Nelson Mandela*. New York: Sever/Henry Holt, 1987, 13–42.

Derrida, Jacques, and Mustapha Tlili, eds., *For Nelson Mandela*. New York: Sever/Henry Holt, 1987.

Dickie-Clark, H. F. *The Marginal Situation: A Sociological Study of a Coloured Group*. London: Routledge and Kegan Paul; New York: Humanities Press, 1966.

Donald, Cleveland, Jr. "Equality in Brazil: Confronting Reality." *Black World* 22 (November 1972). In David J. Hellwig, ed., *African-American Reflections on Brazil's Racial Paradise*. Philadelphia: Temple University Press, 1992.

Douglass, Ramona E. "A Multiracial's Dissent." *New People*, July/August 1994, 4.

Du Bois, W. E. B. *Dusk of Dawn: An Essay toward an Autobiography of a Race Concept*. New York: Harcourt Brace, 1940.

———. To Edward Weeks, October 2, 1941. In David J. Hellwig, ed., *African-American Reflections on Brazil's Racial Paradise*. Philadelphia: Temple University Press, 1992.

Du Pre, Roy H. *Separate but Unequal: The "Coloured" People of South Africa—A Political History*. Johannesburg: Jonathan Ball Publishers, 1994.

Dvorin, Eugene P. *Racial Separation in South Africa: An Analysis of Apartheid Theory*. Chicago: University of Chicago Press, 1952.

Early, Gerald, ed. *Lure and Loathing: Essays on Race, Identity, and the Ambivalence of Assimilation*. New York: Penguin, 1993.

Fabricius, Peter, and Chris Whitfield. "Rapturous Reception for Mandela Speech at United Nations." *Argus* (Cape Town), October 4, 1994, 11.

———. "Guru Needed to Be More of a Capitalist." *Star* (Johannesburg), October 13, 1994, 16.

———. "You'll Never Walk Alone: Clinton's Pledge to SA." *Argus* (Cape Town), October 5, 1994, 17.

Fanon, Frantz. *Black Skin, White Masks*. Trans. Charles Lam Markmann. New York: Grove, 1967 [1952].

Fernandez, Carlos A. "La Raza and the Melting Pot: A Comparative Look at Multiethnicity." In Maria P. P. Root, ed., *Racially Mixed People in America*. Newbury Park, Calif.: Sage, 1992.

———. "Justice in Alabama?" *New People*, July/August 1994, 8.

Frazier, E. Franklin. *The Negro Church in America*. New York: Schocken, 1974.

Fredrickson, George M. *White Supremacy: A Comparative Study in American and South African History*. New York: Oxford University Press, 1981.

———. *Black Liberation: Comparative History of Black Ideologies* (New York: Oxford University Press, 1995).

French, Mary Ann. "The Triumph of Nelson Mandela." *Washington Post*, October 5, 1994, C1, C11.

Funderburg, Lise. *Black, White, Other: Biracial Americans Talk about Race and Identity*. New York: William Morrow, 1994.

Gabriela. "What It Means to Be Bi-Racial." *Interrace*, September/October 1992, 24.

Gates, Henry Louis, Jr. *"Race," Writing, and Difference*. Chicago: University of Chicago Press, 1986.

Gay, Kathlyn. *The Rainbow Effect: Interracial Families*. New York: Franklin Watts, 1987.

Giliomee, Hermann. "The National Party's Campaign for a Liberation Election." In Andrew Reynolds, ed., *Election '94 South Africa: The Campaigns, Results and Future Prospects*. Cape Town: David Philip, 1994.

Gilliam, Angela M. "From Roxbury to Rio—and Back in a Hurry." In David J. Hellwig, ed., *African-American Reflections on Brazil's Racial Paradise*. Philadelphia: Temple University Press, 1992.

Graham, Susan. "I'm Not an 'Other.'" *New People*, March/April 1992, 9.

Green, Heather. "This Piece Done, I Shall Be Renamed." In Carol Camper, ed. *Miscegenation Blues: Voices of Mixed Race Women*. Toronto: Sister Vision Press, 1994.

Greenhouse, Steven. "Mandela Asks U.S. to Help in the Rebirth of His Nation." *New York Times*, October 5, 1994, A9.

———. "Mandela Says U.S. Must Aid World's Poor." *New York Times*, October 7, 1994, A3.

Hall, Christine C. Iijima. "Coloring Outside the Lines." In Maria P. P. Root, ed., *Racially Mixed People in America*. Newbury Park, Calif.: Sage, 1992.

———. "Please Choose One: Ethnic Identity Choices for Biracial Individuals." In Maria P. P. Root, ed., *Racially Mixed People in America*. Newbury Park, Calif.: Sage, 1992.

Hellwig, David J., ed. *African-American Reflections on Brazil's Racial Paradise*. Philadelphia: Temple University Press, 1992.

Hernandez-Ramdwar, Camille. "Ms. Edge Innate." In Carol Camper, ed., *Miscegenation Blues: Voices of Mixed Race Women*. Toronto: Sister Vision Press, 1994.

Hickman, Novella Ann. "Biracial Parenting." *Interrace*, January/February 1993, 29.

"Hogarth." *Sunday Times* (South Africa), October 9, 1994, 24.

Hollis, Daniel. "Just What Does Afrocentrism Mean?" *New People*, September/October, 1993, 15–17.

Hollis, Yvette Walker. "Shades of Jazz." *New People*, September/October 1991, 14, 16.

Jackson, Richard L. "'Mestizaje' vs. Black Identity: The Color Crisis in Latin America." *Black World* 24 (July 1975). In David J. Hellwig, ed., *African-American Reflections on Brazil's Racial Paradise*. Philadelphia: Temple University Press, 1992.

Jamoo. "Where Are All the Dark-Skinned Black Women?" *Interrace*, May/June 1992, 14–15.

———. "Interrace People." *Interrace*, September/October 1992, 20–21.

"Jimi Hendrix Ignited Rock for '60s Minorities." *New People*, November/December 1992, 11.

Johnson, Deborah J. "Developmental Pathways: Toward an Ecological Theoretical Formulation of Race Identity in Black-White Biracial Children." In Maria P. P. Root, ed., *Racially Mixed People in America*. Newbury Park, Calif.: Sage, 1992.

Jones, Hettie. "Moma's White." *Essence*, May 1994, 79, 151–52, 154, 158, 160.

Jones, Lisa. "Mama's White." *Essence*, May 1994, 78, 80, 150–52.

———. *Bulletproof Diva: Tales of Race, Sex, and Hair*. New York: Doubleday, 1994.

———. "The Blacker the Berry." *Essence*, June 1994, 60–62, 114–16.

Joseph, Allison. "Whitewashed: The Effects of Racism on White-Appearing Children of Integrated Marriages." *Interrace*, May/June 1992, 27–32.

Kaufman, David C. "Biracial Experiences in the United States." *Interrace*, April 1994, 15–19.

Keller, Bill. "Mixed-Race S. Africans Riot Over 'Favoritism.'" *News and Observer* (Raleigh), September 16, 1994.

Kifner, John. "'No to Vengeance.'" *New York Times*, October 16, 1994, 1.

Lample, Paul, and Marcia Lample. "The Baha'i Faith and the Oneness of Humanity." *Interrace*, July/August 1992, 16–18.

Lee, Sharon M. "Racial Classification in the U.S. Census: 1890–1990." *Ethnic and Racial Studies* 16, no. 1 (January 1993): 75–94.

Lemon, Anthony. *Apartheid: A Geography of Separation*. Westmead, U.K.: Saxon House, 1976.

Leslie, Connie. "The Loving Generation: Biracial Children Seek Their Own Pride." *Newsweek*, February 13, 1995, 72.

Letters to the Editor. *Interrace*, May/June 1992, 5–7.

Letters to the Editor. *Interrace*, November/December 1992, 4–8.

Letters to the Editor. *Interrace*, January/February 1993, 4–5.

Letters to the Editor. *Interrace*, September/October 1993, 4–10.

Letters to the Editor. *Interrace*, November 1993, 5, 7–8.

Letters to the Editor. *Interrace*, March 1994, 2–3.

Letters to the Editor. *Interrace*, August/September 1994, 4.

Lewis, Desiree. "'Race': South Africa's Censored Four-Letter Word." *Political and Economic Monthly* (Harare) 7, no. 7 (April 1994): 38–39.

Lewis, Gavin. *Between the Wire and the Wall: A History of South African "Coloured" People*. Cape Town: David Philip, 1987.

MacCrone, I. D. *Race Attitudes in South Africa: Historical, Experimental and Psychological Studies*. London: Oxford University Press, 1937.

Mandela, Nelson. *Long Walk to Freedom: The Autobiography of Nelson Mandela*. Boston: Little, Brown, 1994.

———. "A Time To Build." Address at Presidential Inauguration, Opening of Parliament, Pretoria, May 10, 1994.

Marais, Ben J. *Colour: Unsolved Problem of the West*. Cape Town: Howard B. Timmins, 1952.

Marais, Johannes Stephanus. *The Cape Coloured People, 1652–1937*. Johannesburg: Witwatersrand University Press, 1957.

Mathabane, Mark, and Gail Mathabane. *Love in Black and White*. New York: HarperCollins, 1992.

Mattes, Robert. "The Road to Democracy: From 2 February 1990 to 27 April 1994." In Andrew Reynolds, ed., *Election '94 South Africa: The*

Campaigns, Results and Future Prospects. Cape Town: David Philip, 1994.

McNamee, Mike. "Should the Census Be Less Black and White?" *Business Weekly*, July 4, 1994, 40.

Melina, Lois. "Advice for Parents of Children of Mixed Racial Heritage." *Adopted Child* (newsletter) 9, no. 5 (May 1990).

Miller, Robin L. "The Human Ecology of Multiracial Identity." In Maria P. P. Root, ed., *Racially Mixed People in America*. Newbury Park, Calif.: Sage, 1992.

Mills, Candace. "Editor Memo." *Interrace*, July/August 1992, 6.

————. "'Multiracial': Worth Fighting For?" *Interrace*, November 1993, 21–28.

"The Minister Who Learnt to Hate, and Love." *Sunday Times* (South Africa), March 9, 1980, 5.

Morganthau, Tom. "What Color Is Black?" *Newsweek*, February 13, 1995, 63–65.

Motlhabi, Mokgethi. *Toward a New South Africa: Issues and Objects in the ANC/Government Negotiation for a Non-racial Democratic Society*. Johannesburg: Skotaville Publishers, 1992.

Nakashima, Cynthia L. "An Invisible Monster: The Creation and Denial of Mixed-Race People in America." In Maria P. P. Root, ed., *Racially Mixed People in America*. Newbury Park, Calif.: Sage, 1992.

"NGK Clerics Sign Statement." *Cape Times* (Cape Town), August 18, 1976.

Njeri, Itabari. "Who Is Black?" *Essence*, September 1991, 65–66, 115–17.

Office of Management and Budget, Public Hearing(s) on Standards for the Classification of Federal Data on Race and Ethnicity, July 7 (Boston), July 11 (Denver), July 14 (San Francisco), July 18 (Honolulu), 1994.

Olney, Wayne, host. "Racial Categories on the Next Census: Should They Be Changed or Should They Be Eliminated Altogether." On *Which Way L.A.?* KCRW Radio, Santa Monica College, California, August 4, 1994.

Ottley, Roi. "5 Million U.S. White Negroes." *Ebony* 3, no. 5 (March 1948): 22–28.

Paschal, Belinda. "Reflections of a Biracial Woman." *Interrace*, January/February 1993, 27–28.

Patterson, Sheila. *Colour and Culture in South Africa: A Study of the Status of the Cape Coloured People within the Social Structure of the Union of South Africa*. London: Routledge and Kegan Paul, 1953.

Paulse, Michele. "Commingled." In Carol Camper, ed., *Miscegenation Blues: Voices of Mixed Race Women*. Toronto: Sister Vision Press, 1994.

Pierce, Lora. "Double Standard?" *Interrace*, May/June 1992, 22.

Poe, Janita. "Multiracial People Want a Single Name That Fits." *Chicago Tribune*, May 3, 1993, 1, 13.

Qwelane, Jon. Editorial. *Tribute*, February 1995, 5.

Ragaza, Angelo. "All of the Above: Mixed Race Asian Americans Are Changing the Look and Meaning of Asian America." *A. Magazine*, 3, no. 1, 21–22, 76–77.

A Rainbow of Color (newsletter of the Cincinnati Multiracial Alliance), September/October 1994.

Raphael, Sally Jessy, host. "I Don't Know Who I Am." *Sally Jessy Raphael Show*, November 16, 1993.

The Reconstruction and Development Programme: A Policy Framework. Johannesburg: African National Congress, 1994.

"Reforming the Dutch Reformed Church." *Challenge* (Johannesburg), December/January 1994/95, 9–10.

Reuter, Edward Byron. *The Mulatto in the United States: Including a Study of the Role of Mixed-Blood Races throughout the World*. Boston: Richard G. Badger/Gorham Press, 1918.

Review of Federal Measurements of Race and Ethnicity. Hearings before the Subcommittee on Census, Statistics and Postal Personnel of the Committee on Post Office and Civil Office and Civil Service, House of Representatives, 103rd Congress, First Session, April 17, June 30, July 29, November 3, 1993. Washington, D.C.: U.S. Government Printing Office, 1994.

Reynolds, Andrew. "The Results." In Andrew Reynolds, ed., *Election '94 South Africa: The Campaigns, Results and Future Prospects*. Cape Town: David Philip, 1994.

———, ed. *Election '94 South Africa: The Campaigns, Results and Future Prospects*. Cape Town: David Philip, 1994.

Rhoodie, N. J., ed. *South African Dialogue: Contrasts in South African Thinking on Basic Race Issues*. Philadelphia: Westminster, 1973.

Rogers, J. A. *Sex and Race: Negro-Caucasian Mixing in All Ages and All Lands*, vol. 1. St. Petersburg, Fla.: Helga M. Rogers, 1952.

Root, Maria P. P., ed. *Racially Mixed People in America*. Newbury Park, Calif.: Sage, 1992.

———. "Within, Between, and Beyond Race." In Maria P. P. Root, ed., *Racially Mixed People in America*. Newbury Park, Calif.: Sage, 1992.

Rosin, Hanna. "Boxed In." *New Republic*, January 3, 1994, 12–14.

Rout, Leslie B., Jr. "Brazil: Study in Black, Brown and Beige." In David J. Hellwig, ed., *African-American Reflections on Brazil's Racial Paradise*. Philadelphia: Temple University Press, 1992.

Russell, Kathy, Midge Wilson, and Ronald Hall. *The Color Complex: The Politics of Skin Color among African Americans*. New York: Harcourt Brace Jovanovich, 1992.

Schlesinger, Arthur M., Jr. *The Disuniting of America: Reflections on a Multicultural Society*. New York: Norton, 1992.

Sharkey, Paulette Bochnig. "Philippa Duke Schuyler: Child Prodigy." *Interrace*, July/August 1992, 10–11.

Silke, Daniel, and Robert Schrire. "The Mass Media and the South African Election." In Andrew Reynolds, ed., *Election '94 South Africa: The Campaigns, Results and Future Prospects*. Cape Town: David Philip, 1994.

Siluma, Mike. "Divisions Wrought by Apartheid Are Still Intact." *Star International Weekly* (Johannesburg), September 22, 1994, 14.

———. "Are We Going Back to an Apartheid Future?" *Star* (Johannesburg), October 13, 1994, 16.

Sirica, Jack. "The Race Question." *Newsday* (Melville, New York), January 16, 1995, B15.

Sisk, Timothy D. "A US Perspective of South Africa's 1994 Election." In Andrew Reynolds, ed., *Election '94 South Africa: The Campaigns, Results and Future Prospects*. Cape Town: David Philip, 1994.

Sono, Themba. *Reflections on the Origin of Black Consciousness in South Africa*. Pretoria: Human Sciences Research Council Publishers, 1993.

Sontag, Susan. "This Man, This Country." In Jacques Derrida and Mustapha Tlili, eds., *For Nelson Mandela*. New York: Sever/Henry Holt, 1987, 49–52.

Spencer, Rainier H. "False Categories: Old and New." *Interrace*, Spring/Summer 1993, 8.

———. "The Melanin Myth." *Interrace*, April 1994, 24–25.

Spickard, Paul R. "The Illogic of American Racial Categories." In Maria P. P. Root, ed., *Racially Mixed People in America*. Newbury Park, Calif.: Sage, 1992.

Spitzer, Leo. *Lives in Between: Assimilation and Marginality in Austria, Brazil, and West Africa, 1780–1945*. Cambridge, U.K.: Cambridge University Press, 1989.

Steele, Shelby. *The Content of Our Character: A New Vision of Race in America*. New York: HarperCollins, 1991 [1990].

Stephan, Cookie White. "Mixed-Heritage Individuals: Ethnic Identity and Trait Characteristics." In Maria P. P. Root, ed., *Racially Mixed People in America*. Newbury Park, Calif.: Sage, 1992.

Stephens, Gregory. "Mixed-Race Children Put Equality Issues in Focus." *Oakland Tribune*, July 2, 1994.

Stewart, Ollie. "The Color Line in South America's Largest Republic." *Baltimore Afro-American*, June 22 and 29, July 6 and 27, 1940. In David J. Hellwig, ed., *African-American Reflections on Brazil's Racial Paradise*. Philadelphia: Temple University Press, 1992.

Still, William Grant. "The Negro and His Music." *War Worker*, October 1943, 15.

———. "A Symphony of Dark Voices." *Opera, Concert and Symphony*, May 1947, 18–19, 36, 38–39.

———. "The Men behind American Music." *Crisis*, January 1994, 12–15, 29.

Stonequist, Everett V. *The Marginal Man: A Study in Personality and Culture Conflict*. New York: Russell and Russell, 1961 [1937].

Strauss, Valerie. "At Howard U., Mandela the Man Lives Up to Mandela the Legend." *Washington Post*, October 8, 1994, A1, A6.

Tenzer, Lawrence R. "The Census—A Target for Recognition." *Interrace*, July/August 1992, 33.

———. "A New Look." *Interrace*, January/February 1993, 38.

Thakur, Shanti. "Domino: Filming Stories of Interracial People." In Carol Camper, ed., *Miscegenation Blues: Voices of Mixed Race Women*. Toronto: Sister Vision Press, 1994.

Thomas, W. H. "Socio-Economic Development of the Coloured Community." In Hendrik W. van der Merwe and C. J. Groenewald, eds., *Occupational and Social Change among Coloured People in South Africa: Proceedings of a Workshop of the Centre for Intergroup Studies at the University of Cape Town*. Cape Town: Juta, 1976.

Thornton, Michael C. "Is Multiracial Status Unique?: The Personal and Social Experience." In Maria P. P. Root, ed., *Racially Mixed People in America*. Newbury Park, Calif.: Sage, 1992.

Van der Merwe, Hendrik W. *Pursuing Justice and Peace in South Africa*. London: Routledge, 1989.

Van der Merwe, Hendrik W., and C. J. Groenewald, eds. *Occupational and Social Change among Coloured People in South Africa: Proceed-*

ings of a Workshop of the Center for Intergroup Studies at the University of Cape Town. Cape Town: Juta, 1976.

Van der Ross, Richard E. "The Coloured People," MS. Talk broadcast over BBC radio, 1957. Richard E. van der Ross Papers, Institute of Historical Research, University of the Western Cape, Cape Town.

————. "The Contribution of the Coloured People, 1652–1971," MS, May 1971. Richard E. van der Ross Papers, Institute for Historical Research, University of the Western Cape, Cape Town.

————. *Myths and Attitudes: An Inside Look at the Coloured People.* Cape Town: Tafelberg Publishers, 1979.

————. *Coloured Viewpoint: A Series of Articles in the Cape Times, 1958–1965, by R. E. van der Ross.* Ed. J. L. Hattingh and H. C. Bredekamp. Bellville, South Africa: The Western Cape Institute for Historical Research/University of the Western Cape, 1984.

————. *The Rise and Decline of Apartheid: A Study of Political Movements among the Coloured People of South Africa, 1880–1985.* Cape Town: Tafelberg Publishers, 1986.

————. *100 Questions about Coloured South Africans.* Cape Town: University of the Western Cape Printing Department, 1993.

————. "Group Identity and the Coloured People," MS. Lecture at the Abe Bailey Institute of Interracial Studies, June 17, 1994. From the files of Jimmy Ellis, University of the Western Cape, Cape Town.

————. "Blacks in the USA and S. Africa," MS, n.d. From the files of Richard E. van der Ross, Cape Town.

Venter, Al J. *Coloured: A Profile of Two Million South Africans.* Cape Town: Human and Rousseau, 1974.

The Vision of Race Unity: America's Most Challenging Issue. Wilmette, Ill.: Baha'i Publishing Trust, 1991.

Vobejda, Barbara. "Categorizing the Nation's Millions of 'Other Race.'" *Washington Post,* April 29, 1991, A9.

Wardle, Francis. "Children of Mixed Parentage: How Can Professionals Respond?" *Children Today,* July/August 1989, 10–13.

————. "Raising Good Biracial Children." *Interrace,* January/February 1990, 20–26.

————. "Tomorrow's Children." *New People,* September/October 1991, 5.

————. "Are Biracial Children and Interracial Families a Threat to the Progress of Blacks in the U.S.?" *Interrace,* September/October 1992, 42–44.

———. "Tomorrow's Children." *New People*, November/December 1992, 10–11.

———. "It's Open Season on Race and Identity." *New People*, May/June 1993, 12–13.

———. "Hindsight Doesn't Count in Racial War." *New People*, July/August 1994, 6, 17.

———. "Seeking Out Biracial Heroes Isn't Always for the Birds—But Sometimes, It Is." *New People*, May/June 1993, 9.

Webster, Yehudi O. *The Racialization of America*. New York: St. Martin's Press, 1992.

Williams, Teresa Kay. "Prism Lives: Identity of Binational Americans." In Maria P. P. Root, ed., *Racially Mixed People in America*. Newbury Park, Calif.: Sage, 1992.

Williamson, Joel. *New People: Miscegenation and Mulattoes in the United States*. New York: Free Press, 1980.

Worthington, Rogers. "Black-and-White Question: Mixed-Race Families Rush for New Race Classification." *News and Observer* (Raleigh), July 10, 1994, 5E.

Wright, Lawrence. "One Drop of Blood." *New Yorker*, July 25, 1994, 46–55.

X, Khoisan. "Why I Changed My Name." IMVO (King Williams Town, South Africa), September 29, 1994, 8.

Zack, Naomi. *Race and Mixed Race*. Philadelphia: Temple University Press, 1993.

———. "My Racial Self over Time." In Carol Camper, ed., *Miscegenation Blues: Voices of Mixed Race Women*. Toronto: Sister Vision Press, 1994.

[INDEX]